TEACHING THE INTRODUCTORY COURSE
IN RELIGIOUS STUDIES
A Sourcebook

SCHOLARS PRESS
Studies in the Humanities

TEACHING THE INTRODUCTORY COURSE IN RELIGIOUS STUDIES
A Sourcebook

edited by

Mark Juergensmeyer

Scholars Press
Atlanta, Georgia

TEACHING THE INTRODUCTORY COURSE IN RELIGIOUS STUDIES
A Sourcebook

edited by

Mark Juergensmeyer

©1991
Scholars Press

Library of Congress Cataloging in Publication Data

Teaching the introductory course in religious studies : a sourcebook /
    edited by Mark Juergensmeyer.
    p. cm. — (Scholars Press studies in the humanities series :
    no. 15)
    Includes bibliographical references.
    ISBN 1-55540-598-3 (alk. paper) ISBN: 1-55540-599-1 (pbk: alk. paper)
    1. Religion—Study and teaching. 2. Religions—Study and
teaching. I. Juergensmeyer, Mark. II. Series.
BL41.T44 1990
291'.07'1—dc20   90-24669
                                            CIP

Printed in the United States of America
on acid-free paper

CONTENTS

III. "How I Teach the Introductory Course": A Symposium

THE BERKELEY-CHICAGO-HARVARD PROGRAM: RELIGIOUS STUDIES IN THE LIBERAL ARTS

This volume is a product of the Berkeley-Chicago-Harvard Program, a five-year series of institutes, workshops and related projects aimed at enlarging the role and scope of religious studies in the undergraduate liberal arts curriculum. The objective was to collect resources to assist teachers of undergraduate courses in religious studies—especially those teachers whose training has been limited to only one religious tradition—and to provide reflection on the changing nature of the liberal arts curriculum, and the role that religious studies plays within it.

These two objectives are linked. The basic courses in religion have within recent years begun to move away from the periphery of the liberal arts to which they have been banished for over a century. Increasingly they have come to occupy a more central location in the college curriculum. In many schools the "world religions" and "introduction to religion" courses serve as integrators for the humanities and the social sciences. These courses give an overview of the history of world civilization, provide a window on the cultural dimensions of global politics, and supply a way of perceiving many of the modern quests for personal meaning. This three-volume sourcebook and other projects related to the Berkeley-Chicago-Harvard Program were created to facilitate this new and expansive vision of religious studies in the liberal arts.

The Berkeley-Chicago-Harvard Program was funded by grants from the National Endowment for the Humanities and was sponsored by the Office for Programs in Comparative Religion at the Graduate Theological Union, Berkeley; the History of Religions Program in the Divinity School of the University of Chicago; and the Center for the Study of World Religions at Harvard Divinity School. The codirectors were John Carman (Harvard), Mark Juergensmeyer (Berkeley), and Frank Reynolds (Chicago).

INTRODUCTION

Mark Juergensmeyer

If you are a teacher of religious studies in a liberal arts college, the introductory course may be the most important one that you will ever teach. Students who will never take another religious studies course—perhaps never another course in the humanities—will take this one. Students contemplating religious studies as a major will take it to see if there is any point in going further. Asian-American Buddhists will take it to gain a sense of their cultural roots; and so will Jewish students, and Protestants and Catholics. Business majors will take it to understand the cultural aspects of a growing international market. Political science majors will take it in hopes of understanding the cultural side of current world tensions. Former philosophy majors will take it in hopes of finding a discussion of questions regarding the meaning of life that they failed to find in Philosophy 1: Current Trends in Linguistic Analysis. And students of all sorts will take it with the expectation that the history of world civilization is best viewed through the lens of the world religious heritage.

These are heady expectations, and the chances are pretty good that you won't live up to all of them. But then, no one ever does. We would like to help you live up to more of them, however, and create a course that is not only useful for responding to this wide range of student interests, but also intellectually exciting to teach.

There is no one way to teach the introductory course, and no perfect syllabus—not even the ones provided here. Teaching is an intimate and personal experience, the creation of a set of relationships between the teacher and the material, and the teacher and his or her students. The way you design your course and the way you teach it will depend upon you: how you understand your role and location in the university, how you perceive religion as a subject to be taught, how you see the relationship between intellectual and spiritual activity, and how you go about the art of teaching. The old world religions parade—"if it's Tuesday, it must be Taoism"—is as likely to be as stultifying to the student as it is to you. Nothing projects a greater sense of vitality than a course that the teacher believes in, one that has integrity, substance and intellectual vision. We hope this sourcebook will help in designing such a course.

This volume is a product of the Berkeley-Chicago-Harvard project on teaching Religious Studies in the Liberal Arts, and our thanks go to the hundred or more scholars involved in the project. The "Berkeley Team" that organized this volume consisted of Karen McCarthy Brown, William Darrow, Ninian Smart and myself, augmented by the twenty five college teachers who participated in the summer institute in Berkeley in 1987 and contributed much to the shaping of this volume by writing articles for it and by providing helpful comments on an earlier draft that was circulated during the institute. The hard work of the staff of the Office for Programs in Comparative Religion and a host of graduate assistants brought this volume to completion. We appreciate especially the labors of Andrew Davis, Gurudharm Singh Khalsa, Darrin McMahon, George McKinley, Natalie Reed, Amelia Rudolph, and Yvonne Vowels. Our thanks to this fine staff, the supportive staff of the NEH, and the many distinguished scholars who have written for this sourcebook who have been motivated by the conviction that the introductory course is truly an important course, and worth all the effort.

I

Types of Introductory Courses

THINKING ABOUT THE INTRODUCTORY COURSE: SOME PRELIMINARY QUESTIONS

Karen McCarthy Brown

Given the richness and complexity of the world's religions, it is assumed that no single course, or even a series of courses, can do it all. Choices must be made, but on what basis? The following list of questions is constructed with the awareness that most teachers of religion do not create their courses *ex nihilo*, but build them around the texts that are available. Many also inherit a particular course focus or structure which they can alter only marginally. Therefore these questions are designed to assist in the assessment of texts as well as in the construction and critique of syllabi. Generally speaking every course has certain structuring principles. It is best to know what they are, identify them at the beginning and remain responsible to them throughout.

1. Which religions are included?

On what grounds were some religions and not others chosen for inclusion in the text or course?

Is this a "World Religions" course in which Judaism and Christianity are left out? Does this omission convey the message that they are essentially different from the rest of the world's religious traditions?

Does the course include African, Native American and other similar religions? If so, are they handled generically? For example under the category "African religion" does one example, or a limited set of disparate examples, pretend to stand for the full range of religions practiced in sub-Saharan African? What of Australian aboriginal religion, ancient Celtic religion and so forth? Are they ignored? Are they grouped under a general rubric which may include Native American and African religions? Is it a rubric such as "extra-civilizational" or "non-literate," one defined by the absence of a particular characteristic? Does the label have a negative valence such as "archaic" or "primitive"? Does the text make a division between so-called major and minor, or big and little traditions? Are some traditions referred to as more or less complex? If so, what is the basis for that distinction?

Is there parity in the material chosen to illustrate each tradition? For example, does a discussion of caste take the central place in the section on Hinduism, while Yoruba religion is presented primarily in terms of an initiation rite and Christianity is handled through Biblical texts and theological treatises?

2. How is the text of the course organized?

Is it organized around themes or concepts, or geographical areas, or some other scheme? What are the strengths and limitations of that particular scheme?

If the text or the course is organized around themes, are these derived mainly from a Christian or Jewish-Christian context? For example, is there an attempt to examine "the quest for salvation" in the world's religions, or are terms such as "messiah" and "prophet" employed in explaining traditions other than Judaism and Christianity? In other words, do Christianity and/or Judaism provide the linguistic norms, so that every other religion is described by a process of re-defining its indigenous terminology?

To take another perspective, it there a double-track in the organizing language of the text or course? Are the sub-headings under Christianity such items as "scripture," "history" and "liturgy," while those under Hinduism are "myth" or "sacred writings," "tradition" and "ritual"? What is the effect, intended and otherwise, of this double-tracking?

Is the course organized historically or synchronically within traditions? If historically, is the movement forward or backward? What are the rationales for these choices and are they clearly articulated and consistently applied? Is there an unexamined assumption that some religions have no history? Are some religions presented only in their ideal past before, for example, European colonial contact?

3. Is there an assumption that religions equal their sacred texts?

If a book or a course is built on selections from different sacred texts, does it deal with the limitations of that approach? Is this limited perspective clearly acknowledged at the beginning and reiterated throughout?

If the intention is not to limit the student's acquaintance with the religions to a study of their texts, how are the other dimensions handled? Is there any attempt at participant observation where that is possible? Are music and film used in the classroom? How else can students be brought to an appreciation of religious act and ethos?

4. *Whose version of a religion is accepted as authoritative?*

Is a religion presented from the perspective of a privileged elite? For example, are there unexamined decisions made about what is orthodox and what is not? The Mormons, for example, wish to be called Christians, as do the members of Reverend Moon's Unification Church. Are these groups labeled Christian because they say they are, or is there another criterion used to exclude them? Are the criteria for such judgements clearly articulated and consistently applied?

Power issues are involved in religious institutions just as they are in any other sort of institution and one of the central powers at issue is that of determining the "official" story of the "authoritative" interpretation. Does the course and/or text take account of women's claims that they have been left out of the picture of Christian and Jewish history? Does that claim raise a cautionary note about accepting the "official" view of other traditions on gender matters? What of race issues? Is the Black Church ghettoized into a single paragraph in the chapter on North American religion? What of issues of social class? The treatment of popular piety is one clue as to how these are handled. Is Krishna piety a colorful footnote in the discussion of the religion of India, and does the Mexican peasant woman even appear in the treatment of Catholicism?

5. *Where is the center of gravity of a religion located?*

Important questions can be raised about the population distribution of the adherents of religions. There are currently more Muslims in Nigeria than in Iran and the center of the Christian population is moving below the equator to Latin America and Africa. Does a particular text or course communicate this important information? How does this sort of information influence the characterization of the present conditions and future directions of religions such as Islam and Christianity?

6. *Does the course or textbook include secular ideologies?*

Is there any attempt at bringing Marxism, secular humanism or scientism—to choose three examples among the many possible ones—into conversation with religious world views? Is this a serious attempt or only a quick nod in the direction of secular ideologies for form's sake? If there is a sustained attempt at making these connections, what is the rationale for it? Is that rationale a good one?

7. Is there a hidden censor at work in the text or course?

Given our heritage of Puritan thought, use of a "proprietary template" may well be a particular problem for scholars from the United States. Sex is religious in some areas of the world. Or to put it another way, some religious acts and images are also sexual. Is there a willingness in the text or the course to deal with that? Similarly, bodily substances such as blood, saliva and urine are sacrilized in some religious traditions. Are they edited out of the classroom? In short, is care taken not to bowdlerize the world's religious traditions?

Conversely, are some aspects of particular religious traditions over-dramatized? For example, is animal sacrifice treated as exotic and violent in a tradition where people perform it routinely?

8. How are the value questions handled?

Are there value judgements made about certain features of religious systems? For example, is the Indian caste system judged to be wrong? If so, is the argument made in an up-front and responsible way or is the judgement implied by the use of certain adjectives, or the selection of particular examples? Are whole traditions negatively caricatured by selective presentation? Does the concept of jihad, holy war, receive such attention in the discussion of Islam that contemporary North American students are liable to dismiss the entire religion as inherently bellicose?

9. What kind of visual images are used and what do they communicate?

Do the pictures in a textbook convey stereotypes and value judgements? Do particular films say one thing and communicate another through the eye of the camera? Does the course create the opportunity for students to become aware of and think critically about the impressions gleaned from visual imagery?

10. What is the mood of the text or course?

Is the overall message of a text or course that religion is a somber and serious affair, always a matter of "ultimate concern"? Are the exhilaration of sacred dance, the excitement of ritual drumming, the gustatory delight of meals shared with the gods, the wonder of masked processions and the alchemy of humor—often bawdy and irreverent—included in the picture of what the people of the world count as religion?

TEACHING RELIGION AND RELIGIONS: THE "WORLD RELIGIONS" COURSE

Ninian Smart

What counts as a "world religion"? There have been moves in the past to claim that Confucianism and Theravada Buddhism are not religions, since they do not correspond to Western definitions of religion. If a religion must give the central place to God or the gods then the Theravada is not a religion. There is, further, disagreement on how we should deal with secular worldviews, such as varieties of nationalism and Marxism. Traditions combine with, and react against, many or all of these ideological forces: consider Buddhist modernism and nationalism in Sri Lanka; Iranian Islamic republicanism; liberal democratic forces within Hinduism in modern India; liberal humanism in its combination with Protestant values; Catholic Marxist liberation theology; and modern themes entering into so many new religious movements whether in the South (e.g. Africa) or in the North (e.g. California).

All this has ancient as well as modern applications. A discussion of early Buddhism needs to take into account other systems of belief and practice, notably Carvaka or anti-ritual materialism. Similarly the history of the religions of the Roman Empire touch on various philosophical systems, from Epicureanism to Neoplatonism, ranging along a spectrum from non-religious to religious (by modern standards of evaluation).

However, the main focus of the world religions course will remain the traditional religions, which stress activities such as worship and concepts such as the transcendent and contain rich symbol systems.

The Believer: Is She Always Right?

We typically wish to present religions as they appear to the believers. The phenomenologist of religion Brede Kristensen had a rule of thumb: "The believer is always right." It is certainly worth bearing this saying in mind. But though we have an obligation in teaching world religions to be fair to the experience of those who belong to a given tradition, there are some dilemmas that need to be resolved.

One is the obvious one that the scholar has already made an important step which most adherents have not made. The student of the field knows something of the richness and variety of a tradition, but this may well be screened from the adherent because she is planted, so to speak, within a particular part of a subtradition, like Scottish Calvinism, with the wider spectrum of the tradition, Christianity, as a whole. Moreover, insofar as a believer is asked to characterize the tradition as a whole she may give a normative definition of it arising from her own particular perspective and from the dictates of her own subtradition. This is especially so if the person is a 'religious expert' (clergyperson, bhikkhu, imam, etc.) since a relatively narrow normative perspective will be assumed as part of his training and as the fruit of his job. It may thus turn out that the more descriptive, historical picture of the scholar will diverge quite substantially from that of the adherent or religious expert from within the tradition.

There are ways in which this tension can be somewhat lessened. The comparative religionist has to include the adherent's own picture of her tradition as part of the data. It is one of the ingredients of her worldview. At the same time as a historian of religion, a scholar may describe what to her appears the likely story among the theories of scholars about the 'real history' of the religion. There will be need for the historian of Christian origins to discuss the composition of the New Testament, say, and such a discussion will be foreign and off putting to some adherents. In my *The Religious Experience of Mankind* I have tried to steer a middle path between the most radical theories and the self-understanding of the traditions.

But we cannot ultimately cancel out the tensions between at least some of the traditional or neo-traditional views of a religious heritage and the latest scholarly efforts at diagnosing the past. But we do not want to let these tensions get in the way of the study of world religions, and this raises the question: who is the reader?

Primarily we are thinking of the student, but students are a very variegated clientele, including as many ethnic groups and religious affiliations as the general public. Our descriptions of religion should therefore be sensitive and as acceptable as is possible (in conformity with scholarly opinion) to most educated adherents. Also, any general account is an approximation, and dissent from the classroom treatment of a tradition should be aired as far as possible. The students themselves may become resource persons for their own traditions and subtraditions. I have usually found that disagreements disappear to a great extent once it is seen that often an adherent is registering her own particular subtradition (or sub-subtradition).

Tied in with all this is the question of the normative account of a tradition. How are we to relate descriptive realism to the normative accounts given by believers, by the Church or other spokespersons? We have to note both sides. The fact that Christianity preaches "Love thy neighbor as thyself" does not at all entail that in Christian countries everyone loves one another. The news is full of such items as 'Christian militia,' 'Christian gunmen,' 'Buddhist resentment at the Tamils,' and so on. We have to include the ideal and the normative as part of the doctrinal and ethical dimensions of a religion, but exhibit some of the actualities as to the degree to which norms are fulfilled or not fulfilled as part of the historical and social description of the tradition. Again, self-understanding may clash with our sober assessments as scholars about the actual nature of a religion. Many modern writers are critical of the modern Hindu ideology which sees Hinduism as a unitary and yet plural system, and sees all religions as pointing to the same Truth. But there is no doubt that his perception of Hinduism, associated with such names as Vivekananda and Radhakrishnan, has proved a potent fore in the history of modern India.

So only up to a point is "the believer always right." But she remains the central focus of attention in the description of religious traditions.

Towards a Rounded View of Traditions

There is a danger, in modern Western treatments of religions, of being overintellectual and too cerebral—too oriented to doctrines, theologies and philosophical accounts, and too little concerned with the social and practical manifestations of religion. This in part stems from comparativists' traditional concern for texts. Because the Bible is important, it is often assumed, e.g. in seminary education, that it should be the main focus of study; and this notion has then been applied to other traditions than Christianity. It is readily thought that we can get at Buddhism through the Pali canonical texts; and at Hinduism through the Veda, Upanishads and Gita; and so on. One has first, however, to determine the place of texts in the other traditions and subtraditions—their importance and actual use. We must know the balance between liturgical, inspirational, intellectual and other uses. Here there is wide variegation among the traditions: The liturgical importance, for instance, of the Qur'an is vastly greater than that of the Pali canon, but two sets of texts are much more equal in their intellectual influence in the respective traditions.

It is obvious from a cursory observation of most religions that the inference from primary scriptures to actual religious practices, whether ancient or modern, is virtually impossible. A religion contains much more than the texts. Shankara's monism and Ramanuja's bhakti (devotional) theology are both based on the same Sanskrit authorities, interpreted differently, but we can scarcely infer from the Upanishads to the rich world of temples, holy men, washings, white-clad widows, hymns, cremations and so forth to be found along the river front, at Banaras. Many very different forms and denominations of Christianity are 'based' on the same New Testament.

So in describing a religion we need to have a rounded view. The contents of the scriptures may be important, but they need to be seen in a full living context. That context will include: (1) doctrines (e.g., the Trinity, the Buddhist doctrine of impermanence); (2) the sacred narratives or myths of the tradition (Christian 'salvation-history', the story of the Buddha Gautama); (3) the ethical and/or legal teachings (as in the Torah, the Shari'a, the Sermon on the Mount, etc.); (4) the ritual and practical side of a religion (the Mass, daily Muslim prayer, Buddhist prescriptions and practices of meditation); (5) the experiential and emotional side of a religion (the nature of devotion to Christ, Paul's religious conversion, the Buddha's enlightenment, and actions to attain nirvana); and (6) the social institutions in which a religion is embodied and the social relations in which it is embedded (the organization and role of the Church of Scotland, the Sangha in Sri Lanka, etc.). And as part of all this, or in addition, it is important to see something of a tradition's artifacts—the Cathedrals of medieval Christendom, the stupas and pagodas of Buddhism, and so on. Some traditions of course put much more emphasis on images and sacred buildings than others. Similarly there may be great variations in the importance attached to the various dimensions of religion listed above. Thus doctrinal and philosophical ideas are very evident in many forms of Buddhism, but are not very important in small-scale and until lately non-literate societies; sacred narrative is more central to Christianity than to Buddhism; ethics and law are more weighty in Judaism than in Shinto; ritual was more complex in pre-Vatican II than after, and is more vital in Catholicism than in Congregationalism; experience is more important for Zen than for orthodox Judaism; the social significance of Hinduism is and was more important than in Neoplatonism; and so on.

Some of the items are, of course, easier to get at in contemporary religions than ancient ones. It is difficult to envisage clearly the social context of Gnostic writings and we have little conception of the religious phenomena underlying a whole lot of older texts. But ancient phases of a religion may nevertheless be important for us, because in one way or another they are part of the consciousness of modern adherents. Also, there are extraordinary and once-powerful religions that need our attention even if they are now dead: they too are part of the spiritual history of the human race.

Terminological Matters and Problems of Comparison

Using such terms as 'theism,' 'liberation,' 'sacred text,' 'sacrifice,' 'mystical experience,' and 'denomination'—to take a few key terms somewhat at random—implies the validity of comparing phenomena from differing traditions (and subtraditions). Indeed it was the hope of many early practitioners of the field that comparative religion could be developed in parallel with such exercises as comparative anatomy and comparative physiology, and guide us to a theory of religious origins and development of religion. Though we may now be rather disillusioned with the older evolutionary assumptions underlying such an approach, the question of similar phenomena in divergent and culturally unrelated religions has an important human and theoretical significance: human, because it opens up religions, helping to prevent a narrow preoccupation with uniqueness, and makes dialogue possible and fruitful; and theoretical, for cross cultural resemblances may tell us something about human nature and the structure of experiential, ritual and other dimensions of the traditions.

The problem of comparisons lies chiefly in contextuality. Any given feature of or concept within a tradition lies within a context, and the context in some degree modifies its meaning. Thus the practice of spiritual meditation, together with breathing exercises, exists both in the Hindu and in the Eastern Orthodox traditions. But the judgments of the different cultures as to the point of meditation vary greatly. So we have here as often a case of similarity and dissimilarity combined; likeness of practice, but unlikeliness of meaning. The resemblance is by analogy. Indeed all general terms used cross culturally can be considered to a greater or lesser degree to be systematically ambiguous. But this should not inhibit us from using such terms, provided that we also remember the divergences of context.

Overwhelmingly the general terms used to classify religion are Western. It is however desireable to have a cross cultural vocabulary with which to talk across boundaries; partly to signal the end of the colonial period in Western religion. The comparativist has to make the familiar strange, as well as the strange familiar. Thus a kind of equality is established, so that we do not just see foreign religions as deviant. We used to presuppose that the main clientele for comparative religions courses is typically Western. This is no longer true—not only because the cross cultural study of religion is taken up in countries such as Nigeria, Sri Lanka and Japan; but also because of the mixed ethnic character in many classes in American and other Western universities. So we might begin to include such terms as bhakti, yoga, dharma, li (ceremonial), etc., in a new world wide cross cultural vocabulary.

Similar remarks apply to terminology sensitive to feminist concerns (without distorting the fact that often the traditional vocabulary of religions themselves—rather than the language of the comparative study of religion—is male-dominated).

Religions of the World

At the present time the globe is becoming integrated into a single economic system, and also to a great degree a single interacting cultural system—in effect a global city. The differing streams of history have flowed into a single river of world history.

In this single world, some broad areas are distinguishable: the North Atlantic, spanning North America and Western Europe, traditionally Christian but with a significant Jewish minority, and now partly secularized; Eastern Europe, the USSR, China, etc., namely the Marxist states with various religions overlain by a spectrum of Marxist orthodoxies; Old Asian countries such as Nepal, India, Sri Lanka, Burma, Thailand, Taiwan, South Korea, Japan—namely countries having important traditional ingredients such as Hinduism, Buddhism, Confucianism, etc.; the Islamic crescent from Indonesia, Malaysia, Bangladesh, Pakistan, Iran, the Arab countries to West Africa and South to the Sudan and Somalia; Latin American, with Hispanic and Portuguese Catholicism overlaying pre-Columbian civilizations and tribal groups, plus African elements in the Caribbean and Brazil; Black Africa, from the Sahara to the Cape, with a mixture of classical African religions, together with Christianity, Islam and new religions, together with Christianity; and Islam and new religious movements in the Pacific, largely Christianized, but with underlying Polynesian, Melanesian and other religions.

It is in the context of these regions that we need to look at the traditions in their various expressions. But we need also to remember that in a different age the arrangement of crucial regions would be different: for a long time Central Asia was an important area of religious and cultural exchange, and Europe in the time of the Roman Empire was divided north-south rather than east-west.

The regional analysis is important because it draws attention to the fact that our treatment of the traditions is often lopsided. For example, the treatment of Christianity deals typically with the Northern and Western varieties (Europe, America) and sometimes gravely underplays Eastern Orthodoxy, and even more the instantiation of Christianity in the South—in Latin America, Black Africa and the Pacific. Again, treatments of Islam usually deal more or less exclusively with Arab Islam. There is thus little treatment of Indonesian, other South-East Asian, South and West Asian Islam.

Also in the modern world so many people have migrated hither and thither that various significant diaspora have emerged, often influencing events 'at home.' So, Sikhs in Canada and Britain have affected events in the Punjab; and there are rich areas for reflection on the differing patterns of Hinduism in Guyana, Fiji, South Africa and so on; of Chinese religion in Malaysia, Indonesia, the U.S.A., etc.; of African religion in the Caribbean, Brazil, etc. Also in the U.S.A. and elsewhere, and especially in such areas as California and New York these diasporas represent great opportunities in teaching, as the world religions are there to be discovered. They represent, in their diaspora manifestation, stepping stones to their 'home' existence. It is thus easy to find in the U.S. groups of Hindus, Buddhists, Muslims, Jews, Eastern Orthodox Christian, new religious movements, Black religions, Hispanic Catholics and so on whose religions are less familiar to the majority of Americans. Provided one uses tact and generosity of spirit in approaching such groups it is possible to use these neighbors as 'teaching materials'. But I emphasize the importance of right attitudes in approaching these groups, for it is important, if you go to a service or meeting, that you are welcome and not overly intrusive.

The comparative study of religion also needs to take stock of the fact that ours is also an age of dialogue between religions, both within the traditions, as ecumenical movements develop within complex traditions long separated into different streams; but also between the major traditions. This dialogical aspect of inter-religious contact is important in that it stresses points of similarity and harmony, especially in regard to the experiential and ethical dimensions of religion. It is liable thus to suggest an important framework for the treatment, in courses, of the various religions, in terms of experiential overlap, i.e. in terms of the recurrence of patterns of experience—numinous, mystical and shamanistic, for instance, together with recurring patterns of attitudes and practices, such as bhakti and dhyana (devotion and meditation). So there are overlaps between Christian mysticism, Sufism and types of Indian Yoga; between Lutheran devotion, Islamic prayer and Ramanuja's religion; and so on. In any case, typology of religious phenomena will be a useful tool in organizing material drawn from the different religions and offers opportunities for reflection.

How far do Jewish and ancient Indian concepts of sacrifice converge? What are the various patterns of belief about the after-life? What are the likenesses and differences between the Christian concept of incarnation and Hindu ideas of avatara? What is the role of the female in the different ways of looking at the ultimate? What are the various kinds of religious specialists? Why is monasticism present so strongly in some religious traditions and not in others? What does lack of visible icons of God in some religions mean in relation to their proliferation elsewhere? What is the difference between Christian love and Buddhist compassion?

Many of these are difficult questions, but they begin to point towards reflection about the nature of the world's religions. Some of them are suggestive from the angle of the student's own thinking about her own approach to her tradition (or non-tradition). But they all help towards a deeper understanding of the religious factors underlying so much of human life and history.

THE "INTRODUCTION TO RELIGION" COURSE: THE TEMPLATE

William R. Darrow

The one-semester course designed to introduce the various dimensions of human religiousness is an increasingly common form. It is characterized by the presentation of a template of classificatory and interpretative categories useful for the understanding of religious expressions, however narrowly or broadly "the religious" is conceived. This type of course is dictated both by the needs of the undergraduate curriculum and by the field of religious studies. Undergraduate general education, for good or ill, has come to be founded upon such one-semester courses. Such courses are designed as introductions to the discourse of the fields of academic departments appropriate for pre- and non-majors. As introductions to the Bible or to theology and ethics have declined as suitable entry courses to the field of religious studies, varieties of template course forms have developed. The reason for this is partly because the sheer bulk of the material of human religiousness makes constructing a balanced and teachable one semester survey of world religions a most daunting task. But more positively, the template course has developed because there is in fact something of a consensus as to what the study of religion should involve, perhaps more of a consensus than many in the field have so far acknowledged.

Within the context of this project, the template courses to be sketched in what follows can be first approximated by contrasting them respectively with the survey, thematic and methodological courses that are discussed elsewhere in these volumes. Negatively put, the template course is not any of these. It is not a survey because it is not organized either in terms of geographical areas or traditions. In addition, it eschews any intention of full coverage of the history of any tradition. Rather the materials of human religiousness are employed as illustrations or case studies of the categories that constitute the template being developed.

Such a course might be seen as a type of thematic course. It necessarily approaches the materials with the same attitude of selectivity as does a thematic course. But here the organizing theme is a general notion of religion that operates at a level of abstraction higher than the thematic options described in the Harvard volume, accompanying this volume, although there is certainly an overlap with them. Finally, although firmly rooted in the issues of a methodological course, such an approach usually pays little attention to the intellectual genealogies of the ideas employed or to the disciplinary and interdisciplinary consciousness that is the focus of a methodological course.

This essay will begin with a treatment of the problems of placing and imaging religion. In many ways, the issues connected with these problems form the agenda of such a course. My purpose here is to gain a modicum of clarity and precision concerning some of these issues. No resolution of them is proposed or is possible. Rather it is the function of the instructor to position himself or herself within the range of issues and options and then to construct a course consistent with the positions taken. Following an initial consideration of the concepts of religion and religiousness, this essay will briefly catalog some of the classificatory and interpretative categories such as religious experience, myth, symbol, ritual, community, and spiritual transformation that might form a template. The third part of this essay will then raise in question-form a set of issues to be decided in structuring such a course. There then follow at the end of this volume two very different syllabi and a list of the more common textbooks that develop a template model.

The Placing of Religion

The development of religious studies in liberal arts colleges and state universities since the Second World War has been predicated on three assumptions that have important implications for thinking about a general introduction to religion course. These assumptions are the difference between theological and religious study; the principle of non-reductionism; and the formation of categories.

Religious studies is defined as an academic study different from theological study. It thus could be argued to have a legitimate place within a secular academic institution. The actual difference between academic and theological study has never been convincingly demonstrated. It is probably better to read this firm differentiation as a piece of American civil religion made necessary politically to secure religious studies safely within academia. Emphasizing norms of objectivity and the avoidance of overt confessional apologetics has been widespread, but a good deal of exciting constructive theological speculation has in fact been conducted within the context of religious studies. The eventual result of this new context of doing theology still remains to be charted, but certainly for our purposes the claim to a radical distinction between the study of religion and theology, while perhaps politically necessary, is disingenuous and counterproductive for three reasons. First, it discourages creative theological construction. Second, it disguises theological assumptions that inform religious studies. Finally, this problematic differentiation tends to downplay the cognitive dimension of religious expression in ways that tie into the strong anti-rationalist currents in post-Enlightenment Western philosophy.

The second assumption that informs religious studies is that of non-reductionism. This is the most significant disguised theological assumption undergirding religious studies. Religion is claimed to be a *sui generis* and irreducible part of human life, or, alternatively religiousness is represented as being an irreducible aspect of human experience. On the face of it, both these positions can be argued to be too deeply mired in the history of Europe and America to be of much use in a cross-cultural perspective. The fact that we have a separate religious institution in Western society needs to be explained by a careful survey of the political and social history of Western civilization. It is by no means clear how useful it is to generalize this experience to other cultures, either small or large, past or present. The fact that we want to consider religiousness to be a separate sphere of human experience needs to be explained by a survey of philosophical anthropology in the West, especially since Kant displaced theology from pure to practical reason and Schleiermacher placed religiousness within an autonomous sphere of human experience. Human beings are seen as religious animals, as well as political, social, rational, working animals. The theological purposes behind establishing an autonomous religious sphere had much to do with securing legitimacy for liberal Christian theology in the modern world, but for the general study of religion this affirmation has provided an overarching category that causes all sorts of conceptual difficulties. We are bedeviled by how we might recognize religion and we engage in silly debates as to whether any number of denominated "isms" are or are not religion. We are puzzled why the Chinese have three religions and why modern or profane humanity seems to have none. These debates are interesting but their substantive hermeneutical implications are only coincidentally greater insight into what we are trying to interpret. The primary benefit of such debates is to underline the limitations inherent in the starting concept of religion about which these debates swirl.

The assumption of non-reductionism also presents two further problems. What sense are we to make of the psychoanalytic and Marxist critiques of religion? Are they to be catalogued as alternatives, subsumed under a general category of possible approaches in a kind of repressive tolerance of interdisciplinary approaches, but dismissed on the rather flimsy ground that they are reductionist. If so, it becomes difficult to take these stances seriously. It also becomes, in a not unrelated way, difficult for non-reductionism to take self-critique within religious communities seriously. There is much about the assumption of non-reductionism that implicitly posits the expectation of a functionalist equilibrium, that religious symbols and rituals will always work to secure the social and cultural order. There will be no internal criticism within religious communities or criticisms of society based upon religious presuppositions. Both doubt and critique are not easily handled as religious phenomena on the assumption of non-reductionism. But without these it is impossible to make sense of the central datum of religious history: change.

The third assumption of religious studies concerns the usefulness of establishing categories of analysis that allow for the classification of "religious" data. Here the most prominent features of the tradition of the phenomenology of religion connected with figures such as Van der Leeuw, Kristensen, Wach and Eliade dominates, and it is from this tradition that the elements of the template developed in a religion course of the sort under consideration commonly derive. Several aspects of the analytical categories in question should be noted. First, the categories focus attention upon modes of expression and behavior typical of "religious" men and women. The structure of the symbolic content of the material is the object of attention. Religion is seen mainly as something humans do or enact. The cognitive dimensions of religion and systematic reflection are given much less attention. This is consistent with the starting point constructed in opposition to theological endeavor discussed above, but also has a vaguely pernicious anti-intellectualist agenda behind it. Secondly, much as is the case with the term "religion" itself, these categories strive to be culturally neutral although they are not. For example, 'the action of the Sacred in revealing itself' (in Eliade's formulation) or 'the experience of the encounter with the Holy' (in the sense that Otto used it) are formulations that do not have an immediate place in the context of Christian discourse, but the roots of these ways of talking still have profound resonance with Christian notions of revelation and experience. Notions of revelation, experience and en-counter are of limited cross-cultural value. Finally, these categories are appropriately seen as ideal types and thus of wide validity, yet when il-lustrative examples are sought, there is a tendency to highlight "simpler" societies where purer forms of the categories are found. This means that the materials dealt with are likely to be from small-scale societies and there may be a rather crude cultural evolutionism lurking within the categories. The student may be left wondering what the relevance of the categories are for his/her own self-understanding, especially when the inexorable processes of secularization and modernization are seen as making religious life impossible in the contemporary world.

Such are some of the dilemmas attendant upon the concept of reli-gion. All of these difficulties should be seen as a challenge to the instruc-tor in formulating his/her course rather than a debilitating handicap making the study of religion impossible.

The Image of Art and Analogy of Language

We have so far considered some of the issues inherent in taking reli-gion or religiousness as an object of study. Within the study there is a major division between those who would underline that it is 'religion' we study versus those who would call it 'religiousness'. We may refer to the first stance as cultural/linguistic and the second as experien-tial/expressive.[1] This distinction is complicated. Most people lie on the spectrum between these two extreme positions. Those who focus upon religion tend to employ the analogy of language. There are several fea-tures to this position. The object of study lies in a space between the gen-eral category of language (there is no language, only languages) and the actual expressions of individual speakers. While there is no such thing as language in the abstract, the fact that human languages exhibit general structural similarities makes the formulation of a systematic portrait of what a language looks like possible. It is possible by comparative analy-sis to survey the whole range of possible linguistic forms and then to document which are used in any particular language. It is also possible to formulate certain general expectations about the nature of linguistic production, meaning and change and to investigate how these general expectations are manifested in particular languages. Those who view religion on the analogy of a language emphasize the structural and sys-

---

[1]Lindbeck, George A., *The Nature of Doctrine: Religion and Theology in a Postliberal Age* (Philadelphia: Westminster Press, 1984).

tematic nature of religious traditions and place them within a cultural context. They might give special emphasis to the respect in which such systems are fabricated, created systems of meaning and values within a culture. Also, they might emphasize that as fabrications, in the sense of being lies, these systems are signs that only represent, and can never make the meaning and value present and fully real.[2] In the gap between the signifiers of the system and the absent signified, the power of symbolization arises.

Those who view religion on the analogy of art are more inclined to view religious expressions as products of religious persons. From the cultural/linguistic stance they may be said to be focusing on the actual speech of language speakers rather than the language. Their task is to elucidate the meaning/intention that lies behind an expression. For them, the category of religious experience tends to play a significant interpretative role. Expressions are seen as arising from a certain experience on the part of a religious persons which is available for recreation within the experience of encountering and interpreting a religious expression. As with certain trends within the interpretation of art, there is likely to be a strong emphasis on the virtuoso, acknowledgement of genius and evaluative judgments according to various criteria. The special place of the religious specialist, mystic, priest or shaman is highlighted. The social and cultural contexts of religion are usually given secondary emphasis and the cognitive stands potentially opposed to the individual religious creativity of the virtuoso. The governing assumption is that there is the possibility of sympathetically 'getting into the head' of the religious person with a confidence that there is something in that head that can be gotten into. Connected with this stance is the notion that it is primarily at the level of the individual that meaning is constructed. Such a stance is construed as being able to challenge the student very effectively in constructing meaning for him/herself.

Categories

We now turn to a brief delineation of some of the standard categories that usually appear within a template course. These are taken from the phenomenology of religion as set forth in the handbooks of Van der Leeuw, Wach, Widengren, Kristensen and Eliade. My purpose will be no more than to focus on certain issues that arise in the treatment of these

---

[2]A formulation most recently made by Jonathan Z. Smith in the context of this project in June, 1985 in Berkeley, California.

categories. Naturally the instructor will select and focus on those which most interest him/her. The template created by these categories is reflected in the first course syllabus that I have included in the end of this volume (syllabus #III). These categories are of a general nature. Many of the themes discussed more extensively in the Harvard volume provide other categories of cross-cultural comparison that should be added to those discussed here.

Sacred and Holy These two categories developed rather independently to denominate the transcendental referent of religion. The sacred may be seen as generally a cultural/linguistic concept, signifying a referent defined dialectically as the opposite of the profane. As such it is a notion that stresses the classificatory network that religious systems predicate. This is its use for Durkheim. For Eliade it becomes itself a source of all power of meaning and in fact an actor. In this Eliade moves closer to the other great name for the transcendent, the Holy, first made standard by Otto, who focused his attention on the experiential encounter with the power of the holy as the starting point of religious expression.

Symbolism A notion of symbol is central to religious studies. There are several standard features of the definition of a symbol within the field. First, symbols are usually contrasted with signs in that symbols are seen as participating more fully in the signified to which they point. In addition, the paradox of the symbol (that it cannot fully be that which it signifies) establishes a further dimension, a tension between what the symbol is, a rock like a bunch of other rocks, and a sacred rock. Third, and finally, the comparative study of actual uses of a symbol allows the development of a lexicon of connotations of a symbol which enriches the interpretation of a specific symbol.

Myth The notion of myth emphasizes the role of narrative in the creation of meaning. Through the story of creation the ordering of a world is represented. The notion of narrative has received significant attention in the field in the past years and work on story and narrative within the theological and literary critical contexts has come to inform the way students of religion read their mythical texts, significantly broadening what might count as myth. In developing the notion of story recently the role of sacred biography has expanded the notion of myth from stories of divine beings to include stories also of normative lives of human beings.

Ritual The other part of the great pair of myth and ritual, the notion of ritual, i.e. the performance or enactment of ritual truth, has recently eclipsed the centrality of myth. Influenced by discussions in anthropology and sociology, ritual has come to take center stage in much contemporary work in religious studies. Rituals can be broadly divided into two categories, rites of passage and rites of recreation. The first category include individually focused rituals of initiation, marriage, and death for example. The latter include seasonal celebrations and sacrifice.

Cosmology The creation and ordering of the world achieved by myth and ritual is cosmology. Cosmologies have both a temporal and spatial dimension and the worlds of meaning created are thus situated both on a distinction in time and in space.

Eschatology Eschatology is the counterpart of cosmology. It addresses the meaning both of individual mortality and that of evil and suffering as well as the end of the world itself. Here especially the beliefs about the nature and meaning of the individual self, its relation to the body and to the community are developed.

Religious Experience The notion of religious experience is central to the experiential/expressive side of approaches to the study of religion discussed above. It stresses the states of ecstasy, non-ordinary reality, or other experiences typical of states achieved after spiritual disciplines. These experiences which stand behind certain expressions are what make such an expression 'religious'.

Sacred Personages The classification of sacred personages involves recognizing the social dimension of religion. The development of ideal types of religious actors such as priests, prophets, shamans, divine kings, ascetics and mystics and their use in the elucidating of particular instances of religious actors provides rich areas of potential cross-cultural comparisons.

Spiritual Transformation The important role of spiritual disciplines of various sorts within most religious traditions provides the need for a heuristic set of concepts to classify and define what might also be called the mystical dimension. The variety of techniques used both in the past and in the present to attain special states of grace are a rich and popular area of investigation.

Religious Communities Typologies of religious communities draw the investigator in the study of the sociology of religion. The typology of different societies and the description of different types of religious institutions within individual societies form the content here. Also of significance here is the encounter between different religious communities over time and their transformation.

Classification of Religions Here taking religious traditions as comparable entities, criteria by which different religious traditions can be classified and modes found to articulate the particular ethoi of individual religious traditions are constructed. For example, doctrinal distinctions between monotheistic and polytheistic or universal vs. ethnically based form the foundations of possible classificatory schemes.

Decisions Checklist

This introduction has raised a number of issues that require decisions in the construction of a course along the lines of the template approach under consideration. The problems in many ways should form the content of the course, but it is worthwhile establishing a checklist of questions to be answered by the individual instructor both within the context of his/her own interests and in the general context of the department and institution in which the course is offered.

1. Is religion to be treated as an irreducible aspect of human culture or experience?

A course that attempts to confirm the irreducible nature of religious expression or experience will be structured quite differently from one that attempts to leave this question to the side and focus instead on the fabrication of meaning and value systems in human community.

2. Where is the course situated on the experience/expressive vs. cultural/linguistic dichotomy?

It is important to stress that this question is separate from the first, although there tends to be a elective affinity between the irreducibility notion and that of expressive/experiential and alternatively between the cultural/linguistic and reductionist positions.

3. What is the stance taken toward theological reflection?

Whether the cognitive content of religion is focused upon depends much on whether constructive theological reflection is seen as a central religious activity or as in some way an aberration. This is an area where the activity of the department is important. If constructive theological work is being conducted, then an introductory course, which is always and quite correctly an introduction to a specific department, should be in the course.

4. Upon what materials will the course draw? Will the focus be one culture or tradition? If not, what background is necessary to provide sufficient context for understanding the material?

This raises the pedagogical problem of movement between disparate sets of materials. To do the creation myths of Genesis, the Maori, and the Winnebago is to leave the student and instructor with a dangerous sense of geographical and cultural vertigo. How much background should be given and does the need to provide background limit the number of sources from which to draw materials?

5. What highlighting will there be of the notion of primary texts?

This question is independent of the last, but connected with it. In addition to the problem of context, there are at least two problems connected with the use of primary texts. The first is that the notion of sacred text is overly emphasized. Studying a description of a ritual, or even better acting one out, may be more useful than studying the text that is recited along with a ritual. Second, if the focus is on primary texts then it is the responsibility of the teacher to alert students to some of the content of critical exegetical readings of most major religious texts. It is difficult to read the Book of Job or the Bhagavad Gita as integral works without at least a nod to their text-histories. Especially if other courses in the department use exegetical methods, groundwork for them should be laid in an introductory course.

6. What sort of practicum might be built into the course?

Involving students in observation or construction brings issues alive. At the very least, use of films and visits to art museums are vital. Visits to religious communities and observation of services are also rewarding. In the area of ritual studies, focus upon apparently non-religious rituals such as modes of meeting people, or ritual insults in a dorm setting can be very effective. To borrow from Mark Juergensmeyer, the actual creation of a religion as a small group project is a very effective strategy.

7. Is there some set of texts, materials or traditions that needs to be covered?

This is also a departmental question. While it would be wrong, given the nature of undergraduate education to think of such an introductory course as designed for majors, it also is important to decide if there are materials with which instructors in more specialized courses might ideally like their students to be acquainted.

8. What attention will be given to the fact of religious change?

There is always a danger given the analytic and generally synchronic focus of such a course of paying insufficient attention to how and why religions change and to the fact that religious traditions are constantly in flux. Attention to the rise of religious movements such as Buddhism and Islam partly addresses this, but leaves the student with the impression that only momentous change matters and that it only occurred sometime long ago. Some attention to the reality of dispute, new formulations and new movements in a tradition seems highly desirable as a way of stressing the religious creativity of each generation.

9. What modes of classification of different religious traditions will be employed?

Will they be divided e.g. by size, historical significance, notions of the ultimate, styles of religious life? Will variety within individual traditions be stressed and for what purpose?

THE "INTRODUCTION TO RELIGIOUS STUDIES" COURSE

Mark Juergensmeyer

One of the most interesting ways to introduce the subject of religion is to introduce the ways in which religion has been studied. Such a course also serves handily to show how religious studies are linked with other areas of the liberal arts. Unfortunately, this course is often pigeon-holed as the "methodology" requirement designed for long-suffering religious studies majors, and it is sometimes thought of as a solely cerebral enterprise in which abstract models of analysis are juxtaposed and scarcely a nod is given to the vivid and interesting subject matter of religion itself.

It is true that a course on the study of religion focusses on ideas and intellectual perspectives. But in doing so it need not neglect the descriptive materials to which they refer. Although this course should cover the major approaches to the study of religion found under the rubrics of the anthropology of religion, sociology of religion, history and phenomenology of religion, philosophy of religion, and the like, it need not be dull.

The first year I was saddled with teaching this course I found it plodding, but it came to be one of my favorites. I found that the subject matter had some special strengths. The ideas presented in this course can challenge some of the basic assumptions students have about objectivity and truth, and the way these notions are thought to be incorporated into modern scholarship. The religious outlook and the perspectives of the academic disciplines are sufficiently different that a comparison of the two points of view, or an encounter between them, can yield interesting results. Each may illuminate the other. By employing the insights of theoretical points of view, examples of religious myths and symbols can be shown to be more intricate and meaningful than they might initially have appeared. And by using the subject matter of religion as the test by which we evaluate a range of analytic perspectives, the assumptions and limitations of those disciplinary approaches can be more easily examined. Religion can be the case study for what is essentially a survey and analysis of some of the major fields within the liberal arts.

Why is this course being taught?

The first questions to ask in designing such a course is what it is intended to do for the student and how it will fit in the existing religious studies and liberal arts curricula. My suggestion is to think big: design a course that will appeal to students from a variety of disciplinary backgrounds, even if the justification for having the course is to provide religious studies majors with a survey of theoretical approaches to the subject. The religious studies majors will profit from having testy young Freudians and reductionist structural anthropologists in the crowd. Optimally, this course might be offered as an upper division seminar. Even though it is an introductory course in theory, it might be better if a previous course in comparative religion is required.

But there are also other possibilities. This course could serve as the lecture course introducing the field of religious studies in general. And it could be an exciting introduction at that, especially if students discover how problematic a subject religion is for some disciplines, and how inevitably it touches on almost all areas of academic life. The problem for beginning students is that some attention has to be given to the subject matter itself, otherwise the course may wander in the air. There are various ways to deal with this. If theories of ritual are what are being discussed, then examples of ritual might well be treated at the same time; or the whole course could begin with a case study (a field trip to a local synagogue or church, for instance) that would set the context for the discussion of theory. For students with no background in comparative religion at all, I have recommended brief introductory textbooks, such as Huston Smith's *The Religions of Man*, or Wilfred Cantwell Smith's *The Faith of Other Men*. It is important for students to have some sense of the history and diversity of religious experience before they set out to discover how it has been dissected, categorized, analyzed and explained. Since theorists often treat religion as a one-dimensional thing, such background is sorely needed.

Should you include the historical development of religious studies?

The most common way of teaching the introductory course in the study of religion is to parade one theory after another without much attempt to connect them together. A danger of this smorgasbord approach is giving the impression that these theories are static things and that they have existed forever, when actually they were products of certain moments in the historical development of ideas. Often these were moments when religion was undergoing great change, so by presenting these ideas from a historical perspective, students may be challenged to see how theory and subject interact. If the course as a whole is to be organized by discipline—anthropology of religion, philosophy of religion, and so forth—it might be useful to begin with several sessions devoted to showing how the by now familiar disciplines of the social sciences and humanities emerged in the last century. At the same time one would want to show how the study of religion emerged from its roots in Jewish scholarship and Christian theology. Then one could chart the historical development of religious studies as a field, looking at the various theoretical writings within their historical and intellectual contexts. I know of no textbook that approaches the study of religion this way, but useful background material may be found in Ninian Smart, et al., *19th Century Religious Thought in the West* (in 3 vols), and Claude Welch's *19th Century Protestant Thought*, especially his chapter on the history of religions. The article by Robert Bellah on "The Sociology of Religion" reprinted in his *Beyond Belief* gives a good sense of the intellectual climate surrounding the emergence of social scientific approaches to the study of religion in the late nineteenth century, and other historical overviews are provided in the essays in Joseph M. Kitagawa, ed., *The History of Religions*.

What theories should be included?

There are many other ways to organize the course besides the smorgasbord and historical approaches. One option is to design a course that focuses on enduring questions of religion. Existential questions such as "what is my real self?" and "what is my purpose in life?" will provide access to studies in theology and philosophy of religion. Questions such as "who are my people?" and "who can I trust?" touch on concerns appropriate to the sociology and anthropology of religion; similar questions lead naturally to the work done in other fields of religious studies.

A criticism often made of the historical approach is that it brings in more extraneous material than introductory students can handle, and the "enduring questions" approach might be faulted for seeming to imply that the best theories are those that answer undergraduate students' questions about life. For these reasons many teachers have returned to the smorgasbord in the interest of serving the widest spread of intellectual tastes.

Regardless of how the course is organized, the heart of it is the exposition of major theoretical positions in the study of religion. But which ones are major? At this point there is no way to escape subjective judgment, and each course will be different depending on the intellectual preferences of the teacher. I have formulated my own list of "musts"— disciplinary fields, seminal thinkers, and specific works to be discussed—which are listed at the end of this sourcebook and which appear in some form whenever I teach this course. (For a sample syllabus based on this approach, see syllabus # V at the end of this book, and the bibliographic essay, "Basic Readings in the Academic Study of Religion.") I tend to include a bit of everything in my syllabuses, but I also know of many excellent courses where only a handful of theorists provide the focus. Even if this "major thinkers" approach is adopted, however, one will want to make reference to other influential theories in each field. The point is to introduce the study of religion in such a way as to show that the issues that theorists grapple with are real: they emerge from personal and historical contexts, and those who deal with them encounter the great intellectual currents of their times.

II

Thinking About the Traditions

THE PROS AND CONS OF THINKING OF RELIGION AS TRADITION

Ninian Smart

It has become a tradition to teach world religions as traditions—entities spoken of as Buddhism, Hinduism, Sikhism, Christianity, Islam and so forth. As we shall see, there are some advantages to this format. But it can attract some obvious and important criticisms.

(1) These names are modern, and for the most part Western ones, and may give the impression of a unitary 'something' when this is not warranted. This is perhaps clearest in regard to Hinduism, which from another point of view is a loose federation of different motifs, movements and cults.

(2) The terminology of "-isms" concentrates too much on beliefs and does not do sufficient justice to the practical, social, ritual character of religious phenomena.

(3) In some areas, the traditions analysis seems to get replaced routinely by regional analysis: e.g. with Chinese and African religions. These are treated as regional, and the task of tracing separate traditions is at least in part abandoned. The case is likewise with such ancient constructs as Greek and Ancient Mesopotamian religion.

(4) The tracing of traditions tends to underestimate regional and other cultural differences: so Sunni Islam, for instance, comes out much more monolithic than the facts, from Morocco to Indonesia, would warrant.

(5) Even where internal variety is admitted there is a tendency to deal with conventional subtraditions—e.g. Christianity and its Roman Catholicism, Eastern Orthodoxy and Protestantism. Obviously, the problems associated with *traditions* also relates to the analysis of *subtraditions*.

(6) Since traditions become easily identified with what is normative or is thought to be normative for the traditions, deviant forms of religion,

e.g. Christian 'heresies,' tend to get undervalued as to their actual power and place in history.

(7) The very idea of a "tradition" may be modeled on the example of Christianity, which incorporates the notion of a continuing Church or community of believers. In a number of cases this model, especially if we think of the centralized mode of Roman Catholic organization, is seriously misleading. Though it may work up to a point with Buddhism, since the Sangha is a core organization having an analogical resemblance to the Church, there is no such counterpart in Hinduism. Religions differ widely in their organizational unity, whether theoretical or actual.

(8) It may be argued that though there are, as W.C. Smith has stated, 'cumulative traditions,' the quality of individual faith and experience is more important. In being drawn to a traditions analysis we may be involving ourselves too much with externals and too little with the 'essence' of religion.

(9) If we look upon the study of religion as concerned among other things with the delineation of worldviews, then when it comes to the crunch every person has her own individual slant on life: so there are in effect four billion worldviews to consider, and writing in terms of traditions is from this point of view a gross simplification.

(10) Treatment of religions in terms of traditions may isolate them from neighboring phenomena. The story of Judaism cannot be told except as intricately interwoven with the stories of Christianity and Islam: nor the story of Indian Buddhism without the story of Hindu, Jain and various other religious and cultural developments. Yet often we have books treating the traditions in relative isolation.

In Defense of "Traditions"

Despite the above problems, there are some important things to be said on the other side, in defense of the tradition of traditions analysis.

(1) In regard to the point that the names—the "-isms"—are modern and that Westerners have in effect 'invented' the religions: whatever the truth of this diagnosis (and it works better with some traditions than with others—e.g. the existence of the Sanskrit term *bauddha* for followers of the Buddha shows that there was long a functional equivalent of the modern term 'Buddhist'), modern religions tend to acknowledge the names. Even if Hinduism is a modern invention, (invented, incidentally, by Western educated Indians such as Vivekananda and Radhakrishnan), it is accepted as an entity by many Hindus today. Other 'invented' reli-

gions such as African religion are being increasingly recognized by their relevant indigenous constituencies.

(2) It is true that the language of '-isms' may sometimes lead us to concentrate too much on the belief aspect of religion, but this need not be the case. Moreover, in the modern period we have the interplay between religions and modern ideologies such as nationalism, Marxism, liberal democracy, etc., leading to an increased intellectualization of religious content. So a comparison of ideas may be useful after all.

(3) There is increased interest in regional analysis, and this represents an alternative to a more strictly traditions approach. There are advantages to treating religions in a single political or cultural milieu: consider courses on religion in American, Chinese religions, Japanese religions, etc. But even in such cases traditions may be important: e.g. Buddhism in China has backward connections to Buddhism in Central Asia and India, and forward connections to Korea and Japan. These connections are important for some developments of Far Eastern Buddhism, and ought not to be neglected in a right regard for the integrity of Chinese religions (i.e. the so-called 'three religions' of China can be looked at also as one interactive thing, namely Chinese religion).

(4) Some of the defects of simplicity mentioned earlier might be cured by a stress on the plural character of each tradition, its regional variations and diversity of schools or movements. We need also to tackle the problem, of which more later on, of the use from within a tradition of a normative perception of the tradition as a unity. A tradition may be actually varied, but seen as a unity. This is part of the wider problem of the relationship between realistic descriptions and normative conceptions in the history of religions.

(5) Regarding the question of individual pieties and the 'four billion worldviews' in relation to the more simplified concept of traditions, of course there are variations of individual belief, commitment and practice, but they are often defined by reference to publicly available traditions of subtraditions. One must recognize that for the most part religious movements are socially manifested as institutions. Where, however, the quantity of data is so enormous, there is an advantage in appropriate simplification. So in this respect the delineation of traditions serves as the use of ideal types of worldviews, patterns of practice, etc.

We can avoid some of the problems of oversimplification by making use of the plural of the "-isms"—Buddhisms, Judaisms, Christianities, etc.—in order to remind ourselves of the internal pluralism of the labeled traditions. Moreover, it is possible, while retaining talk of the traditions, to treat them also on a regional basis, e.g. South-East Asia, Japan, Black Africa, etc.

So, though there are valid criticisms of older ways of dealing with the traditions, the concept of traditions analysis is not without merit and there are conveniences in adopting this approach in introductory courses on world religions.

In general the modern world rightly or wrongly sees religions as distinct traditions. In some degree the religions themselves have adopted the categories of Western historians, orientalists and missionaries, tending to model non-Christian religions on the example of Christianity. So the comparative study of religions becomes in a way self-verifying. Organizations like the World Fellowship of Buddhists reinforce the ecumenical solidarity of Buddhists and therefore the idea of a unitary and identifiable thing called Buddhism; and so on with analogous movements in other traditions. Modern travel makes it much easier to travel to Mecca and for the Pope (himself a traveling Mecca) to visit many regions of the world which would have been virtually inaccessible a couple of generations earlier. Such forces of easy communication help to solidify both traditions and subtraditions.

From these perspectives it is probable that we shall continue to need courses which cover the traditions, or at least some selection of them. The following essays discuss some of the issues that should be considered when each of these traditions are included in an introductory course.

TEACHING THE HINDU TRADITION

John Stratton Hawley

Christians and Jews, even those relatively seasoned in ecumenical affairs, often have difficulty knowing quite what to make of Hinduism. A recent encounter in that most ecumenical of places, the Cathedral of St. John the Divine, illustrated the point for me. It was Pentecost, and Dean Morton, the man chiefly responsible for opening St. John's to an involvement with adherents of faiths, was speaking about the outpouring of the Holy Spirit that he had experienced at a world day of prayer convened by the Pope in Assisi. To hear him tell it, just about everyone was there: the Pope himself, the Archbishop of Canterbury, the Head Rabbi of Israel, the head of the Buddhists, the head of the Hindus—a great day indeed, and one could hardly fault Dean Morton's enthusiasm in recalling it. Only one caveat: the last two figures do not exist.

Hinduism lacks a single authoritative figure—even one whose centrality is confirmed by being disputed, as the Pope's is—and that fact gives an important hint about the shape (or shapelessness) of the Hindu tradition as a whole. For all their attention to hierarchy, it is uncharacteristic for Hindus to array themselves in a single hierarchical order—so uncharacteristic that there used to be some very unpleasant scuffles every twelve years when the occasion demanded it. The issue was who got to be the first to bathe at the point where the holy Ganges joins her sister divinity, the River Jumna, and a third river, the invisible Sarasvati, at the auspicious astrological moment that serves at the focus of the Great Kumbh Mela in Prayag. It took a decision handed down by the British colonial court to resolve the matter, and although current participants still follow the rank order that the British established, few would agree that it is a true representation of the relative authority of major Hindu leaders and organizations.

Similarly, while Hindus emphasize the importance of submitting oneself to a teaching authority (a guru—literally, a "heavy") they have little interest in specifying a single line of teaching authority that ought to be embraced by all. As Diana Eck has recently put it,

> ...for Hindus, matters of great importance are thought of, quite naturally, not in the singular, but in the plural. Singularity is not at all the sign and signal that something is significant. On the contrary, if something is truly significant, it is significant enough to be repeated, duplicated, seen from many angles.[1]

The effect of this is plain: if ever there was an "ism" that isn't an "ism," Hinduism is it. So whatever we teach when we teach Hinduism, it ought not be an "ism."[2] Hinduism has no central authority, no unifying scripture, no verbal formula to which all its adherents give regular assent. The rite of initiation that makes a loose community of many male Hindus—investiture with the sacred thread—extends only to members of the upper castes, and these days is honored in the breach even by most of them. The very word "Hindu," in fact, is an outsider's word, and until recently was not a term that Hindus themselves felt comfortable in using. The term "Hindu" is really just a permutation of the name of the Indus River, and was originally used by travellers from the West to refer to anyone who lived near or beyond the Indus. It was a geographical or at best cultural designation, not one that referred to a system of doctrine or a well-articulated tradition. "Hinduism," in its origins, was just India-ism, and the ethnographies written by visitors from afar were quick to point out the remarkable array of differences they met in travelling through the Indian subcontinent.

Yet we still speak of Hinduism as a unified entity, and most scholars have held that even if "it" fails the tests that might appropriately be applied to define one of the religious traditions that originated in the Near East, it still has a coherence that separates Hindus from other religious people. In teaching Hinduism, our problem is how to present this necessarily elusive coherence without bending too much to our own systematic habits of mind or, even more powerfully, to our students' demand for what is usually called "good organization." "Isms" are the convenience food of the intellectual industry—its containerized cargo—

---

[1] D. Eck, "Darsana and Incarnational Theology," *Harvard Divinity Bulletin* 17:2 (1986), 10-11.

[2] Cf. Wilfred Cantwell Smith, *The Meaning and End of Religion* (New York: Macmillan, 1962).

and it is very hard to operate without them. How can we do so in studying Hinduism?

The Historical Approach

Oddly, one way of doing this is to take what is to Westerners the most familiar approach of all: the historical one. With India, the span of time involved is so long, and the range of material so wide, that a sense of the diversity of the Hindu tradition is bound to emerge even as the student is prodded into seeing elements of continuity that tie it together. Many texts can be used to buttress such an approach, among which perhaps the best known is Thomas Hopkin's *The Hindu Religious Tradition*. K. M. Sen's Penguin paperback, called simply *Hinduism*, also takes a basically historical approach, but prefaces it with a section in which the author attempts to isolate the integrative "Nature and Principles of Hinduism." A.L. Basham's *The Wonder That Was India* is another example of a hybrid approach with an historical base, but this time the hybridization is more ambitious, including politics, society, daily life, and the arts.

One of the difficulties with the historical approach, unfortunately, is that one inevitably begins at the beginning. All too easily one falls prey to what Wilfred Cantwell Smith has called the "originist" fallacy: one supposes that things are best explained by showing where they came from. This means that the earlier centuries—particularly those in which the first great religious texts appear—tend to receive a proportionately greater emphasis than more recent ones. In Hopkin's book, for example, the second to last chapter is called "Late Puranic Religion: The Full Tradition." The subtitle indicates the importance of the period, which begins in about the fifth century C.E. and extends to the nineteenth, but to call it "late" indicates where the writer's emphasis has fallen nonetheless. Fourteen centuries is a long time to compress into a single chapter, and after that is achieved only one short chapter on the modern period remains.

Basham's title, *The Wonder That Was India*, would seem to indicate that he too succumbed to the originist disease, for he concludes with "the coming of the Muslims," as he explains in the subtitles. Actually the reason for this truncation is that the book was originally commissioned for a series conceived in nostalgic "wonder that was" terms. Basham is not, therefore, culpable; the remarkable thing is that so many readers have found the scope of his survey perfectly adequate to the task of introducing Indian civilization and its religious component.

The "originist" problem is a serious one in the study of Hinduism—
so serious that several scholars have refused to apply the term Hinduism
to anything more than about two millennia old. Their feeling is that if
one goes back farther than that, one enters a world in which the patterns
of social organization, the canons of religious thought and practice, and
the gods themselves are so different from the "India-ism" visible in more
recent centuries that one cannot rightly designate them by a single name.
The "originist" offenders are not just Western scholars but Indians themselves, who particularly since the nineteenth century, have emphasized
the Vedic roots of their own religious heritage. In part this is a response
to Western classicism and biblicism, but the fact remains that among
Hindus scarcely anyone studies the Vedas.[3]

If one bases one's teaching approach on a textbook like Hopkin's,
then, one would be well advised to supplement it with other materials
that provide some balance—especially by presenting Hinduism as it has
looked in recent centuries. Two possible sources are Philip Ashby's *Modern Trends in Hinduism* and Lawrence A. Babb's *Redemptive Encounters*.
Both books survey communities that have come to the fore in Hindu life
since the nineteenth century. Another possibility is *Songs of the Saints of
India*, by Mark Juergensmeyer and myself, a book that introduces six
poet saints whose legacy has been pivotal in establishing the tone and
organization of religious life in North India over the last five hundred
years.

The Ethnographic Approach

Ethnographic studies of the Hindu world aim at interpreting the
Hindu universe as it seems from the inside, and can be used to supplement or even replace the historical approach to Hinduism. The difficulty
of using ethnographies in an introductory class, however, is that so few
of them dare to extrapolate from a particular village to India at large. An
array of village studies is available, of which my favorite is perhaps the
Wisers' *Behind Mud Walls*, but for good reason none of them pretends to
describe Hindu life as lived throughout the subcontinent—a notoriously
diverse phenomenon.

Two books stand out as exceptions. One is L.A. Babb's *The Divine
Hierarchy*. Babb uses his field experience in the Chattisgarh region of
east-central India as the basis for generating a picture of "Hinduism" as

---

[3]For a contrary perspective on this matter, see Brian K.Smith, "Exorcising the
Transcendent: Strategies for Defining Hinduism and Religion," *History of Religions*
27:1 (1987), pp. 32-55.

it is actually lived. He deduces the "real" pantheon and the central ritual vocabulary of the people of Chattisgarh, noting differences of usage and perception that accompany social station, and outlines the rites that demarcate the passage of time, both in individual lives and in the passing of public time: days, weeks, months, and years.

Diana L. Eck's *Darsan: Seeing the Divine Image in India* is also ethnographic in that it takes the city of Banaras as its point of departure. But it too has a general thrust. By uncovering the many associations of a central Hindu religious experience, that of witnessing (and being witnessed by) God in image form, Eck attempts to interpret a facet of Hindu life that is radically different from the iconoclastic predilections of the monotheistic religions that grew up in the Fertile Crescent. In the course of doing so, she calls into question an approach to the study of Hinduism that relies too much on print. She urges us to understand that much of the grammar of Hinduism is visual, not aural. And though Hindus revere a plethora of texts—many, too many to make biblicists happy—the vast majority of Hindus (being illiterate, for one thing) have not approached their religion in primarily textual terms. The first edition of *Darsan* included a brief guide to some of the best audio-visual resources for studying Indian religion.

Systematic Approaches

Of course, the ethnographic approach has seemed grievously partial to some, and perhaps somewhat lacking in grandeur. So there have also been great synthetic statements of what Hinduism is all about. Many of these could be called systematic theologies, though some of the practitioners of this approach would be surprised to see their efforts described in this way. One of the most elegant and influential statements about Hindu tradition, R.C. Zaehner's *Hinduism*, falls in this camp, as does that more self-consciously philosophical classic, Sarvepalli Radhakrishnan's *The Hindu Way of Life*. Another fine attempt is Paul Younger's *Introduction to Indian Religious Thought*. Numerous studies of a Vedantic inspiration could be added to the list: if they take an interest in the diverse practical realities of Hindu life, they do so in the belief that all of them are ultimately superseded by an apprehension of a higher, "nondual" level of truth. One should also make mention of the new attempt to describe a unitive pattern in Hindu reality that is emerging from the pen of Madeleine Biardeau. What Louis Dumont's *Homo Hierarchicus* has been to the study of Hindu society, her emerging *ouevre* may become for the study of Hindu thought.[4]

From the point of view of teaching Hinduism, the difficulty with such systematic syntheses of Hindu thought is twofold. First, they tend to be more concerned with ideas than practice, and second, they almost inevitably focus more on aspects of high culture than on what one might see if one actually went to India. We will never know how many readers of such books have been totally bewildered when they set foot on the steamy subcontinent. Zaehner, it is said, did so only once. The experience was enough to persuade him never to return.

Such books do, however, have their virtue. They attempt to provide a sense of what is unitive about "Hinduism," and at least in the Vedantic genre they adopt a Hindu point of view in the course of doing so. But *which* Hindu point of view?, one may well ask, and the answer would usually have to be: the perspective of a tiny learned minority. Even they are by no means in agreement. Of course, this is a problem that one faces in speaking about any religious tradition as if it were a single, coherent entity, but in the Hindu case it can be argued that this is a sufficiently pressing problem that it ought not be ignored at any level.

An Aspectual Approach

Several recent attempts to provide an introduction to Hinduism have tried to avoid the pitfall of oversystematization. A relatively early effort in this direction is Richard Lannoy's *The Speaking Tree*. Its subtitle identifies it as "A Study of Indian Culture and Society," so one knows from the outset that if this is a work on Hinduism, it is Hinduism in the sense of India-ism. To the more traditional preoccupations of "The Social Structure," "Value Systems and Attitudes," and "Sacred Authority" (Parts 3-5), Lannoy adds discussions of "The Family System" (Part 2) and "The Aesthetic Factor in Indian History" (Part 1). It is significant that he uses the latter two to set the stage for the more "systematic" concerns that follow, and particularly helpful that he gives his historical introduction a visual twist.

David Kinsley's *Hinduism: A Cultural Perspective* forms part of the recent series mounted by Prentice-Hall in which all religions are portrayed against the background of the cultures that give them sustenance. In far briefer compass, Kinsley takes up some of the issues that make

---

[4]M. Biardeau, *L'Hindouisme: Anthropologie d'une civilisation* (Paris: Flammarion, 1980). Cf. Alf Hiltebeitel, "Toward a Coherent Study of Hinduism," *Religious Studies Review* 9:3 (1983), pp. 206-212.

Lannoy's book worth reading—the Hindu social structure and the meaning of Hindu art, for example—and in addition he provides an account of "Dissent within the Hindu Religious Tradition." One of the purposes of the series is to strike a balance between an overall description of a tradition and a depiction of ethnographic and historical examples that enable the reader to encounter it in a less (and more) than systematic form. This emphasis and the provision of a section having specifically to do with dissent help the student appreciate that if there is such a thing as Hinduism, it must be seen from many angles. A book like Kinsley's encourages students to think of Hinduism in terms of the old parable of the elephant and the blind men, or indeed to go farther and ask if the blind men were right in asking whether the behemoth they touched could usefully be understood as a single entity at all. Kinsley's personal interest in the goddess Kali helps him give voice to Hindus' own suspicion that human experience—certainly Hindu experience—is not entirely orderly or comprehensible.

Another way of conveying the typically Hindu conviction that things need to be seen in plural terms and from more than one angle is the approach taken by Norvin Hein in his chapters on Hinduism that form a part of the general textbook called *Religions of the World* (Nielsen *et al.* 1982). Hein organizes his material in accordance with the Hindu perception that what we might call "religion" has at least three distinct expressions: *jnana*, that is, knowledge or insight; *karma*, that is, action; and *bhakti*, that is, love of God, devotion. I have often used this tripartite framework to structure courses on Hinduism that I have taught. One of the advantages of adopting a Hindu grid for the teaching of Hinduism is that it suggests, somewhat paradoxically, that this is a view not specifically of Hindu religious experience but of all such experience. As Wilfred Smith has pointed out, this is the characteristic perspective of most religious traditions: they describe the human condition, not just the situation of one community within it. Certain shortcuts are therefore required to adapt this tripartite outlook to a description of Hindu religion specifically—the *karma* section of the course, for instance, is made to focus on ritual action more than on action in general—but I hope the distortions are not too great. In the *jnana* section it is possible to inject an historical element, focusing on the evolution of major Hindu texts and ideas, so I have typically begun there. In the *bhakti* section historical issues again emerge, and special attention can be given to sectarian, class, and gender variations in Hindu religion—all issues that emerge elsewhere as well.

Resources for exploring those variations are increasingly available. For getting at sectarian perspectives and identities, one might want to make use of A.K. Ramanujan's *Speaking of Siva*, David Kinsley's *The Sword and the Flute*, or my *At Play with Krishna*. For exploring the Hindu world as it appears to Untouchable and other low-caste Indians—from the bottom up rather than from the top down, as is usual—one might consult Mark Juergensmeyer's *Religion as Social Vision*, James Freeman's *Untouchable*, or the chapters on Kabir and Ravidas in *Songs of the Saints of India*.

To get a picture of how Hinduism seems to women, one can turn to Doranne Jacobson and Susan Wadley's *Women in India* or to their chapters in *Unspoken Worlds*, a collection of essays edited by Nancy A. Falk and Rita M. Gross. An array of other studies is fast appearing, of which two are perhaps worthy of special mention since they emerge from the mouths of Hindu women themselves: *Inside the Haveli*, a novel by Rama Mehta, and *In Search of Answers*, an anthology of "Indian Women's Voices from [the publication] *Manushi*" edited by Madhu Kishwar and Ruth Vanita. Finally, there are two general books on the goddesses of India: David Kinsley's *Hindu Goddesses* and *The Divine Consort*, edited by Donna M. Wulff and myself.

Hindus Abroad

One of the great things about teaching Hinduism in New York is that students can come to know Hindus first-hand. Not only do Hindus appear in one's classes—a resource not to be missed—but they are increasingly visible as a part of New York's prodigious ethnic mix. I always ask students to separate into groups and study several Hindu communities in New York: typically a temple patronized by Indian families from a variety of backgrounds, the Vedanta society, the International Society for Krishna Consciousness (the Hare Krishna movement), and sometimes, to get a sense for the borders of "Hinduism," a Sikh gurdwara or a Ravidas temple. The issue of "aspect" emerges instantly in an involvement with such diverse expressions of the Hindu tradition, as does the question of whether in the Hindu case we are dealing with an "ism" that can be separated geographically from India itself. But perhaps the most valuable feature of such a project is that it enables students to come to know actual people whose lives are shaped by what in the classroom inevitably appear as abstractions.

In part because such encounters leave deep traces in students' memories, it is important to make some use of audio-visual materials about

Hinduism in its Indian context that can serve as a balance to these more immediate involvements. (The South Asia films produced by the University of Wisconsin provides an excellent starting point.) Even in a city like New York there is a danger that many students will experience expatriate Hindu groups or American Hindu converts as minorities—representatives of something strange—and fail to let it sink in that hundreds of millions of people actually see the world in ways that are profoundly different from the habits of mind to which they themselves are accustomed. One of the advantages of teaching Hinduism in the context of a course in which other religious traditions, including the more familiar ones, are also taught is that it creates a natural opportunity, through comparison, to press the point that if you look carefully enough, the familiar is scarcely less strange than the strange.

Yet for strangeness unalloyed, India can hardly be beaten. If ever there was a religion that refused to fit nicely into the categories of analysis that we normally use to expound the religions of the West, Hinduism is it.

BIBLIOGRAPHY

I. Books and Articles

Ashby, Philip. *Modern Trends in Hinduism*. New York: Columbia University Press, 1969.

Babb, Lawrence A. *The Divine Hierarchy: Popular Hinduism in Central India*. New York: Columbia University Press, 1975.

_____. *Redemptive Encounters: Three Modern Styles in the Hindu Tradition*. Berkeley: University of California Press, 1986.

Basham, A. L. *The Wonder That Was India: A Survey of the Culture of the Indian Sub-Continent Before the Coming of the Muslims*. London: Sidgwick and Jackson, 1954.

Eck, Diana L. *Darsan: Seeing the Divine Image in India*. Chambersburg, PA: Anima Books, 1981. Revised edition, 1985.

Falk, Nancy A., and Rita M. Gross. *Unspoken Worlds: Women's Religious Lives in Non-Western Cultures*. San Francisco: Harper and Row, 1980. Second edition, Belmont, CA: Wadsworth, 1988.

Freeman, James. *Untouchable: An Indian Life History*. Stanford: Stanford University Press, 1979.

Hawley, John Stratton. *At Play with Krishna: Pilgrimage Dramas from Brindavan*. Princeton: Princeton University Press, 1981. (In association with Shrivatsa Goswami.)

_____, and Donna M. Wulff, eds. *The Divine Consort: Radha and the Goddesses of India*. Boston: Beacon Press, 1986. Original edition, 1982.

_____, and Mark Juergensmeyer. *Songs of the Saints of India*. New York: Oxford University Press, 1988.

Hopkins, Thomas J. *The Hindu Religious Tradition*. Encino, CA: Dickenson, 1971.

Jacobson, Doranne, and Susan S. Wadley. *Women in India*. Columbia, MO: South Asia Books, 1977.

Juergensmeyer, Mark. *Religion as Social Vision: The Movement Against Untouchability in 20th-Century Punjab.* Berkeley: University of California Press, 1982.

Kinsley, David R. *The Sword and the Flute: Kali and Krsna, Dark Visions of the Terrible and the Sublime in Hindu Mythology.* Berkeley: University of California Press, 1975.

_____. *Hinduism: A Cultural Perspective.* Englewood Cliffs: Prentice-Hall, 1982.

_____. *Hindu Goddesses: Visions of the Divine Feminine in the Hindu Religious Tradition.* Berkeley: University of California Press, 1986.

Kishwar, Madhu, and Ruth Vanita, eds. *In Search of Answers: Indian Women's Voices from Manushi.* London: Zed Books, 1984.

Lannoy, Richard. *The Speaking Tree: A Study of Indian Culture and Society.* London: Oxford University Press, 1971.

Mehta, Rama. *Inside the Haveli.* New Delhi: Arnold-Heinemann, 1977.

Nielson, Niels, et al. *Religions of the World.* New York: St. Martin's Press, 1982.

Radhakrishnan, Sarvepalli. *The Hindu View of Life.* London: George Allen and Unwin, 1927.

Ramanujan, A. K. *Speaking of Siva.* Baltimore: Penguin Books, 1973.

Sen, K. M. *Hinduism.* Harmondsworth: Penguin Books, 1961.

Wiser, William and Charlotte. *Behind Mud Walls, 1930-1960.* Berkeley: University of California Press, 1969.

Younger, Paul. *Introduction to Indian Religious Thought.* Philadelphia: Westminster, 1972.

Zaehner, R. C. *Hinduism.* Oxford: Oxford University Press, 1962.

II. Films and Visual Resources

American Committee for South Asian Art Color Slide Project. John Listopad, Project Coordinator. Department of the History of Art, Tappan Hall, University of Michigan, Ann Arbor, MI 38109 (313-763-0517).

Contemporary South Asian Film Series. South Asian Area Center, 1242 Van Hise Hall, University of Wisconsin, Madison, WI 53706 (608-262-9690).

Dell, David, *et al. Focus on Hindusim: Audio-Visual Resources for Teaching Religion.* New York: Council for Intercultural Studies and Programs (60 East 42nd Street, New York, NY 10017), 1977.

Eck, Diana L. *Darsan: Seeing the Divine Image in India,* Appendix I: "Audio-Visual Resources". Chambersburg, PA: Anima Books, 1981.

THE SIKH TRADITION

Mark Juergensmeyer

In planning for an introductory course in religion, the Sikh tradition may not immediately come to mind. Sooner or later, however, anyone who plans such a course will have to come to terms with it, not only because it exists, but because it is the main tradition of expatriate Indian communities throughout the world, and has played an important role in contemporary Indian politics. Even though the Sikh community claims less than 2 percent of the Indian population, there are over 10 million Sikhs worldwide. The majority live in their homeland, the North Indian state of Punjab, where they comprise the majority. Their significance, however, is larger than their numbers. This is in part because they are fiercely independent as a community and easily recognizable: the men are not allowed to shave or cut their hair, which is bound in bright and distinctively-tied turbans. Moreover, the Sikh community has occupied a unique place in South Asia's complex religious history.

Finding that place has been a major theme in the 500 years that the tradition has evolved. At critical moments in its history, the matter of the distinctiveness of Sikhism as a tradition separate from Hinduism and Islam has turned into a rallying cry.[1] It was in defense of this separate identity that some Sikhs recently turned to violence, precipitating the spiral of tragic events which led to the Indian government's invasion of the central shrine of Sikhism, the Golden Temple, in the summer of 1984, and which culminated later that year in a violent response: the assassination of Mrs. Gandhi by Sikh members of her bodyguard.

Locating the Sikh community's place in history is not only a problem for Sikhs; it is also a problem for scholars and teachers. Such questions as where to locate the Sikh tradition in a course syllabus, and how to describe it, puts the teacher face to face with issues that are culturally

---

[1]For an excellent discussion of this: W.H. McLeod, *Who is a Sikh? The Problem of Sikh Identity*, Oxford's Clarendon Press, 1989.

sensitive to many Sikhs, and matters of puzzlement and debate among scholars who specialize in the field. At the heart of the problem are issues that are critical in the case of the Sikh tradition, but should be considered when teaching any religion: what makes a tradition? when does a tradition become a tradition, and how is it related to other traditions from which it emerges and with which it historically interacts?

In surveying a number of textbooks in world religion I have looked at the ways they have tacitly answered these questions with regard to Sikhism. One way, unfortunately, is to ignore Sikhism altogether. Sikhism is not a religious tradition, as far as Huston Smith is concerned in *The Religions of Man*. In the English translation of Hans-Joachim Schoeps' *The Religions of Mankind*, the existence of Sikhism is acknowledged, but barely, in only five lines: and most of these are inaccurate. According to Schoeps, the founder of the faith "built this combined Hindu-Moslem religion around the god Rama."[2] (In fact, Sikhism rejects all names and anthropomorphic forms of God, including Rama; and as we shall see, it is not a combination of Hinduism and Islam at all.) The main problem with ignoring Sikhism, aside from insulting the Sikhs, is that is gives a false impression of Indian religious culture: that it is composed solely of a monolithic Hinduism, and that minor and schismatic movements do not exist.

A second way of dealing with the problem is to present Sikhism as a tradition, but to present it as if it had no relationship to any other tradition whatsoever. This is essentially the approach that Noss takes in *Man's Religions*, which is typical of his way of dealing with each of the world's religious traditions: as discrete, and relatively uniform entities. While this approach has the practical value of making the material easy to summarize and present, it gives a misleading view of the way in which history actually works. Traditions evolve and change over time, and the changing character of traditions is an important fact to present in an introductory course.

Often textbooks will opt for a third approach to the presentation of Sikhism which will be revealed in the way they organize the chapters: the section of Sikhism will be sandwiched in between those on Hinduism and Islam, giving the appearance of what many will actually (but erroneously) state to be fact: that Sikhism is a syncretic amalgam of these two faiths. Ninian Smart, whose two pages on Sikhism in *The Religious*

---

[2]Han Joachim Schoeps, *The Religions of Mankind*, Garden City: Doubleday & Co. Anchor Books, 1966 (translated from the German: *Religionen: Wesen und Geschichte*, Gutersloh: C. Bertelsmann Verlag, 1961), p. 167.

Experience of Mankind are otherwise fairly accurate, describes it as a "faith designed to bring men of goodwill in Islam and Hinduism together."[3] The Jesuit scholar, John A. Hardon, in *Religions of the World*, starts out well by admitting that Sikhism is "sometimes lightly dismissed as a hybrid of two old religions, Islam and Hinduism, made into one" but then he unaccountably decides to label Sikhism as "conscious syncretism, one of the few that has ever been successful."[4] Noss, taking a different tack, claims that the Sikhs' is a spontaneous rather than a calculated fusion: "the religion of the Sikhs is not to be confused with the rationalistic syncretisms whose adherents have been engaged in a reworking of philosophy rather than in a revival of religion, properly conceived".[5]

The syncretist notion is not wholly based on fiction, for the Muslims have certainly had some influence on Sikhs during their years of cultural contact. The reverence that Sikhs accord their sacred book, the *Adi Granth*, and the emphasis they place on congregational worship may have resulted, in part, from early Sikh interaction with Islam. Guru Nanak, the first of the ten founding leaders of the faith, mentioned Muslim teachers among the yogis, Brahmans, and other religious people with whom he was in contact. Yet these contacts and influences do not constitute syncretism, and the credit for the promotion of that idea must go to a Sikh scholar, Khushwant Singh, who for years was the major source of information on Sikhism for Western scholars, and who was quite fond of the Hindu-Muslim syncretic view—a position which, unfortunately, no other major scholar of the tradition has held before or since.

Most other scholars, including W.H. McLeod, the most reliable contemporary historians of the tradition, hold to the notion that the Sikh tradition evolved from medieval Hinduism. They derive its origins from the *sants*, the poet-saints among whom the Sikhs' own Guru Nanak is numbered, and whose verses are included in the *Adi Granth*. Many textbooks that are devoted solely to Hinduism will quite properly mention the rise of Sikhism in the context of their discussions of the medieval *sant* movement. But although they avoid the error of classifying Sikhism as a

---

[3]Ninian Smart, *The Religious Experience of Mankind*, New York: Scribner's, 3rd edition, 1983 (1976, 1969) p.152.

[4]John A. Hardon, S.J., *Religions of the World* (2 vols.), Garden City: Doubleday, Image Books, 1968 (1963) vol. I, p.224.

[5] John B. Noss, *Man's Religions* (5th edition), New York: Macmillan Publishing Co., 1974 (1st edition, 1949), p.226.

synthesis, these textbooks are not altogether satisfying in their presentations of Sikh tradition. They are, after all, determined to present Hinduism as a distinct and separate tradition of its own; and the Hindu aberrations and offshoots, such as Sikhism, tend to receive short shrift.

Several examples will illustrate the problem. In an otherwise thoughtful and lengthy section on the medieval *sants*, A.L. Basham, in his chapter on Hinduism in *The Concise Encyclopedia of Living Faiths*, edited by R.C. Zaehner, dismisses Nanak and the Sikhs in seven sentences. K.M. Sen's *Hinduism*, which in its Penguin paperback version is perhaps the most familiar of the introductory textbooks in that tradition, is subtitled "The World's Oldest Faith," and the text appears determined to keep it that way, since all but twenty pages are pre-medieval. The two sentences on Nanak and Sikhism in Sen's book are buried in a paragraph on another *sant* figure, Kabir. The previous edition of the two-volume *Sources of Indian Tradition*, compiled by a team of scholars under the general editorship of Wm. Theodore deBary, excluded Nanak and the Sikhs altogether. This glaring omission was corrected in the present revised edition being prepared by Ainslie Embree, but again the concentration is on Nanak and the early Sikh tradition, rather than a fuller exposition of the history and later-evolved tenets of the faith.

For a full and accurate portrayal of the Sikh tradition, then, one must turn to the scholarship devoted solely to the Sikhs and their historical interactions with other traditions. Quite a bit of work has been done on Sikhism since 1948, largely due to the Indian government support of Sikh educational institutions and research projects. Notable among the works by Indian scholars are J.S. Grewal's *Guru Nanak in History* and Harbans Singh's *The Heritage of the Sikhs*. Other research has been conducted by scholars from abroad, the most prominent of whom is a New Zealand historian, W.H. McLeod. McLeod lived in the Punjab for some years, and has produced several ground-breaking books in the field, including *Guru Nanak and the Sikh Religion*, and *Early Sikh Tradition*. McLeod also has a brief and readable introduction to Sikhism in *The Penguin Dictionary of Religions*, and the title essay in his collected essays, *The Evolution of the Sikh Community* is a classic. A British scholar, Owen Cole, has done several important works as well, including *The Guru in Sikhism* and *Sikhism and its Indian Context, 1469-1708*. An overview and assessment of the current state of scholarship on Sikhism may be found in Mark Juergensmeyer and N.G. Barrier, eds., *Sikh Studies: Comparative Perspectives on a Changing Tradition*.

The current state of thinking about the origins of the Sikh tradition is that Nanak and the other 16th century medieval sants were influenced by Vaisnava devotionalism and Nath mysticism: the former stressed the importance of loving the Lord, and the latter provided a formless, almost gnostic view of the Lord, and a series of meditation practices aimed at achieving higher states of consciousness. The nine gurus who followed Nanak were increasingly concerned with keeping their young community together and dealing with the Moghul military authorities.

The most radical changes in the Sikh tradition occurred toward the end of the 17th century when the community was joined by large numbers of people known as the Jats, who were influenced by the culture in the hilly areas near the Punjab. They were warriors whose religious beliefs reflected their militant lifestyle, and were also believers in the potency of nature and in the force of special words, colors, metals and sounds. A number of the symbols that are now identified with Sikhism probably came into the tradition via the Jats: the metal band that all Sikhs wear on their wrists, the notion that long hair and beards are expressions of potency, and the ubiquitous swords that appear not only in Sikh garb, but in the insignia of the faith.

After the tenth Guru, Gobind Singh, brought the line of guruship to an end, the power of spiritual authority was thought to continue in the presence of the *Adi Granth* and the community itself, which was dubbed the *Dal Khalsa*, the "army of the faithful." The feeling of community solidarity was enhanced by the five symbols that all Sikhs are enjoined to wear—long hair, a wooden comb, a sword, breeches, and the metal wrist band—and by their names. Most faithful Sikhs took Gobind Singh's own last name as their own. And since last names in India often reflect community and caste identities, this act is tantamount to the creation of a new community of Singhs.

In the 18th and 19th centuries this militant community had the opportunity of testing its mettle against a formidable opponent: the British. The kingdom of Ranjit Singh, "the one-eyed lion of the Punjab," was one of the last to fall to British control. Eventually, however, the Sikhs became allied with their former foes, and when the Hindus and Muslims joined in mutiny against the British in 1857, the government increasingly turned to the Sikhs for aid in manning their armies. The British, in turn, supported the Sikhs. With the help of the government, a political structure was established in the last decades of the 19th century which enabled representative delegates of Sikhs to control the community's various shrines throughout the Punjab, many of which had fallen into the hands of Hindu families. This political organization has been the main arena for Sikh politics in the 20th century, and after India's independence, it spawned a political party, the Akali Dal, which has on several occasions garnered enough votes to displace the Congress Party in controlling the legislative assembly of the Punjab.

Sikh religious organizations have probably never been stronger than they are at present, and the community is thriving in the Punjab and in immigrant communities of Sikhs throughout the world, principally in Fiji, Singapore, Kenya, England, and several locations in Canada and the United States: Northern California, Vancouver, Toronto, New York and Washington, D.C. Although Sikhs do not proselytize, a number of Americans have converted to the tradition, most of them associated with the Sikh Dharma ashrams established by a Sikh missionary to the United States, Yogi Bhajan, and his 3-HO organization.

Local communities of Sikhs are a rich resource for classes in world religion. Sikhs enjoy talking about their beliefs and customs, and a classroom visit from a Sikh, or a field trip to a local Sikh temple (which Sikhs call a *gurdwara*, "the doorway to the Guru,") will enliven a presentation of the Sikh tradition. Americans who have joined a Sikh Dharma ashram are usually quite knowledgeable about Sikh history and customs as well, but their perspective on the tradition is somewhat different from that of the Punjabis who have grown up with the faith, and many of the American Sikhs' practices (such as wearing only white garb, and undertaking yogic meditation) are not followed by the rest of the Sikh community. The best introductory book on Sikhism for classroom use is Owen Cole and P.S. Sambhi, *The Sikhs*, which has incorporated the best of recent scholarship on the origins of Sikhism into a readable account that details actual Sikh religious practices more thoroughly than any other book available.

BIBLIOGRAPHY

W.H. McLeod, *Guru Nanak and the Sikh Religion*, Oxford: Clarendon Press, 1968. The most influential and controversial book of Sikh scholarship written in this century.

W.H. McLeod, trans. and ed., *Textual Sources for the Study of Sikhism*, Manchester: University Press, 1984. These are selections and translations from the Sikh scriptures, rituals, and other writings.

W.H. McLeod, *Evolution of the Sikh Community: Five Essays*, Oxford: Clarendon Press, 1976. Each essay is a gem. The title essay alone, which succinctly describes the Sikhs own view of their history and replaces it with a new theory from modern scholarship, is worth the price of the book.

W.H. McLeod, *The Sikhs: History of Religion and Society*, New York: Columbia University Press, 1989. A brief and straightforward introduction to the history, literature and religious practices of Sikhism.

Khushwant Singh, *A History of the Sikhs* (2 vols.) Princeton: Princeton University Press, 1966. Although flawed by the author's biases, it is still the most complete history of the tradition.

Mark Juergensmeyer, *Sikh Studies: Comparative Perspectives on a Changing Tradition*, Berkeley, CA: Berkeley Religious Studies Series: Graduate Theological Union, 1979. These are essays by Western scholars on various aspects of the tradition including a large section on Sikhs abroad.

Mark Juergensmeyer and John Stratton Hawley, *Songs of the Saints of India*, Oxford: Oxford University Press, 1988. Has one section on Guru Nanak, including translations of his poetry and discussion of the significance of his life.

Karine Schomer and W.H. McLeod, ed., *The Sants: Studies in a Devotional Tradition of India*, Berkeley, CA: Berkeley Religious Studies Series, 1987. This is a collection of essays on the medieval tradition that is a context for the origins of Sikhism. Includes three articles on the origins and development of Sikhism.

Mark Tully and Satish Jacob, *Amritsar: Mrs. Gandhi's Last Battle*, London: Pan Books, 1985. The best description of the tragic confrontation between the Sikhs and the Indian government in the mid-1980's.

tradition that is a context for the origins of Sikhism. Includes three articles on the origins and development of Sikhism.

Mark Tully and Satish Jacob, *Amritsar: Mrs. Gandhi's Last Battle*, London: Pan Books, 1985. The best description of the tragic confrontation between the Sikhs and the Indian government in the mid-1980's.

CHINESE RELIGIONS

Judith A. Berling

China has had a long and complex religious history, dominated primarily by the developments and interactions of three main traditions: Confucianism, Taoism, and Buddhism. Both the length of the historical tradition and its plurality pose challenges to a balanced selection of topics in designing courses or units on China. Many teachers resolve the problem by limiting the treatment of Confucianism and Taoism to the classical period of late Chou China. This is tempting because the primary sources of that period have a universal appeal as "classics" and can readily be taught as teachings on basic human issues. However this approach obscures the religious dimension of both Confucianism and Taoism, and treats them basically as "thought," not religions. More seriously, it tends to ignore the crucial impact of sociocultural changes in shaping the religious developments of the Chou. These connections are well established in the eminently readable and short volume by Frederick Mote, *Intellectual Foundations of China* (New York: Alfred A. Knopf, 1971).

The texts on Chinese religions leave something to be desired. The best textbook treatment is in John Fenton et al, *Religions of Asia* (New York: St. Martin's Press, 1983). A very brief treatment for shorter units or students who must be assigned very little reading is in Joseph Kitagawa, ed., *Religions of the East* (Philadelphia: Westminster Press, 1960). Laurence Thompson's *Chinese Religions: An Introduction* (Belmont, CA: Wadsworth, 1975) is quite good, although I have found that students have problems following these readings.

There are a wealth of source books which can be used to supplement textbook assignments or as resources for faculty lectures. The oldest and best known is perhaps Wm. Theodore deBary, ed., *Sources of Chinese Tradition* (New York: Columbia University Press, 1960). There are still some fine selections in this volume, but it contains too much on political philosophy to make it suitable for most Religious Studies courses, and it lacks anything on later Taoist sources. Wing-tsit Chan's *A Source Book in Chinese Philosophy* (Princeton: Princeton University Press, 1963) is just what the title suggests, although it too is very light on Taoist thought and philosophy. Patricia Ebrey's *Chinese Civilization: A Source Book* (New York: Free Press, 1981) contains some marvelous selections on family regulations and popular religion.

Literary sources (poems and stories) are a marvelous supplement to philosophical or doctrinal texts. An easily accessible collection of fine translations may be found in Cyril Birch's *Anthology of Chinese Literature* (New York: Grove Press, 1965 and 1972). Moreover, *Journey to the West* is an excellent and popular reading for courses or units on Chinese religions. Anthony Yu's four volume translation is now definitive (Chicago: University of Chicago Press, 1977-1982), and an excellent source of fuller annotation on various themes, but Arthur Waley's one-volume of selections, *Monkey* (New York: Grove Press, 1958) is more practical if the time that can be allotted is severely limited.

It is always difficult to find readable translations of primary sources. Many people find the excerpts of Confucius, Mencius, Lao Tzu, and Chuang Tzu in the *Sources of Chinese Tradition* or *Source Book in Chinese Philosophy* preferable to the entire book because they are briefer and arranged nicely by categories. However, there are good readable translations of the whole texts; I especially recommend those by D.C. Lau (Penguin editions) for use with undergraduates, although these Penguin editions have not been consistently available in the past few years. Burton Watson's *Chuang Tzu: Basic Writings* (New York: Columbia University Press, 1964) is reasonably priced and readable, although A.C. Graham's *Chuang Tzu, The Seven Inner Chapters* (London: Allen and Unwin, 1981) is a more authoritative translation. In addition, there are translations of Taoist texts by Wing-tsit Chan in *The Great Asian Religions: an Anthology* (New York: Macmillian, 1969).

Very few of the books mentioned to date treat the institutional and practical side of Chinese religions, which is both important and of considerable comparative interest. Courses centered around religious institutions, ritual practices, monastic life, or life cycle rituals will have to turn elsewhere for comparable material on Chinese culture. Unfortunately, there are few texts readily available in this area for student use, but there are a number of resources for faculty lectures or reserve readings. A classic is C.K. Yang's *Religions in Chinese Society* (Berkeley: University of California Press, 1967), which is an overview of the religious system of Chinese culture. This is readily available in paperback. Holmes Welsh's volume *The Practice of Chinese Buddhism* (Cambridge: Harvard University Press, 1967) is a gold mine of information about monastic life and discipline in recent Buddhist history. Yoshioka Yoshiotoyo did an article on monastic routines in Taoist temples in Welch and Seidel, ed., *Facets of Taoism* (New Haven: Yale University Press, 1979)

The study of Chinese ritual practice has experienced a breakthrough in recent years. Michael Saso's *Taoism and the Rite of Cosmic Renewal* (Pullman: Washington State University Press, 1972) is useful for undergraduate instruction since it provides concrete description and an anthropological analysis in clear and simple terms. His *Taoist Master Chuang* (New Haven: Yale University Press, 1978) is also readable, although it has been criticized for the claims he makes about the history of the tradition; it is most useful as a portrait of a contemporary Taoist priest. One of the finest sources of Chinese ritual is the anthropological collection *Religion and Ritual in Chinese Society* (Stanford: Stanford University Press, 1974), edited by Arthur Wolf. Particularly interesting is Wolf's article "Gods, Ghosts, and Ancestors," which relates the attitudes toward different classes of spiritual beings with the position of people in the society.

The sheer volume of material on Chinese religions mandates very conscious selectivity in teaching a unit or course on Chinese religions. Although many people opt for teaching a few of the classical thinkers, if the teacher is more likely to organize his or her courses around intellectual or phenomenological themes, the resources cited make it possible to do so. Even if you choose a textbook to organize your course or unit around you will still need to know what aspects you want to stress and choose supplemental materials for lectures and readings which represent your interests and emphases.

Beyond the general sources outlined above, you can locate more specialized materials in any of the following bibliographies: 1) Wing-tsit Chan, *Outline and Annotated Bibliography of Chinese Philosophy* (New Haven: Yale University Press, 1961; supplement 1965), 2) Laurence Thompson, *Chinese Religion in Western Languages* (Tucson: University of Arizona Press, 1985) 3) Frank Reynolds and John Strong, *Guide to Buddhist Religion* (Boston: Hall, 1981), 4) Michel Soymie, *Bibliographie du Taoism Etudes lans les Langues Occidentale* in *Dokyo Kenkyu*, 3 and 4 (1968 and 1971); 5) *Bibliography of Asian Studies,* under the categories of religion, anthropology, and philosophy.

JAPANESE RELIGIONS

Miriam Levering

On setting out to teach about Japanese religion in an introductory course, there seem to be two choices. One can select specific examples without regard to whether or how what is selected is in some sense "representative" of Japanese religion as a whole. Then one can look at those in detail as part of whatever inquiry one is pursuing. Or, one can formulate some generalizations about Japanese religion as a whole or in part, and select examples to illustrate those.

If one opts for generalizations about Japanese religion as a whole, then one needs guidance. In what follows, I will offer some reflections on certain generalizations that have been put forward about Japanese religion. And I will suggest some sources that give fuller presentations. In addition, I will offer thoughts about pitfalls that lie in one's path no matter how one chooses to teach Japanese religion.

GENERALIZATIONS

Generalization #1: "Absolute phenomenalism"

Where religious dimensions of culture are concerned, a highly influential moment was the publication of Hajime Nakamura's early book, *The Ways of Thinking of Eastern Peoples*, first published in Japan in 1947.[1] Japanese scholars had often sought to draw broad distinctions between their own national genius and that of India and China—or, to put it more accurately, India and China as they construed them as entities over against which what was "Japanese" could be defined. Nakamura introduced this discussion to the West.

Nakamura proposed that the Japanese habit of thought is to affirm "this world" so completely that no separation can exist between the ab-

---

[1]A revised version published in 1964 is still available in paperback from the University of Hawaii Press.

solute (ultimate reality) and the manifest world. One term he used for this was "absolute phenomenalism."

Recently leading scholars have revisited the issue of "absolute phenomenalism" as a characteristic of the Japanese mind. A leading scholar of Japanese Buddhism, Yoshio Tamura, has put forth a thesis similar to Nakamura's "absolute phenomenalism." He has suggested that Japanese versions of Buddhism are marked by a deep feeling that the world, and within that particularly the world of Nature, is already both the world of illusion and the perfect manifestation of Buddha-nature itself. While the Mahayana Buddhist philosophical grounding for this (known as *hongaku* thought) was already well advanced in China, it was in Japan that it was taken to the point of saying that the very grasses and trees are enlightened.[2]

This line of thinking has an important corollary. If the Japanese see no separation between the absolute and the manifest world, then the human and the artistic task would be to see the divine in Nature, or, to put it another way, to see Nature as it really is.

Incorporating this line of thought, William LaFleur has made a grand proposal concerning the shape of what he calls the episteme of medieval Japan (a period from 700 to 1600 C.E.).[3] A significant shift is indicated, however, by the fact that his proposed worldview (or episteme) is time-limited. An even more important shift is that his worldview is characterized by tension between "absolute phenomenalism" and another Buddhist cosmology which emphasizes the need for transcendence. Specifically, this worldview was characterized by a tension between the literati's involvement in the symbols of Buddhism, including most notably those of the cosmology of the "six courses" of existence (*rokudo*), which includes the need to escape from or transcend the six courses, on the one hand, and that of "dialectic Buddhism" on the other, which asserts and seeks to experience a total integration or identification of the absolute and the relative, theoretically expressed in *hongaku* thought. Because this total identity or integration is believed to be immediately perceivable, there is so far as this half of the worldview is concerned no need for a symbolizing process, and so a critique of symbols in introduced.

---

[2]"*Hongaku* thought" is skillfully discussed in a non-technical manner in the introduction to William R. LaFleur, *The Karma of Words: Buddhism and the Literary Arts in Medieval Japan* (Berkeley: University of California Press, 1983), pp. 20-25.
[3]In LaFleur, *The Karma of Words*.

This approach finds an echo in a recent textbook, *Japanese Religion*, by Robert S. Ellwood and Richard Pilgrim.[4] Their chapter on "descriptive realities and worldview" proposes "two relatively distinct religious paradigms" that cut across traditions "as well as across the distinction between religion and culture" (p.97). One is a "vertical" paradigm that emphasizes hierarchy and separation between the divine powers and the human world. Early Yamato clan myth, Pure Land *mappo* (degeneration of the dharma) thought, and what LaFleur calls the "six courses" cosmology are examples of this paradigm. The horizontal paradigm, on the other hand, "tends to deemphasize any distance or distinction between realms of being and to deemphasize hierarchical structures. It collapses ontological distance and hierarchy and emphasizes a closeness between the human and the sacred realms. It emphasizes the sacrality of *this* world and time rather than the sacrality of other worlds and times on some great chain of being." (p. 101) This sums up current thinking, and provides a framework useful in teaching.

Generalization #2: "Limited social nexus"

In *The Ways of Thinking of Eastern Peoples*, Nakamura argued that the Japanese characteristically emphasize a limited social nexus over the individual and over universal values. Under this heading he noted that the Japanese tend to give absolute devotion to a specific individual symbolic of the social nexus (such as the emperor, or a founder of a sect). He also noted that close relationships between religion and the state are taken for granted in traditional Japanese thought.

a. Nakamura's idea that a close relation between religion and the state characterizes Japanese religion still seems valid. But, as with the others, one has to be careful with this generalization. For example, the notion that there is a natural bond between the imperial family and its religious symbols on the one hand and the Japanese nation and people on the other is a theme that appears from time to time in Japanese history. But we must teach our students to look carefully at each set of circumstances under which this bond has been portrayed as important and natural. We must show them that there have been times when the emperor was not an important symbol, times when the emperor as symbol was not exclusively linked to Shinto, etc.

b. It does seem to be characteristic of Japanese religion that social institutions such as family and village are the locus of, and are intimately

---

[4]Englewood Cliffs, N.J.: Prentice Hall, 1985.

connected with, religion. For examples, the cosmologies of ancestor veneration seem to be pervasive in Japanese religious movements even today, whatever their degree of organization or their label as Shinto, Confucian or Buddhist. And much of what is significant in Japanese religious life occurs on the level of local festivals and small cults.

Nakamura's observation that a single human figure can become an object of devotion as a symbol of the social nexus (e.g., the emperor sect founder Kukai or the founder of a "new religion") is still accepted as a valuable insight into a characteristically Japanese phenomenon.

c. Another way of putting Nakamura's point is to say that, as compared to the universalism of Islam and Christianity, Japanese religion often seems to be characterized by particularism. This is a distinction I often find useful to make in an introductory course.

d. Yet another way of putting Nakamura's point is to say that Japan's group orientation contrasts with Western individualism: Japanese value and seek the harmony and success of the groups to which they belong, more than they value independence and individual attainment. To this Chie Nakane has added the insight that Japanese groups are formed around a vertical structure of loyalties and ties: for example, one's loyalty is to one's professor, rather than to students of one's own. Because these generalizations are now coming under criticism, and are overemphasized in the popular media, class presentation of them is tricky—see below.

Generalization #3: "Intuition rather than logic"

Nakamura argued that the Japanese lack interest in logic and favor truths revealed to intuition and emotion. This generalization is presented in updated form in Ellwood and Pilgrim's *Japanese Religion* in their section on "Poetic Realities." For another interesting treatment of the same theme, now cast as a way in which the Japanese understood what "Japaneseness" was, see David Pollack, *The Fracture of Meaning*.[5]

---

[5]Princeton, N.J.: Princeton U. Press, 1986.

Generalization #4: "Inseparability of the religious and the aesthetic"

Nakamura, and later the historian of religion Hideo Kishimoto, suggested that compared to the West, religion in Japan was more closely related to aesthetic and more separated from ethical values.[6]

The generalization that intuitive, poetic, aesthetic feeling is valued especially highly in Japan and is often found at or near the center of religious life has been widely accepted. A distinction such as Kierkegaard's between the aesthete and the man of faith has for the most part been alien to Japan, although at times some tension was felt.[7] Beyond this, the study and practice of a number of arts has been given a religious valuation. Arts are of course also valued for their own sake; and yet the conviction that the arts provide a way both to find and to express the most profound dimensions of character and the deepest insights gives them a close relation to their forms of religious cultivation.[8]

Generalization #5: "Embodiment"

There is another general point that I like to make that I have not seen discussed as such. This insight, common to many Japanese religious teaching and practices, is that if one wants a Way to become one's own, one needs to embody it. Nichiren tells his disciples that they must read the *Lotus Sutra* with their bodies. Dogen instructs his not to sleep spreadeagled on their backs, but rather in a particular position on their sides. In the tea ceremony, one brings the mind and spirit to serenity, openness and harmony by practicing the gestures of hand and foot that such a mind and spirit would spontaneously produce. One can begin spiritual work with the body; if the body changes, conforms itself to harmonious and serene activity, the spirit will follow. One can proceed from the body to the mind, as well as vice versa.

---

[6]See Hideo Kishimoto's discussion of this point in "Some Japanese Cultural Traits and Religions," in Charles Moore, ed., *The Japanese Mind* (Honolulu: U. of Hawaii Press, 1967).

[7]LaFleur points out that during the medieval period the question of whether writing poetry should be shunned as a distraction by those committed to a monastic path to enlightenment was a live issue. Cf. LaFleur, *The Karma of Words*, pp. 7-8.

[8]Cf. Richard Pilgrim, *Buddhism and the Arts of Japan* (Chambersburg, Pa: Anima Press, 1981). Also, D.T. Suzuki's *Zen and Japanese Culture* (Princeton: Princeton University Press, 1970) is still valuable.

Generalization #6: "The high tradition in Japan is the folk tradition"

Religion which is not centrally organized or rationalized and is not primarily text-based has certainly maintained a high degree of vitality and impact throughout Japanese history, becoming for long periods almost the primary content of such text-based "high" traditions as Soto Zen. Scholars such as Ichiro Hori and Carmen Blacker have established the importance of knowing folk religion for understanding the so-called "high" traditions in Japan by showing how shamanism, mountain asceticism, divination and the like pervade all the traditions, large and small, high and low.[9]

Generalization #7: "Religious traditions in Japan are often not the focus of exclusive participation"

H. Byron Earhart made a major contribution by asking us to understand Japanese religion as the ongoing stream of synthesis of elements from Buddhism, Shinto, Taoist, Confucian and less organized folk practices into a variegated set of religious lives, movements and worldviews. This flow of syntheses is where Japanese people really live and find their identity, far more often than as members of any one of the traditions.[10]

Pitfalls

A number of pitfalls lie in wait for the unwary teacher.

1. A thorny problem that Japanese religion presents is that, with the exception of Shinto, the traditions that we think of as "religious" in Japan, that is, the Buddhist, Taoist, and Confucian, were imported. To speak of the Japanese versions seems to be to speak of matters which, though adopted and adapted in Japan, were already fully and classically developed elsewhere. This leads to two kinds of distortions. The first is a tendency to view Japan without a culture of its own, an empty vessel into which was poured Chinese culture. The second is to think only of Shinto and Zen when one thinks of Japanese contributions to world religion. This distortion has plagued introductory textbooks and courses, particularly ones using the "traditions" approach. (Zen of course also

---

[9]Ichiro Hori, *Folk Religion in Japan: Continuity and Change* (Chicago: University of Chicago Press, 1968); Carmen Blacker, *The Catalpa Bow: A Study of Shamanistic Practices in Japan* (London: George Allen and Unwin, 1975).

[10]Earhart's contribution is easiest to find in his textbook, *Japanese Religion: Unity and Diversity*, now in its third edition (Belmont, California: Wadsworth, 1982), a book everyone should read.

reached full development in China, but since our Western knowledge of Zen came through the Japanese, who presented it as a creation of their own culture, we usually do not require ourselves to take account of that fact.)

2. A second pitfall is a temptation to overdraw the contrast between Japanese group orientation and Western individualism. One danger here is that one may inadvertently present Japan as a wonderfully harmonious society without mentioning the fact that one can find very real conflicts at many levels in Japan. Another danger is to leave the impression that, since Japanese do not emphasize the need for individuals to define themselves over against the expectations of the group, adults in Japan are typically dependent, lacking in full maturity or adulthood, or lacking in strong personality or character development. Such a picture is far from accurate. The Japanese put a considerable and successful emphasis on developing strength of character, individual judgment, and the mature balance of personality that will enable a person to face any difficulty successfully.[11]

3. A third pitfall results from our own Western tendency to privilege ideas and beliefs over actions, and ethical over ritual actions, and thus to see Japanese religious expressions as inferior to Indian, Chinese or Western ones. For example, it is frequently noted that in the Heian period few elite Japanese were interested in Buddhist ideas, but many were strongly attracted to Buddhist ritual. Some scholars and teachers are tempted to say that this shows that their grasp of Buddhism, and their religious sensibilities, were superficial. This reflects a questionable tendency to see ritual as an inferior form of knowledge.

4. A fourth is a tendency to overemphasize the importance of Zen as a living religious force and as an influence on Japanese culture. The student who completes an introductory course should realize that when she arrives in Japan, she will not see Zen temples on every corner.

5. Fifth, one has to be very careful about how one presents Japanese understandings of the relations between *kami*, humans and nature. A lot of oversimplified nonsense has been written about the topic. *Kami* do not lurk in every tree and rock (or, to put it differently, "*kami*"-ness does not characterize every waterfall); Japanese like to preserve the grain in wood, but they also like lacquer and brocade; and a successful flower arrangement or Zen garden is not "natural" in the sense that flowers

---

[11]On this point, see especially David Plath, *Long Engagements: Maturity in Modern Japan* (Stanford: Stanford University Press, 1980).

growing in a meadow are natural. It is "natural" in some other sense, and the relation between those two senses needs to be explored.[12] The subject calls for one's most profound and paradoxical insights.

6. Shinto as a topic presents pitfalls. The early clan myths and the Ise shrine are splendidly appealing religious documents which seem to reflect a "Shinto" untainted by Buddhist influences. And of course the government in the nineteenth century created a Shinto that was separate from Buddhism by forcibly separating the two. But for most of the course of Japanese history it is not accurate or useful to think of Shinto as having been a separate religious tradition. When one is taking the "traditions approach" one must be particularly careful on this point, as textbooks mislead.[13]

7. Earhart, Helen Hardacre and other students of the recent Japanese "new religions," have successfully focused attention on the importance in this century of these non-elite movements as a principal locus of religious creativity.[14] Their impact is shown in the fact that several of the current "world-religions intro texts" devote considerable space to the new religions.

There are many reasons why one wants to teach about the new religions. They are vividly alive. They were often founded or led by women. The almost total interpenetration of the folk and the "high" (or text-based) in Japanese religion is well illustrated in the "new religions," where healing and shamanic gifts are typically important. And one can explore sociological generalizations about new religious movements.

It is the temptation to reductionist sociological explanation that opens a pitfall in teaching this subject. Precisely because these are non-elite movements, and because as teachers we sympathize with elite worldviews, we must be very careful to give full attention and respect to the testimony of participants that their lives have been changed by the religious worldview and transforming religious experiences that these movements have opened up to them.

---

[12]Cf. Royall Tyler, "A Critique of 'Absolute Phenomenalism'," *Japanese Journal of Religious Studies*, 9:4 (1982), p. 261.

[13]Cf. Toshio Kuroda, "Shinto in the History of Japanese Religion," translated by James C. Dobbins and Suzanne Gay, *Journal of Japanese Studies*, 7:1 (Winter, 1981), pp. 1-21.

[14]See most recently Helen Hardacre, *Kurozumikyo and the New Religions of Japan* (Princeton: Princeton U. Press, 1986); H. Byron Earhart, *Gedatsukai and Religion in Contemporary Japan* (Bloomington: Indiana University Press, 1989.)

8. Finally, of course, generalizations themselves, particularly those leading to a sense that there is a unified Japanese worldview, are themselves a pitfall.

INTRODUCING BUDDHISM

Frank E. Reynolds

There is no one appropriate way to introduce students of the liberal arts to Buddhism. There are, however, a number of inappropriate ways in which this introductory process is often carried out. It may be best to begin this communication of friendly advice (to use Mark Juergensmeyer's characterization in his instructions to the authors of these essays) by mentioning four very common approaches or tendencies that religious studies teachers of Buddhism should be careful to avoid.

First, those who introduce Buddhism to students in religious studies and/or liberal arts programs should avoid transmitting an overly simplistic notion of what "Buddhism" *really is*. At the outset a certain amount of oversimplification may well be necessary. I myself, for example, have rather successfully assigned Walpole Rahula's very readable though subtlety dogmatic *What the Buddha Taught* (rev. ed., Bedford: G. Fraser, 1967) as one of the first books for students to read. But, before the course or course segment is completed, students must be made aware of the fact that it is impossible to provide an historically defensible description of what the Buddha actually said or did. Moreover, students must be confronted with the fact that who the Buddha was, what he said, and what he did (as well as virtually all of the other aspects of Buddhism as an historical tradition) have, over the centuries, been continually contested by Buddhists of different backgrounds, persuasions and temperaments. Unless the teacher wishes to assume the mantle—and the responsibility—of a Buddhist "theologian", he or she will do well to present Buddhism in terms of various orientations that Buddhists have historically generated, and the various problems and possibilities that Buddhists have historically grappled with, rather than providing (either explicitly or implicitly) a philosophically or religiously normative notion of what "Buddhism" really is.

A second, closely related tendency that needs to be resisted by those who introduce Buddhism in a religious studies or liberal arts curriculum is the temptation to interpret Buddhism as a tradition that has followed a uni-directional trajectory that is characterized either by progressive evolution or progressive degeneration. Both of the most common versions of this kind of approach tend to identify early Buddhism with the Theravada or Hinayana tradition; they then move on to Mahayana Buddhism as the successor to the Theravada tradition; and—in some cases at least—continue with discussions of Vajrayana (or Zen) as the successor or culmination of the Mahayana tradition. In the first of the two scenarios, this uni-directional process in which each new version of the tradition effectively relegates to oblivion the one that preceded it, tends to be presented as a process of degeneration in which the true message of the Buddha is increasingly lost. In the second of the two scenarios this same process of a one-dimensional sequential movement from early/Theravadada tradition to Mahayana tradition to Vajrayana (or Zen) tradition appears as a gradual unfolding of the true essence of Buddhist insight and practice. Either way, a confessionally-oriented Buddhist "theological" position is taken, and the continued existence *and the continued creativity* of the "earlier" tradition(s) is ignored.

A third temptation that needs to be resisted when teachers introduce students to Buddhism is the tendency to romanticize the tradition. Perhaps more than any of the other great religions (especially, perhaps, Christianity and Islam), Buddhism has often been presented by modern interpreters, including many purveyors of contemporary popular culture, in terms that can best be described as idyllic. Those aspects of Buddhism that can be made attractive to disaffected western intellectuals (e.g. Buddhism's emphasis on meditational praxis, its supposedly non-judgmental and "therapeutic" orientation toward the problematics of the human condition, and the supposed compatibility of Buddhist doctrine and modern science) have been highlighted in ways that are not always consistent with the historically discernable teachings and practices of actual Buddhist peoples. On the other hand, many very prominent doctrinal, practical and sociological aspects of Buddhism that are less attractive to contemporary sensibilities (for example, sectarian conflicts, traditional Buddhist attitudes towards wealth and poverty, Buddhist notions of heavens and hells, and the care and regard for ancestors) are often ignored.

Finally, a fourth temptation which teachers of courses that introduce Buddhism would do well to avoid is the temptation to present Buddhism as an "other-worldly" religion that has little or no concern or involvement with those aspects of reality that we ordinarily designate as "social", "political" or "economic." This is a temptation that is fueled by one very venerable strand of modern western scholarship that has interpreted Buddhism in general, and Theravada Buddhism in particular, in exactly this way. However, the best contemporary scholars (see, for example, the work of Stanley Tambiah) have clearly demonstrated the inadequacy of this kind of approach. These studies have demonstrated, beyond any reasonable doubt, the need to take seriously into account the character that Buddhism has often assumed as a "total religio-social fact."

Positive advice for how a course might best be structured is more difficult to give. There are a variety of appropriate ways of proceeding in order to introduce students to Buddhism in a religious studies or liberal arts context. The appropriateness of a course will vary depending on the background, the interests and the style of the teacher, as well as the background, the academic capacities and the motivations of the students. But one principle applies across the board: students should in every case be apprised, as precisely and forcefully as possible, of the specific advantages *and the specific limitations* of whatever approach is taken. Any approach that is viable will necessarily involve a very high degree of selectivity, both in terms of the particular Buddhist traditions that are considered and the particular aspects of those traditions that are highlighted. Students should be made aware that this kind of selectivity is being exercised; they should be apprised of the reasons informing the choices that the teacher has made; and they should be explicitly apprised of the existence and importance of those aspects of the tradition that are—for whatever reasons—being given short shrift.

Keeping this very important preliminary point in mind, my own more substantive (and perhaps more controversial) suggestion is that the most adequate kind of introduction to Buddhism is one that acquaints students with some of the characteristic ways in which three complexes of correlated elements have been expressed and functioned in a variety of different Buddhist contexts. The arguable presupposition on which this kind of approach is based is that wherever Buddhism has been well established, at least until very modern times, these three complexes of elements have been "in place"; that in virtually every instance they have been central to the structure of Buddhism as a holistic religious tradition; and that, taken together, they have encompassed the most typically Buddhist aspects of Buddhist life.

The first of these three complexes of elements consists of a corpus of Buddhist teachings on the one hand, and a symbolic representation of the Buddha's "presence" on the other. Generally speaking, most academic studies of Buddhism focus on the corpus of teachings that are recognized in particular Buddhist contexts, spelling out in considerable detail their form and their content. In some instances this emphasis on content is supplemented by a presentation of the various ways in which these teachings are communicated to the members of the relevant Buddhist community. This emphasis is required, as no discussion of any form of Buddhism at any period in its history will be even minimally adequate if this focus on teachings (including doctrines, stories, aphorism and the like) is not given its proper due.

At the same time, however, both the explicit testimony of the tradition and the overwhelming evidence of historical research and observation indicate very clearly that in situations in which Buddhism has been fully established and operative, the relevant corpus of Buddhist teachings has coexisted with equally valorized symbolic representations of the person of the Buddha: These symbolic representations include relics, stupas (funerary monuments), images and the like which serve as reminders of his accomplishments and as appropriate loci for the veneration and devotion of the faithful. Any treatment of Buddhism that hopes to provide an adequate account of the tradition must attend very closely not only to the relevant corpus of Buddhist texts, but also to these very central Buddhist symbols, and to the rituals that give these symbols their religious life and meaning.

The second complex of elements that has been constitutive of various Buddhist traditions from India to Japan is more specifically communal or ecclesiastical in character. Once again, there is one component in this complex—namely the monastic component—that teachers tend to single out for extended presentation and discussion. And, once again, this tendency is not totally unwarranted. It is certainly true that Buddhism developed a unique kind of monastic community that must be properly understood in order to understand the distinctive character of Buddhist life and practice.

However, just as a focus on Buddhist texts must be complimented by a focus on Buddhist symbols, so too a focus on Buddhist monasticism must be complimented by a focus on the Buddhist laity. From the very earliest times about which we have any knowledge, the Buddhist community included not only monks and nuns who had given up the household life, but also lay men and women who continued to participate in the structures of ordinary society. Throughout Buddhist history these lay men and women have had very specific and important responsibilities and functions that have been crucial to the process of constituting and maintaining the Buddhist world.

Buddhist monks (and sometimes nuns) have been the primary bearers of Buddhist teachings, the primary practitioners of Buddhist meditation and ascetic practice, and the primary loci of saintly charisma; yet, Buddhist lay men and women have generally been recognized as co-participants in the tradition who have had a special responsibility for the proper maintenance of the social order and for the kind of gift-giving that supported the monks (and nuns) and the monastic establishments over which they presided. Following their own particular vocations, the monastics and the laity have pursued their own soteriological and practical interests. But those vocations have been so structured that a remarkably symbiotic relationship has been maintained. As a result, a distinctive form of Buddhist communal life has continually been constituted and reconstituted.

The third complex of elements that should be highlighted in an adequate religious studies or liberal arts introduction to Buddhism is the hierarchically organized conception of cosmology and society that is characteristic of most classical forms of Buddhist tradition. Though the position of the monastic community in relation to the cosmic and social orders is often problematic, the cosmic and social orders themselves are usually conceived in terms of a hierarchy in which beings are situated in accordance with the law of *karmic* reward and retribution (the law according to which good deeds are rewarded and evil deeds are punished, primarily in future lives). Thus, Buddhism has generally provided a legitimating basis for political orders headed by Buddhist monarchs (presumably great beings who have performed innumerable good deeds in their previous lives), and for modes of social organization structured in terms of rather widely differentiated hierarchies of prestige and wealth.

A good religious studies or liberal arts introduction to Buddhism should—in one way or another—acquaint students with these very basic complexes of elements that have been central to most Buddhist traditions through the course of Buddhist history. Such an introduction should also provide examples of the very different ways in which these complexes of elements have appeared and functioned in different Buddhist contexts. In addition, such an introduction should not neglect contemporary developments.

In presenting contemporary Buddhism, the teacher should make it clear to students that in most parts of the Buddhist world the three complexes of elements that have been basic to Buddhism in the past remain basic to the structure and dynamics of the tradition as it is presently practiced. (This is a point which many teachers tend to ignore in their enthusiasm to describe new developments that have been occurring in the 19th and 20th centuries.) On the other hand, the teacher should also point out some of the most important ways in which traditional patterns and practices are being called into question by contemporary Buddhists. For example, students should be apprised of the efforts of Buddhist modernists (both in Asia and in the West) who have espoused a kind of "protestant" Buddhism that affirms reformist versions of Buddhist teaching and meditational practice, but is skeptical of the value of Buddhist relics, images and related ritual activities. Similarly, they should be apprised of the fact that there are important contemporary Buddhist groups particularly, but not exclusively, in Japan and the West, that have rejected Buddhist monasticism and generated new forms of Buddhism that are oriented almost totally toward the laity. Finally, students should be apprised of the fact that there has been a widespread movement among both Asian and Western Buddhists to develop Buddhist political and social orientations that are more democratic and egalitarian in character.

So far as I am aware, there is not presently available any single, overall treatment of Buddhism that explicitly focuses attention on the three complexes of elements that I have identified. However, there are a number of books and articles that discuss these complexes of elements and their interrelationship, and would prove helpful for structuring an introductory course and for developing a correlated reading list for students.

My own attempt to provide a well balanced historical overview is an essay entitled "Buddhism" in Niels Nielson, ed. *Religions of the World* which was republished in John Fenton, ed. *Religions of Asia*. Both books are available in paperback in second editions published by St. Martin's Press (New York, 1988).

More recently and with a differently organized presentation, I have covered the same ground in an article published jointly with Charles Hallisey as the major "Buddhism" entry in Mircea Eliade, ed. *Encyclopedia of Religion* (New York: Macmillan, 1987). This essay and an accompanying essay on "Buddha" (also co-authored with Charles Hallisey) have just been included as the lead essays in a collection of *Encyclopedia of Religion* entries edited by Joseph Kitagawa and Mark Cummings entitled *Buddhism in Asian History* (New York: Macmillan, 1988).

For those seeking a free-standing introductory textbook, I recommend two books. The first is the Kitagawa/Cummings *Buddhism in Asian History* collection mentioned above. Written by top experts in various areas of Buddhist studies, it provides students with a reasonably comprehensive account that is both authoritative and readable. My other recommendation is William LaFleur's *Buddhism: A Cultural Approach* (Englewood Cliffs, N.J.: Prentice Hall, 1988). This is a shorter book that has both the advantages and disadvantages of a single-author presentation.

Teachers who wish to gain more background for themselves, or to provide additional readings for their students, should consult the excellent and up-to-date bibliographies that are attached to the various essays in the Kitagawa/Cummings collection. In addition, extremely helpful bibliographies are included in various other essays on Buddhism that are included in the *Encyclopedia of Religion*.

Anyone who wishes to pursue in-depth investigations into more specialized areas of Buddhological concern should take advantage of the 415 page *Guide to Buddhist Religion* (Boston: G. K. Hall, 1981) which I compiled in the mid 1970's with the assistance of John Strong and John Holt. Originally designed for use by college teachers, this fully annotated bibliography is organized in terms of twelve major topics: Historical Development of Buddhism; Religious Thought; Authoritative Texts; Popular Beliefs and Literature; The Arts (Art, Architecture, Drama, Music, Dance, etc.); Social, Political and Economic Aspects; Religious Practices and Rituals; Ideal Beings, Hagiography and Biography; Mythology (including Sacred History), Cosmology and Basic Symbols; Sacred Places; and Soteriological Experience and Processes—Path and Goal. This *Guide to Buddhist Religion* also contains an extensive index which enables the teacher or student to locate important books and articles that deal with more precisely identified Buddhological topics.

Placing Islam

William R. Darrow and Richard C. Martin

Islam in the Introductory Survey Course

Scholars of religious traditions like to claim that the tradition in which they specialize has received too little attention in religious studies scholarship. Islamists are notoriously plaintive in this regard. The softer form of this argument has it that *Religionswissenschaft* in the nineteenth century and phenomenology in the twentieth century failed to contribute relevant categories that apply to Islam.[1] The stronger form of this argument claims that Islam can be known and understood only through specialized study of its history and texts.[2] This litany of complaints may be suspected of being a benign bias of specialists, but it is an important indication of the endemic problem of religious studies concerning the relation of the whole (religion) to its parts (religions). In any case, the teacher in the introductory course presumably intends to help students discover in the Islamic materials problems in the study of religion. How does the study of Islam contribute to the study of religion, and vice versa?

In the spiritual geography of contemporary America, Islam is invariably accorded a marginal place. Like everything presumed to exist in the cultural margins these days, to talk about Islam even in the academic

---

[1]The locus classicus for the Islamists' version of this argument is Charles J. Adams, "The History of Religions and the Study of Islam" in *The History of Religions: Essays on the Problem of Understanding*, ed. by Joseph M. Kitagawa with Mircea Eliade and Charles Long (Chicago and London: University of Chicago Press, 1967). The issue was raised more constructively by Adams and younger historians of religions two decades later in *Approaches to Islam in Religious Studies*, ed. by Richard C. Martin (Tucson, Ariz.: The University of Arizona Press, 1985).

[2]For an intelligent discussion of this issue, see Leonard Binder, "Area Studies: A Critical Reassessment" in *The Study of the Middle East: Research and Scholarship in the Humanities and Social Sciences*, ed. Leonard Binder (New York: John Wiley & Sons, 1976), pp. 1-28.

setting encounters inflammatory rhetoric at worst and biases that must be deconstructed at best. Geographically, Islam is neither East nor West and chronologically it is the "last" of the Big Seven[3] world religions to appear in history. Islam is often categorized as one of the monotheistic religions, however. The result is that inevitably in an introductory course Islam comes just before the mid-term (as the third of the "Western" monotheisms) or at the end of the course (the last to appear in history) and all too often receives rushed attention, or simply gets dropped, to make way for the rest of the course or the final examination. The political and cultural reasons for this placing of Islam at the margins perhaps have deeper causes in the Euro-American historical consciousness, as Edward W. Said has argued.[4]

That Muslims themselves regard the Qur'an as the final and complete revelation of God's Word and Muhammad as the "Seal" of the prophets provides a different (one might say "emic") reason for placing Islam last (or alternately, first) among the religions of humankind. In an Islamic religious context, one would start with Islam and the cosmological claim that everyone is born Muslim. Societies after Creation were "sent" messengers with the message of divine unity. Judaism and Christianity can be dealt with in that framework, leading to Islam in history as the completion of the revelatory process. The religions of Asia would fall under the category of pagan polytheism against which the Qur'an and Prophet took such a strong exclusivist stand. This primordial sense of Islam as the original and ultimately the final "submission" of humankind to the will of Allah shapes an Islamic view of other religions as well as Islamic political and social views. In this view, otherness has to do with the characteristic human forgetfulness of and disobedience toward the universal divine message, embodied in the Islamic religion. Thus, the very decision by "outsiders" to place Islam as the last (and expendable unit of study if too much time is spent on other religions) has "theological" implications for Muslims and is often seen as an implicit polemic against Islam. We do not suggest that Islam need, or even

---

[3]For most textbooks these include Hinduism, Buddhism, China (Confucianism/Taoism), Japan, Judaism, Christianity, and Islam—and usually in that order.

[4]The discourse against "orientalism" by the Poststructuralist critic Edward W. Said (*Orientalism* [New York: Random House, 1978]) is perhaps worth considering in class discussions. At some point quite early in the course it needs to be asked: How (in what historical and political circumstances) did European and North American scholars come to construct a body of knowledge about "other" religions?

should, be taught from a Muslim doctrinal point of view, but we do suggest that it is time to rethink the place of Islam in the introductory course.

Islam in Comparative Studies in Religion

Leonard Binder has argued in the case of the human sciences in area studies "that the logic of their discourse is synthetic, that their evidence is always incomplete, that analysis is comparison, and that the first principles are normative."[5] If the survey course amounts to being most students' first acquaintance with world religions—or their first significant noetic encounter with other civilizations of any kind—it is probably also their first opportunity to struggle with comparative studies. Does the introductory course teach students how to engage in comparative studies? The answer is: probably not. The Big Seven religions get treated differentially in the introductory course because the bodies of respectable scholarship that have produced our knowledge and textbooks about them over the past century and a half have produced synthetic discourses largely in isolation from one a other; East Asian studies, South Asian studies and Middle Eastern studies had little influence upon one another until recently. Introductory textbooks are either edited volumes that draw on the expertise of diverse area specialists or a single author's attempt to structure all religions according to an idiosyncratic scheme. Even the latter approach does not necessarily amount to comparative studies, however. Let us return, then, to the question of Islam in the introductory course in light of possible approaches to comparative studies.

In global terms—and not just in modern times—Islam is just as much an Asian as a Mediterranean/Middle-Eastern religion. Of the nearly one-billion human beings who adhere in some form to Islam in the world today, the majority live east of Karachi—the lands of Hindu, Buddhist, local animist (and some very densely Islamic) cultures. Although even non-Arab Muslims have idealized the so-called pure Arabic and other aspects of Bedouin culture, Islam has spread and thrived readily in the rural, agricultural areas of South and Southeast Asia. Comparatively, it is important to see the history of Islam in relation to Buddhism, Hinduism and Asian civilizations. In this regard, too, it is important to recall that Salman Rushdie, the author of the notorious *Satanic Verses*, is not an Arab but a South Asian. The Asian experience of Islam has in many ways transcended the East/West dichotomy—through religious pilgrimage and post-Colonial dislocations—and Asian Muslims have consequently

---

[5]Binder, "Area Studies," p. 15 (emphasized in the original).

come to epitomize the global and universal migrations of Muslims to Europe and the Americas as well as to other parts of Asia.

Another way to construct a comparative framework for Islam is to place it among the universal missionary religions that include Buddhism and Christianity. The introductory survey course might divide between those religions strongly identified with a particular region, ethnic group, or community (Confucianism, Taoism, Shinto, Hinduism, and Judaism) and those that have retailed a more universal impetus.

Still another way to construe the comparative study of world religions is to start from the North American cultural experience. From various ancient migrations of Native Americans, through the Europeans, African slaves, on down to the Boat People, Levantine immigrants and Japanese and Arab investors (and Engineering students), North America hosts (not always graciously) all of the world religions—some in surprisingly large and growing numbers. In the North American context, Islam is the fastest growing religious tradition. Understanding religion in America is no longer effectively structured around a tripartite consideration of "Protestant, Catholic, and Jew." This "start from where the students are" approach might well incorporate projects that involve visiting local religious communities and focus on how these communities construct their religious identities in the American cultural context (the comparative axis). That many Muslim and Buddhist communities conduct instructional "Sunday Schools" can provide an important heuristic insight into how religions adapt communal group identities to local cultural patterns. This approach also allows the instructor to give an important place to Asian, Middle Eastern and other "foreign" students in the discourse on religions in relation to Jewish and Christian students of Euro-American background. This much they share in common: they are all what they are religiously in a local American context. Finally, it forces the deconstruction of religious "traditions" as essentialist, isolated systems of beliefs and rituals that somehow have an existence apart from the other traditions. Such a view of religious traditions exists only in textbooks, not in historical reality.

How might an introductory course be structured so as to invite the raising of comparative issues? One central issue around which to develop common sets or stages of comparative studies is to focus on the symbols and rituals of the social formation of communal identities and the process of drawing and maintaining (and ultimately negotiating across) the boundaries with "Other" traditions. This kind of focus can be subdivided into a common set of studies: 1. *beginnings* (founders, authoritative texts, authentic communities), 2. *world view* (cosmologies, core rituals, law), 3. *society* (issues of gender, sexuality, ethnicity, festivals, power, and violence), and 4. *modernity* (responses to colonialism, secularism and globalism). In this approach, it is important in the case of Islam, for example, to continually bring such core matters as Qur'an, Sunna, religious duties (Five Pillars) into each stage in order to show that they are many-faceted symbols that pervade religious life.

The Problem of Sources

However one decides to construct the introductory course and to place Islam within it, sources for the teacher and for the student present problems that are slowly being resolved. For both the teacher and the student, encyclopedias, dictionaries, and bibliographic databases can be extremely important. In addition to the many well-known encyclopedias, such as *Britannica* and the new *Encyclopedia of Religion*, we would call the reader's attention to the *Encyclopaedia of Islam* (Leiden: E.J. Brill), now in progress in its second edition in many volumes and the single-volume *Shorter Encyclopaedia of Islam*, which focuses on religious, cultural, and institutional topics from the first edition. The scholarship, however, is dense and often makes for tough sledding over numerous protruding technical terms from Arabic and other foreign languages.[6] Both the teacher and the student may want to consult J. D. Pearson, et. al., *Index Islamicus*, a database bibliography that includes a highly differentiated set of listings on Islamic religion, covering books and journal articles published in Western languages. Also useful to both teacher and student is *Islamic Book Review Index* (Berlin, 1982-).

Audio-visual aids for Islamic religion and culture are growing in numbers and quality. An older review of materials prepared by the American Council of Learned Societies is *The World of Islam, Images and Echoes: A Critical Guide to Films and Recordings,* ed. Ellen-Fairbanks Bodman (1980). A slide collection prepared for the ACLS on all aspects of Islamic religious and cultural life, accompanied by a useful text and commentary on each slide by Frederick M. Denny and Abdulaziz A. Sachedina is titled *Islamic Religious Practices.* Another important source of materials is the Middle East Studies Association (MESA, Department of Oriental Studies, Tucson, AZ 85721; 602/621-5850). Recently MESA has produced *MEOC Middle East Materials for Teachers, Students, Non-*

---

[6]Even the article titles are mostly transliterated Arabic terms, so that the article on the mosque, for example, is found under the Arabic term "masjid."

Specialists and *MEOC Middle East Resource Guide for Teachers, Students, Non-Specialists.*

A number of general introductions to the full range of Islamic materials available for use as introductory textbooks exist for use in lieu of a single world religions textbook. H.A.R. Gibb's *Muhammedanism* is among the oldest still in print, but it continues to be the best short introduction that lends itself to repeated profitable rereadings. Fazlur Rahman, *Islam* (Chicago paperback), is longer and not so introductory for students, but useful to teachers and advanced students who will realize something of the background of his many arguments with Western and Muslim scholars about interpretation. Seyyed Hossein Nasr, *Ideals and Realities of Islam* (Beacon Paperback) in six essays introduces students to comparative studies of Islam vis a vis Christianity, mysticism, and Shi'ite expressions of Islam. Kenneth Cragg, *The House of Islam* (Wadsworth paperback) is a very perceptive and appreciative Christian evaluation of Islam. Written from a history of religions perspective are Frederick M. Denny, *An Introduction to Islam* (Macmillan paperback) and Richard C. Martin, *Islam: A Cultural Perspective* (Prentice-Hall paperback).

Many teachers prefer to rely on primary texts in translation, especially in classes that emphasize discussion and writing. A useful guide to Islamic texts in translation is Margaret Anderson, *Arabic Materials in English Translation* (Boston, 1980). Among the more popular anthologies are Kenneth Cragg and Marsden Speight, *Islam from Within*; Marilyn R. Waldman and William McNeill, *The Islamic World*; John A. Williams, *Themes of Islamic Civilization* (with very short selections); A. J. Arberry, *Aspects of Islamic Civilization*; A. J. Jeffery, *A Reader on Islam*; and Andrew Rippin and Jan Knappert, *Textual Sources for the Study of Islam.*

Many teachers will want to focus class discussion on the Prophet Muhammad and/or the Qur'an when they come to Islam in the world religions course. Of the many works available on the Prophet, we recommend for the beginning student W. M. Watt, *Muhammad: Prophet and Statesman*, and, from a more psychological perspective, Maxime Rodinson, *Muhammad*. Also, one might consult Annemarie Schimmel, *And Muhammad is the Messenger of God*. On the Qur'an, the standard introductory work is W. M. Watt, *Introduction to the Qur'an*, although from a comparative religions perspective we highly recommend William A. Graham, *Beyond the Written Word: Oral Aspects of Scripture in the History of Religion*. Another important single focus in the study of Islam (especially in comparison with Judaism) is Islamic law, for which the most accessible work for beginners is N. Coulson, *A History of Islamic*

Law. For a biographical approach to religious thinkers in Islam, one might use S. H. Nasr, *Three Muslim Sages*. Although we do not recommend that the single focus on Islam be Sufism (mysticism), nonetheless mysticism makes a good comparative category; among the several works available, the most definitive is Annemarie Schimmel, *Mystical Dimensions of Islam*. Finally, the study of Islamic ritual is not aided by a good overall introductory study; still usable, however, is Gustav von Grunebaum, *Muhammadan Festivals*.

Final Thoughts

In the 1990s, Islam is no longer a religion that should be "introduced" to students as something that is intrinsically foreign and alien to the American cultural experience. Nor, for that matter, are Buddhism, Hinduism, and other Asian religions. We believe that the introductory course on world religions must find a place for Islam that recognizes not only its Middle Eastern origins and its dramatic spread to Asia and Africa, but also its place within the religious and cultural pluralism of the Americas. A growing number of good textual and audio-visual sources exist to aid the teacher in presenting Islamic religion to students.

The comparative structure of the introductory course remains the greatest challenge that most of us face in the classroom. And in this regard the classroom is still the crucible of success and the syllabus is the conceptual guide that must be carefully constructed. Any predetermined construction is arbitrary; none is "essential" to the understanding of religion. What the teacher needs to decide is how best to see religions alongside each other and in their encounters with one another, especially in the modern period. We hope the few brief suggestions made in this essay will be useful in bringing Islam into the introductory course in a way that is dynamic and illustrative of comparative studies in the best sense of the term.

ANCIENT MEDITERRANEAN AND NEAR EASTERN RELIGIONS

William R. Darrow

The religions of the peoples of the Mediterranean and the Near East play a multifaceted role in the history of European culture and thus in the history of the study of religion that developed in that milieu. The religious traditions of Greece and Rome stand in the background of the development of classical civilization and the humanist strands of European thought that found sustenance in those traditions. The religions of the Ancient Near East came to provide insight into the context in which the religion of the Israelites developed, sometimes to provide contrasts and at other times to provide parallels. The rise and spread of Christianity united these two worlds, but also defined the very different contexts in which Christianity developed from Iran and the Fertile Crescent to Spain.

In approaching these traditions the teacher thus faces some unique problems if s/he chooses to include materials from them in a survey course, especially since they are likely to be covered elsewhere in the Classics and History departments. The first question is why include any material from these traditions. Are they to be included on the argument that cultural literacy requires some familiarity with selected monuments of these traditions? This is a sufficient argument and some of the treasures of these cultures such as *The Epic of Gilgamesh*, the Babylonian New Year's festival, Homer and Hesiod, Euripides' *The Bacchae* or Aeschylus' *Orestian Trilogy* and *Prometheus Bound* and the architectural remains of Egypt certainly merit the attention of a survey of human religiousness and deserve to be recaptured from the Classicists.

There are at least three issues that must be addressed in the decision to focus on such materials. Why these traditions rather than other ancient traditions of Asia, Africa and the Americas? The argument of cultural significance needs to be contextualized and historicized. We focus on these materials because they have been significant in the history of European culture. Any further claim raises the dangers of provincialism and ethnocentrism.

A claim to larger cultural significance of these traditions, even if modestly maintained, has the further problem of ownership. Materials from these traditions are thought in some sense to be ours. Especially for Americans, the post World War II myth of the rise of civilization, freedom and individuality beginning in Sumeria and moving inexorably west until it is now safely enshrined in the United States, provided an evolutionary timeline in which materials from these peoples could be safely placed and owned. This myth was the latest version of Christian universal triumphalism and provided a conceptual grid in which the religious traditions of these peoples could be appropriated and interpreted. But the undisguised evolutionism left interpretation of these traditions loaded with unexamined assumptions. This is inevitable in the interpretative process, but in the study of these traditions it meant the tendency to assume these 'others' were more familiar to us than other peoples; that each tradition was frozen into a fixed significance and that the confident evolutionism that justified our cultural superiority was secured.

The study of the religious traditions of these areas and the use of materials from them in an introductory religion course is in fact a highly charged issue, but there are still several very compelling reasons to include materials from these areas in an introduction to religion course. These include:

• Religious evolutionism—the issues alluded to in the preceding paragraphs can be a very useful focus. What assumptions do we make about the direction and content of human religious evolution and why do we make them? What roles have been played by the religious traditions we are concerned with here in the formulation of these assumptions? Robert Bellah's classic article "Religious Evolution" contained in his *Beyond Belief* read in conjunction with materials from these areas would be a very useful classroom exercise to explore the character and effects of an evolutionary progressive view of history.

• Polytheism and Mythology—all the traditions we focus on here were polytheist. What did it mean to live in a polytheist world? What are the assumptions that have lead us to distinguish between monotheism and polytheism? David Miller's *The New Polytheism* (1974) is an interesting place to start with this issue. Polytheism is reflected in mythology.

The study by G.S. Kirk *Myth:Its Meaning and Functions in Ancient and Other Cultures* is a structuralist approach to the mythology both of Greece and the Ancient Near East that raises a number of interesting issues in the study of mythology.

• Religion and the Political Order—One of the most striking features of the interpretation of Ancient Near Eastern religions is the assumption of the close identity between political and religious order, most specifically the notion of the divine king, a mode of interpretation that dominates Henri Frankfort's *Kingship and the Gods: A Study of Ancient Near Eastern Religion as the Integration of Society and Nature.*

• The Character of Religious Belief—The study of Greek religion has been informed by an interesting tension between students of literature and students of religion that has posed the fundamental question captured in the title of Paul Veyne *Did the Greeks Believe in Their Myths?* The relation between mythology and belief normally assumed by religionists is rather essentialist, myths are believed literally by their makers, except for the Greeks. The interesting question posed by Greek and Roman religion about different modes of appropriating religious traditions serves as a useful corrective to too simple an assumption of the literalness of belief in human religious history.

• Comparative Religion—It is in comparison to the materials of this area along with the new materials that came into Europe in the eighteenth century from China, India, Africa and the Americas that the foundation of modern comparative religions was laid. The exercises in comparison between mythological figures, cults and art are rich and numerous. The kind of comparative treatments represented by Henri Frankfort ed., *Before Philosophy: The Intellectual Adventure of Ancient Man: An Essay on Speculative Thought in the Ancient Near East* is still a very enjoyable text to teach. For comparative ritual studies, Theodor Gaster *Thespis, Ritual, Myth and Drama in the Ancient Near East* is still useful. In the area of literature, Auerbach's essay "Odysseus' Scar" in his *Mimesis* belongs on the short list of works that every student of religion should read.

• Cultural Encounter—Less attended to, but still a very rich theme is the materials on cultural encounters to be found in the long history of interaction between the peoples of these regions. The identification of divinities, the spread of cults and the development of syncretic practices and the issues posed by cultural pluralism are all directions that might be followed. On the last issue the recent book by Francois Hartog *The Mirror of Herodotus: The Representation of the Other in the Writing of History* is an excellent place to start. It is with Herodotus that the foundation for the description of other cultures was laid.

In the remainder of this essay I will briefly discuss the traditions of the Ancient Near East: Mesopotamia, the Levant and Egypt and the traditions of Greece and Rome. I will mention some of the more significant works on religion in each of the areas and what materials might be especially appropriate in an introductory survey course.

The Ancient Near East

The vast majority of work on the peoples of the Ancient Near East has been done in the context of the comparative study of the history of the Israelites. Readers should refer to references in the entry on Judaism for materials related to the Hebrew scriptures. The most convenient summary of the history both of Mesopotamia and Egypt is William W. Hallo and William Kelly Simpson, *The Ancient Near East: A History*. The place of women in the area is the focus of Ilse Seibert, *Women in the Ancient East*. The standard collection of texts is James Pritchard, ed., *Ancient Near Eastern Texts Relating to the Old Testament* which is abridged as *The Ancient Near East: An Anthology of Texts and Pictures*. These texts are scholarly and thus require careful classroom preparation. There are several more literary translations of the Epic of Gilgamesh that work very well in class. One is by Herbert Mason, one by Sanders and the third by John Gardner and John Maier.

Mesopotamia can roughly be divided into two regions, the northwest that came to be called Assyria and the southeast Babylonian region. Both areas were characterized by urban settlements that were in competition with one another as well as with settlers on the Iranian plateau. (On Iran see the separate entry on Iranian religions.) These cities were the seat of religious identity. Broadly speaking there were two peoples who left significant cuneiform records, the Sumerians and the Semitic speaking peoples: the Akkadians, Babylonians and Assyrians.

For the study of Sumerian culture, which is the earliest well attested culture in the south, the works of Samuel Kramer including *Sumerian Mythology, History Begins at Sumer*, and *The Sumerians: their History, Culture, and Character* are the place to begin. Thorkild Jacobsen, *The Treasures of Darkness: A History of Mesoptamian Religion* provides a rich interpretation of the religions of the different peoples. Both contain extensive translations of texts. Diane Wolkstein and Samuel N. Kraemer, *Inanna, Queen of Heaven and Earth: Her Stories and Hymns from Sumer* have recently studied the chief goddess in the area and J.V. Kinnier Wilson,

The Rebel Lands: an Investigation into the Origins of Early Mesopotamian Mythology has provided an interpretation of some of the main themes in the mythology.

For the Levant, the culture of Canaan has become clearer to us since the discovery of the Ugaratic texts that have provided vital insight into the wider context in which the Hebrew scriptures developed. G.R. Driver, *Canaanite Myths and Legends* and John Gray, *The Legacy of Canaan; the Ras Shamra texts and their relevance to the Old Testament* are useful collections of texts. William F. Albright, *Yahweh and the Gods of Canaan; a Historical Analysis of Two Contrasting Faiths* and F.M. Cross, *Canaanite Myth and Hebrew Epic: Essays in the History of the Religion of Israel* contain attempts at comparing and contrasting the god of the Hebrew scriptures from the world of the Ugaritic texts. For a very full treatment of the later history of the region and the spread of peoples from the levant cf. Sabatino Moscati, *The Phoenicians*.

For Egyptian religion the best place to start is still Henri Frankfort, *Ancient Egyptian Religion: An Interpretation*, which is suitable for undergraduates. Miriam Lichtheim, *Ancient Egyptian Literature* is a useful collection of texts. There is a nice brief discussion of funerary practice in Catharine Roehrig, *Mummies and Magic: an Introduction to Egyptian Funerary Beliefs*. For a general introduction to the art history, William Stevenson Smith's *The Art and Architecture of Ancient Egypt* is the most useful reference and B. G. Trigger et al. *Ancient Egypt: A Social History* is the most recent full historical survey.

Greece

Greek mythology and religion is, of course, a huge field of inquiry and one in which a number of modes of the interpretation of religions have been developed. The two best available surveys in English of the archaic and classical periods are Martin Nilsson's *A History of Greek Religion* and Walter Burkert's *Greek Religion*. Nilsson's studies focus especially on popular religious practice. They include *The Minoan-Mycenaean Religion and Its Survival in Greek Religion, Greek Piety, Greek Popular Religion*. Burkert has come to be especially interested in ritual as in his *Structure and history in Greek Mythology and Ritual, Ancient Mystery Cults*, and *Homo Necans: The Anthropology of Ancient Greek Sacrifical Ritual and Myth*. E.R. Dodds, *The Greeks and the Irrational* is also an excellent introduction to popular belief and practice. The most useful collection of texts for Greek religion is David G. Rice and John E. Stambaugh, *Sources for the Study of Greek Religion*. For the art and archaeology of Greece W.R. Biers, *The Archaeology of Greece: An Introduction*.

Greek mythology has in particular been the scene of a very rich and diverse interpretative enterprise. W.K.C. Guthrie's *The Greeks and Their Gods* and G.S. Kirk's *The Nature of Greek Myths* are useful places to start. Mark P.O. Morford and R.J. Lenardon, *Classical Mythology* is the most useful handbook of the Greek myths. For a Jungian inspired approach to the Greek gods the works of Karl Kerenyi are the place to begin. These include studies of Dionysius, Zeus and Hera, Prometheus, Asklepios, and the Eleusinian mysteries. More recently the works of two French students of Greece, both influenced by structuralist trends have revolutionized the approach to Greek mythology. These are Jean Pierre Vernant and Marcel Detienne. Vernant's works in English translation include: *Myth and Tragedy in Ancient Greece* (with P. Vidal-Naquet), *Myth and Thought Among the Greeks*, *Myth and Society in Ancient Greece* and *The Origins of Greek Thought*. Detienne's works in translation include *Dionysus Slain*, *The Gardens of Adonis: Spices in Greek Mythology*, *Dionysus at Large*, and *The Creation of Mythology*. Together they have written *Cunning Intelligence in Greek Culture and Society* and edited *The Cuisine of Sacrifice*.

Roman Religion

Roman religion has always been less attended to than Greek religion. In English three solid starting points are W. Warde Fowler, *The Religious Experience of the Roman People from Earliest Times to the Age of Augustus*; H.J. Rose, *Ancient Roman Religion*; and H. Liebeschuetz, *Continuity and Change in Roman Religion*. There is no collection of texts on Roman religion, but N. Lewis and M. Reinhold, *Roman Civilization* (2 vols.) is the most commonly used collection of texts. The one exception to the general neglect of Roman religion has been the comparative Indo-Europeanists who have considered Roman religion much closer to the hypothesized Indo-European religion. Several works of the founder of this scholarship Georges Dumezil focus specifically on Rome. These include *Archaic Roman Religion* and *Camillus: a Study of Indo-European Religion as Roman History*.

The imperial period is, of course, one of rich and fascinating religious developments relevant both to the histories of Judaism and Christianity. Peter Brown, *The World of Late Antiquity* is the most readable introduction to the whole period. Ramsay MacMullen *Paganism in the Roman Empire* and *Christianizing the Roman Empire, A.D. 100-400*; Robin Lane Fox, *Pagans and Christians*; E.R. Dodds, *Pagan and Christian in an Age of Anxiety*;

John Holland Smith, *The Death of Classical Paganism*; and Robert Grant, *Gods and the One Gods* are some of the more excellent recent studies.

For syncretic cults during the time period R.E. Witt, *Isis in the Graeco-Roman* and Friedrich Solmsen, *Isis Among the Greeks and Romans* is useful and a reading of Apuleius' *The Golden Ass* is always a delightful classroom exercise. Arthur Darby Nock's *Conversion: The Old and New in Religion from Alexander the Great to Augustine of Hippo* remains standard. For the most recent large scale introduction to gnostic movements Kurt Rudolph, *Gnosis: The Nature and History of Gnosticism* is the place to start. The collection of Coptic Gnostic texts found at Nag Hammadi in Egypt have been translated in *The Nag Hammadi Library in English*.

IRANIAN RELIGIONS

William R. Darrow

Although the primary focus of this essay will be on Zoroastrianism, brief attention will be directed toward the two "honorary" Iranian religions of Manichaeism and Mithraism. These religious traditions command interest for students of the history of religion disproportionate to the number of living representatives of those traditions. There are at least three reasons for this. First, Persia was for the Greeks and later the Roman empire the most significant cultural enemy during large portions of their history. Hence in reflecting on the formulation of the Western tradition, it is useful to remember that the spectre of Persia was always on the horizon (and still is!). Second, the influence of Iranian religious currents on the development of both Judaism and Christianity, as well as on gnostic and mystery religions in the Hellenistic period and later on the history of Islam, while often debated in individual cases, continues to be recognized as multifaceted and significant. At least in the areas of angelology and eschatology the influence of Iran seems unmistakable. Finally, the survival of Iranian cultural identity in the face of the major cultural as well as military conquests by Alexander and then by Islam, allows us to recognize Iran as one of the world's major cultural areas. To be sure it has transformed and changed throughout its history, but it has always survived.

In this essay I will briefly address the current state of studies on pre-Islamic Iranian religions, with specific attention to their relevance for conceiving the tradition as a whole. I will then turn to some specific issues that might be included in an introductory course, with reference to specific sources available. I will conclude with a brief discussion of Manichaeism and Mithraism.

Zoroastrianism

The term Zoroastrianism is of course a modern one, but it has a close resonance to the tradition's own self definition as the worship of the Ahura Mazda according to the teachings of Zoroaster. Zoroaster is now considered by most scholars to have lived sometime around 1000 B.C.E. or earlier in Eastern Iran. He is the author of seventeen hymns called the *gathas* composed in an Avestan dialect that are preserved in the text of the high liturgy of the tradition. The exact content of his life and teaching are lost to any secure historical record, but it appears quite certain that Zoroaster was a creative and perhaps reforming priest of the ancient Iranian religious tradition. This tradition was similar to its sister tradition in India represented by the Rg Veda. Zoroaster's stance toward that tradition was in some ways reformist, although his stress on the worship of the high god Ahura Mazda may already have been a more general feature of the tradition. The movement of Zoroaster's date backwards by a half-millenium or more has been accepted by most contemporary scholars marking a significant break from scholars of the last generation. The problems connected with extending the period between the foundation of the tradition and its first historical record have not been fully explored, and probably can never be very satisfactorily filled in unless new evidence is discovered.

Zoroastrianism is the name we give to the official religion of the two great pre-Islamic Iranian dynasties, the Achaemenids (550-330 B.C.E.) and the Sasanians (224 C.E. - 651 C.E.). The appropriateness of the single term may be debated, especially with regard to Achaemenid religious identity, since the Achaemenids never mentioned Zoroaster in their inscriptions. Nevertheless they worshipped Ahura Mazda and other divinities in the Zoroastrian pantheon. It is only in the Sasanian period that we can speak with much evidence about the institutional identity of the tradition. It was also only in this period that the texts composed in Avestan were canonized. These include the texts of the liturgy, other hymns of praise and other texts discussing a wide range of religious issues. Of the latter materials only a text dealing mainly with ritual pollution survives. The composition of a variety of other texts in Pahlavi, Middle Persian, began under the Sasanians and continued after the Islamic conquests. The best historical introductions to this period are Richard Frye's *Heritage of Persia* and *The History of Ancient Iran*. The latter work contains extensive and wide-ranging bibliographical comments as well as a narrative survey of the entire period.

For textual resources, most of the Avestan and Pahlavi texts were translated in the *Sacred Books of the East*. These are, however, dated and not immediately intelligible. There are two good modern English translations of the *gathas* by J. Duchesne-Guillemin and by Stanley Insler. More useful for the instructor and students are collections of texts. There are three that cover rather different materials. The fullest is edited by Mary Boyce, *Textual Sources for the Study of Zoroastrianism*. This contains selections from all the genres of Zoroastrian religious literatures, including the range of literature by modern Parsis. The selections are annotated. The work provides the best overview of the textual remains of the tradition. William Malandra has selected Avestan literary remains primarily from the hymns of praise in his *An Introduction to Ancient Iranian Religion*. Although more limited in focus this work is of special use for students of comparative Indo-European mythology. Third, R.C. Zaehner edited *The Teaching of the Magi*, which contains selections from the Pahlavi literatures organized around a number of theological issues. There is finally *Persian Mythology* by J.R. Hinnells which does not contain texts, but provides a good introduction to the mythology found in the tradition and later reflected in the Iranian epic as well as introduction to the major archaeological and artistic evidence. A fuller introduction to art history is E. Porada, *Ancient Iran, the Art of Pre-Islamic Times*.

The two most significant contemporary scholars of the tradition are Mary Boyce and Gherardo Gnoli. Boyce is the author of the major modern history of the tradition of which two volumes have appeared in the *Handbuch der Orientalistik* under the title *A History of Zoroastrianism* covering until the fall of the Achaemenids with two further volumes expected. The major themes of her interpretation are contained in her *Zoroastrians, Their Beliefs and Practices*, which is available in paper and is the best introduction available. The great merit of Boyce's interpretation is the sweep of her view. She rejects the view of Zaehner, contained in his earlier standard English introduction, *The Dawn and Twilight of Zoroastrianism*, that the twilight of the tradition took place with the fall of the Sasanians. She knows the living tradition in both India and Iran better than anyone and has published a separate account of Iranian Zoroastrianism in the middle 1960's in *A Persian Stronghold of Zoroastrianism*. Several themes dominate Boyce's interpretation which are contested. First, she stresses the unchanging continuity of the tradition suggesting that the teachings of Zoroaster are faithfully reflected in the contemporary community. Second, her work stresses the central role of ritual in the survival of the tradition and tends to underplay the significance of doctrinal issues. This allows her to maintain the priestly character of Zoroaster rather than presenting him as an anti-ritualist ethical thinker. However her interpretations of the rituals of the tradition are not very nuanced and her neglect of thought contrasts rather starkly with the earlier generation represented by Zaehner and Widengren. While the interpretations of these two should not always be accepted, they still serve as a supplement to Boyce in the area of doctrinal history. Finally her overwhelming stress on continuity obscures the reality of change in the history of the tradition.

Gnoli's main English work is *Zoroaster's Time and Homeland* which accepts the recent redating of Zoroaster championed first by Boyce and mainly tries to prove his long held view that Zoroaster was active in south-eastern rather than north-eastern Iran. Gnoli is also the author of all the essays in Mircea Eliade's *Encyclopedia of Religion* dealing with Zoroastrianism. There are several other short introductions available in English. These include, J. Hinnells, *Zoroastrianism and the Parsees* which is a judicious introduction, two works by J. Duchesne-Guillemin, *Zoroastrianism Symbols and Values*, which deals primarily with symbolism and *The Western Response to Zoroaster*, which contains positive reflections on the relevance of the theories of Dumezil for the study of Iranian religions. The best brief introduction by a Parsi is Rustom Masani, *Zoroastrianism: The Religion of the Good Life*.

Themes

It is unlikely that Zoroastrian materials would compose a large part of most introductory religion courses, nevertheless there are six specific areas where Iranian materials provide unique resources that would be appropriate in introductory courses.

• Religious expression—The *gathas* of Zoroaster, opaque though they are, remain a monument of religious expression that can profitably be read with the roughly contemporary and linguistically related Vedic hymns. Attention to these hymns provides a useful introduction to modes of interpretation, including the multifaceted notion of *mantra*. James Boyd's contribution in Fred Denny's *The Holy Book in Comparative Perspective* is a useful introduction to these issues.

• Prophecy—The historical Zoroaster will always elude our grasp, but we do have enough collateral material and material from the later tradition to use the figure of Zoroaster as a case study in the use of the category of prophet. We can explore the usefulness of the cross-cultural category in elucidating what we can surmise about Zoroaster's activity and thought and in turn use that material to criticize aspects of the general concept of prophecy. My article in *History of Religions* on "Zoroaster Amalgamated" discusses some aspects of how the tradition conceived their founder.

• Ritual—The central liturgy of the tradition, the *yasna*, is documented in a film produced by James Boyd and myself, available from Audio-Visual Services at Colorado State University in Fort Collins, Colorado. It contains commentary on the major ritual actions and gestures and a teacher's guide that introduces the tradition. The place of ritual is debated in the contemporary community in both Iran and India. The fact that the tradition has survived because of the active role played by the priesthood whose primary activity was the performance of the sacred rituals contrasts with the view of many laymen that these rituals represent unwanted superstition that detracts from the life affirming, ethical message of the tradition.

• Dualism—In Western spiritual geography the uniqueness of Zoroastrianism lies mainly in its dualist solution to the problem of evil. The connection between our textual evidence and dualist interpretations is complicated and it is by no means clear that the tradition was always a thoroughgoing dualist one. It does appear fairly clear that Sasanian orthodoxy was, although we should be suspicious of Zaehner's proposed Zurvanite heresy in contradistinction to Sasanian orthodoxy. With these caveats in mind and the recognition that we are mainly speaking of an ideal type, the character of Zoroastrian dualism as a solution to the problem of theodicy had a wide ranging impact on monotheistic systems. Zaehner remains the best introduction to the issues connected with dualism.

• Pollution—The Zoroastrian pollution system is an extraordinarily interesting one founded as it is on a division of the world into good and evil forces and the recognition that the struggle against evil is very much a struggle to keep the good creation pure. The specific role played by death as the ultimate pollution and the concomitant development of the famous Zoroastrian mode of disposal of the dead makes graphic for students the interconnection between beliefs and actions in this area. Boyce's discussion of the pollution system at the end of the first volume of her *History* is probably the best place to start.

• Survival and Influence—We have already alluded to the debate among contemporary Zoroastrians about the significance of ritual activity. The larger issues connected with the survival and self-definition of the tradition are wide-ranging both in the Iranian and Indian contexts. Until Boyce finishes her history the best place to start are the final chapters of her *Zoroastrians Beliefs and Practices*. In addition to the issues indigeneous to the tradition there is also the question of influence of one tradition on the other. The influence of Iranian concepts, assumptions and doctrines in Judaism and Christianity open a wide area familiar to students of the inter-testamental and new testamental periods. Alternatively the effect of Zoroastrianism's encounter with Hellenism, Islam and Hinduism also provide interesting examples of the role of adaptation by the tradition to changed contexts.

Manichaeism

An earlier generation of scholarship considered Iranian dualism the source of much of Manichaean doctrines. This position is still reflected in Widengren's *Mani and Manichaeism* (Holt, Rinehart and Winston, 1965), which remains the most easily available introduction. More recent scholarship has almost universally moved away from interpreting Manichaeism specifically and Gnosticism more generally as a products of Iranian religious currents. The publication of a Greek codex concerning the life of Mani by Henrichs and Koenen fifteen years ago has provided tremendously important insight into the baptist context out of which Mani arose. It is available in an English translation by Ron Cameron and Arthur Dewey entitled *The Cologne Mani Codex* (Scholars Press, 1979). However, a large portion of Manichaean texts were written and survive in Iranian languages and the Sasanian emperor was one of Mani's main missionary targets, so the designation of Manichaeisma as an Iranian is not entirely inappropriate. The best collection of texts in English is by Jes Asmussen, *Manichaean Literature: Representative Texts* (Caravan Books, 1975).

The history of Manichaeism is of extraordinary fascination both for its tremendous geographical and cultural breadth and for the specific issues of the interaction between Manichaeism and Christianity in late antiquity as source of at least some Christian heretical movements, and original faith of Augustine. The most recent and convenient introduction to the history of Manichaeism that has the great merit of attempting to cover both the Mediterranean, Middle Eastern and East Asian materials is by Samuel N.C. Lieu, *Manichaeism in the Later Roman Empire and Medieval China*.

Mithraism

I have included a brief word on Mithraism here to draw attention to the fact that recent scholarship has drastically called into question the Iranian origins of this widespread mystery cult in the Roman world. Franz Cumont's proposal at the end of the last century that Mithraism could best be explained as an Iranian cult of Mithra with Iranian antecedents has held the field for seventy-five years. Cumont's theory (most conveniently summarized in English in *The Mysteries of Mithra*) was never well founded since there was no evidence for a Mithraic cult on Iranian soil, although Mithra was an important Iranian divinity (cf. Gershevitch, *The Avestan Hymn to Mithra*) and Cumont had to alter the content of the Zoroastrian myth of the death of the primordial bull rather drastically to make Mithra the agent of the bull's death. Cumont's theories have recently been called into question by a number of scholars who recognize instead the astral connections of much of Mithraic iconography. There is a convenient introduction to this debate in David Ulansey, "Mithraic Studies: A Paradigm Shift", *Religious Studies Review* 13:2 (April, 1987) pp. 104-110. The use of astral symbolism also has entered into the discussion of Zoroastrian beliefs in the work of Gernot Windfuhr at the University of Michigan. What still remains to be explained is the dynamics of the identification between the hero/constellation Perseus, obviously identified with Persia and Mithra that was likely made in Cilicia in Asia Minor from whence the Mithraic cult was carried by Roman soldiers. What also needs further rethinking is the actual sources, if any, of competition that the Mithraic cult posed to the Jesus cult in the late antique world.

JUDAISM IN THE INTRODUCTORY COURSE

William Scott Green

> The interest of the historian of religion in [Judaism] cannot depend on apologetic, historical, or demographic reasons. That is to say, the interest in Judaism for the imagination of religion cannot be merely because it is "there," because it has played some role in our collective invention of western civilization, or because some students of religion happen to be Jews. Rather it is because of the peculiar position of Judaism within the larger framework of the imagining of western religion: close, yet distant; similar, yet strange; "occidental," yet "oriental"; commonplace, yet exotic. This tension between the familiar and the unfamiliar, at the very heart of the imagining of Judaism, has enormous cognitive power. It invites, it requires comparison. Judaism is foreign enough for comparison and interpretation to be necessary; it is close enough for comparison and interpretation to be possible. By virtue of its tensive situation between the near and the far, Judaism provides an important test case for central methodological issues such as definition and comparison besides illuminating the larger issues of imagination, self-consciousness, and choice crucial to the academic study of religion.
>
> —*Jonathan Z. Smith (1982:12)*

The problem of misrepresentation that affects any religion taught in an introductory religion course—especially a survey course—has a particular edge and complexity in the case of Judaism. The tendency—since Paul—to explain Christianity in terms of its differences from (and superiority over) Judaism has obscured Judaism's autonomy. Indeed, conceptions of Christianity often depend so heavily on the contrast with Jewish religion that "Judaism" itself becomes only a comparative category—the term for "not-Christianity."

Teaching Judaism in the introductory course thus imposes a double duty. On the one hand, as Jonathan Smith rightly observes, Judaism's "tensive situation between the near and the far" makes it an ideal vehicle for raising larger theoretical issues in the study of religion. On the other hand, the popular inclination to conceive Judaism in the terms of

Christianity makes correcting established misconceptions about Judaism a necessary part of teaching it in the introductory course. Because fulfilling the first duty depends on fulfilling the second, learning about Judaism may require some students and faculty to do some un-learning as well. Let us turn to some specific issues.

Perhaps the most common error we make in the presentation of Judaism is to equate or identify Jewish religion with the Hebrew Bible. This mistaken conception, which serves theological and polemical claims in both Christianity and Judaism, typically takes three forms. On the Christian side, either Judaism is relegated to the boundaries of the canon and denied any vitality beyond it, or Judaism's contents are reduced to scripture. On the Jewish side, Judaism is depicted as the direct continuation of the Israelite religion described in the Bible.

In different ways, each of these views confuses Judaism with the Bible and mistakes scripture for religion. All of them make it difficult for students to perceive Judaism as a discrete religion. Especially at the introductory level it is important for students to understand that Judaism is a religion with biblical antecedents but with an autonomous morphology and history. It is a post-biblical religion.

It therefore is not helpful to introduce Judaism in religion courses by assigning readings in the Hebrew Bible. Although the Hebrew Bible is called scripture in Judaism, and although the scroll of the Pentateuch, the *Sefer Torah*, is treated as a sacred object, reading the Hebrew Bible will reveal nothing essential about Jewish religion. There is almost no theme, symbol, or idea in the Hebrew Bible that is not equally but differently evocative in both Judaism and Christianity. The texts that give Judaism its distinctive cast and shape are the rabbinic documents, all of which are post-biblical and none of which has the status of scripture in Judaism. The Talmuds and the exegetical literature (midrash) represent, define, and determine the character of Jewish religion more than does anything written in the Hebrew Bible.

The survey of Judaism in the basic introductory course thus can afford to slight the Bible in favor of attention to classical Judaism—often called rabbinic or talmudic—the form of Judaism that dominated Jewish religious life and shaped the essential structures of piety from the seventh to the nineteenth century.

In teaching about rabbinic Judaism, however, it is helpful to avoid two popular misconceptions. The first of these is a variation on the biblicist error discussed above. It holds that rabbinic Judaism, and therefore later forms of Judaism as well, is a religion of interpretation in which piety and theology are the consequence of biblical exegesis. This model effectively reduces religion to reading and depicts talmudic Judaism as a kind of Protestantism. The model itself is denied both by the form and content of rabbinic literature, which is only partially exegetical in form, and by statements within rabbinic literature itself that claims the rabbis have their own traditions, which are independent of scripture. Indeed, the distinctive doctrine of the sanctity of the Torah scroll is a creation of rabbinism, but rabbinism is not the creation of scripture.

A second error we commonly make when teaching rabbinic Judaism is to reduce it to legalism. The application of the category of "law" to rabbinic piety—another consequence of the mutual embeddedness of conceptions of Judaism with conceptions of Christianity—blocks students' understanding of the character of rabbinic piety. In this history of western religion, "law" and "legalism" are hardly terms of neutral description.

In this regard, it may help to describe rabbinic Judaism as a levitical religion, a religion that—on the model of the Temple cult—conceived the interaction with God to entail a system of concrete and disciplined behavior. As heirs of a priestly legacy, ancient rabbis sought to preserve the contours of a levitical system even when the Jerusalem Temple had been destroyed for good. This effort entailed an enormous labor of rethinking and reinterpretation, but it also guarateed that Judaism as a religion would engage the body as much as the head. In place of "law," therefore, it may help students to explore rabbinic piety under the rubric of "ritual."

As important as classical Judaism is for understanding the morphology of the tradition as a whole, it is misleading to reduce all of Judaism to it or to focus, in the introductory course, solely on that period in the religion's history. Indeed, the history of Judaism beyond the Talmud is often presented in the introductory course as a kind of afterthought, a mere appendage to an essential classical structure, which is assumed to represent Jewish religious authenticity. This sort of approach begs many important questions about Judaism and misrepresents its overall shape.

In this regard, it may be useful for an introductory section on Judaism to consider that, unlike the other major literate religions, Judaism has persisted for nearly its entire history (so far) without a native center. Consequently, it has been alienated from the general culture of the societies in which it has existed, and it has developed unnurturted by the homology of surrounding political, economic, and social institutions. Under such conditions, Judaism has had to perform more functions than we ordinarily associate with religion. It has had to form the basis for society and to constitute a culture.

As a result of Judaism's history, particularly in the West, the study of Judaism in modern times provokes important questions about the relationship of religion to politics and to culture. For instance, is Zionism a religious movement or a political one? Do the activities of modern Jewish organizations represent an extension of Judaism or a neglect of it? The ways Judaism has and has not shaped the social and cultural basis of Jewish collective life can be a distinctive focus for teaching Judaism in an introductory course.

One caveat is apposite here. Although the presentation of Judaism in the introductory course should not emphasize the classical at the expense of the modern and contemporary, it is important not to confuse Jewish religion with Jewish history or Jewish ethnicity. That is, not everything Jews did or do to maintain the identity of their group or community is pertinent to the study of Jewish religion. Indeed, it is precisely the need to distinguish religion from history and ethnicity that makes Judaism such a good vehicle for testing definitions of religion.

By design, these brief caveats fall short of offering concrete suggestions about how to teach Judaism in introductory religion course. They suggest what teachers should avoid rather than what they should include. No initial treatment of Judaism—or any other religion—can hope to achieve any kind of coverage or exposure, and it is folly to try. Rather, the introductory course should raise central issues of description and interpretation, and give students a preliminary sense of what it means to study religion. If the course is issue-oriented rather than information-oriented, Judaism may turn out to be especially useful as a case study for some central questions. The appended bibliography provides a selective set of reliable works on various issues and areas within Judaism to which non-specialists can turn to build a solid foundation for including Judaism in the introductory religion course.

One final recommendation may be useful. If time in the introductory course is short, or if teachers prefer—as many now do—to assign students brief reading assignments that can be studied closely and reviewed, for Judaism some texts are more useful than others. If there is time only for one or two works, I recommend the use of the *Authorized Daily Prayerbook* (Hertz) and Jacob Neusner's *The Enchantments of Judaism*. In the prayerbook, study of the prayers recited during the morning and evening service will reveal the essential religious structure of Judaism. *Enchantments* provides an elegantly analytical, religiously sensitive, and strongly contemporary interpretation of that structure. Since the basic form of the liturgy is shared by all sectors of contemporary Jewish religion, these two works are an ideal place to begin.

SELECT BIBLIOGRAPHY

Blau, Joseph L. 1964 Modern Varieties of Judaism (New York: Columbia University Press

Cohen, Arthur A. 1979 *The Natural and the Supernatural Jew: An Historical and Theological Introduction.* Second Revised Edition. (New York: Behrmann House)

Cohen, Martin A. 1987 "Synagogue: History and Tradition." *ER* 14:210-214

Cuddihy, John Murray 1974 The Ordeal of Civility: Freud, Marx, Levi-Strauss and the Jewish Struqgle with Modernity (New York: Basic Books)

ER 1987 The Encyclopedia of Religion. 16 Vols., Mircea Eliade, Editor-in-Chief (New York: MacMillan)

Feldman, Seymour 1987 "Premodern [Jewish] Philosophy." ER 8:56-70

Fishbane, Michael 1987 Judaism: Revelation and Traditions (San Francisco: Harper & Row)

Goldin, Judah, ed. 1976 The Jewish Expression (New Haven: Yale University Press)

Goldscheider, Calvin, and Jacob Neusner, eds. 1990 *Social Foundations of Judaism* (Englewood Cliffs, NJ: Prentice-Hall)

Goldin, Judah 1987 "Midrash and Aggadah." *ER* 9:509-515

Goldenberg, Robert 1987 "Talmud." *ER* 14:256-60

Goldscheider Calvin, and Alan S. Zuckerman 1984 *The Transformation of the Jews* (Chicago: The University of Chicago Press)

Green, Arthur 1987 "Hasidism." *ER* 6:203-212

Green, Arthur, ed. 1986 *Jewish Spirituality: From the Bible through the Middle Ages* (New York: Crossroad). 1987 *Jewish Spirituality: From the Sixteenth Century Revival to the Present* (New York: Crossroad)

Gutmann, Joseph 1987 "Synagogue: Architectural Aspects of." *ER* 14:214-218

Heilman. Samuel C. 1976 *Synagogue Life: A Study In Symbolic Interraction* (Chicago: The University of Chicago Press). 1983 *The People of the Book: Drama, Fellowship, and Religion* (Chicago: The University of Chicago Press)

Hertz, Joseph H., ed. 1959 *The Authorized Daily Prayer Book* (New York: Bloch Publishing Company)

Idel, Moshe 1988 *Kabbalah: New Perspectives* (New Haven: Yale University Press)

Katz, Jacob 1962 Exclusiveness and Tolerance: Jewish-Gentile Relations In Medieval and Modern Times (New York: Schocken Books). 1971 Tradition and Crisis: Jewish Society at the End of the Middle Ages (New York: Schocken Books). 1973 Out of the Ghetto: The Social Background of Jewish Emancipation (Cambridge, Mass.: Harvard University Press)

Liebman, Charles "Orthodox Judaism." ER 11:114-23

Marcus, Ivan G. 1987 "Ashkenazic Hasidism." ER 1:458-61

Mendes-Flohr, Paul 1987 "Modern [Jewish] Thought." ER 8:70-82

Mendes-Flohr, Paul, and Jehuda Reinharz. eds. 1980 The Jews In the Modern World: A Documentary History (Oxford: Oxford University Press)

Meyer, Michael 1987 "Reform Judaism." *ER* 12:254-63

Neusner, Jacob 1974 *The Life of Torah: Readings in the Jewish Religious Experience* (Encino, California: Dickenson Publishing Company). 1978 *There We Sat Down; Talmudic Judaism In the Making* (New York KTAV). 1981 *Stranger at Home: "The Holocaust," Zionism, and American Judaism* (Cicago: The University of Chicago Press). 1984 *Invitation to the Talmud: A Teaching Book.* Revised and Expanded Edition. (San Francisco: Harper & Row). 1986 *The Oral Torah: The Sacred Books of Judaism: An Introduction* (San Francisco: Harper & Row). 1986a *Judaism In the Matrix of Christianity* (Philadelphia: Fortress Press). 1987 *Death and Birth of Judaism: The Impact of Christianity, Secularism, and the Holocaust on the Jewish Faith* (New York Basic Books). 1987a *Self-Fulfilling Prophecy: Exile and Return in the History of Judaism* (Boston: Beacon Press). 1987b *The Enchantments of Judaism: Rites of Transformation from Birth Through Death* (New York: Basic Books). 1987c "Rabbinic Judaism in Late Antiquity." ER 12:185-192. 1987d "Mishinah and Tosefta." *ER* 559-63. 1988 *From Testament to Torah: An Introduction to Judaism In its Formative Age* (Englewood Cliffs, NJ: Prentice-Hall). 1988a *The Way of Torah.*

Fourth Edition (Belmont, CA: Wadsworth). 1989 *Invitation to Midrash: A Teaching Book* (San Francisco: Harper & Row). 1989a *Foundations of Judaism* (Philadelphia: Fortress Press). 1990 *Torah Through the Ages* (New York: Trinity Publishing House)

Neusner, Jacob, ed. 1983 *Take Judaism, For Example: Studies toward the Comparison of Religions* (Chicago: The University of Chicago Press)

Neusner, Jacob, ed. and trans. 1987 *Scriptures of the Oral Torah* (San Francisco: Harper & Row)

Neusner, Jacob, William Scott Green, and Ernest S. Frerichs, eds. 1987 *Judaisms and Their Messiahs at the Turn of the Christian Era* (Cambridge: Cambridge University Press)

Neusner, Jacob, with William Scott Green 1989 Writing with Scripture (Philadelphia: Augsburg Fortress)

Porton, Gary G. 1985 *Understanding Rabbinic Midrash* (New York: KTAV)

Raphael, Marc Lee 1984 *Profiles In American Judaism* (San Francisco: Harper & Row)

Rosenblum, Herbert 1987 "Conservative Judaism." *ER* 4:62-69

Samuelson, Norbert M. 1989 *An Introduction to Modern Jewish Philosophy* (Albany: SUNY Press)

Scholem, Gershom G. 1961 *Maior Trends in Jewish Mysticism* (New York: Schocken Books) 1971 *The Messianic Idea in Judaism: And Other Essays on Jewish Spirituality* (New York: Schocken Books). 1974 *Kabbalah* (New York: Quadrangle Books). 1976 *On Jews and Judaism in Crisis* (New York: Schocken Books).

Schulweis, Harold M. 1987 "Reconstructionist Judaism." *ER* 12:225-28

Stern, David 1987 "Afterlife: Jewish Concepts." *ER* 1:120-124

Segal, Alan F. 1986 *Rebecca's Children: Judaism and Christianity In the Roman World* (Cambridge: Harvard University Press)

Smith, Jonathan Z. 1982*Imagininq Religion: From Babylon to Jonestown* (Chicago: The University of Chicago Press). 1987*To Take Place: Towards Theory In Ritual* (Chicago: The University of Chicago Press)

Steinberg, Milton 1939*As A Driven Leaf* (New York: Behrman House)

Wilken, Robert 1987 "Christianity and Judaism." *ER* 3:431-38

TEACHING THE CHRISTIAN TRADITION

Carol Zaleski

For those of us whose religious background is Christian or who have been raised in a predominantly Christian society, the prospect of introducing undergraduates to Christianity can call forth doubts and questions that we may not experience as acutely when we consider other traditions.

I usually try to raise such questions as explicitly and frankly as possible, and invite student response, at the very beginning of class meetings on the Christian tradition. What do students expect to hear when they show up for class: a sermon? a scholarly confirmation—or debunking— of cherished beliefs? What do they expect to learn? Do we feel obliged either to disclose or conceal our own religious affiliations? Do we feel more uncomfortable about covering Christianity in two weeks than we did about giving the same brief treatment to other traditions? If so, what does this tell us?

One senses a palpable change in mood when the class first ventures into Christian material. There are the dewy eyes: students who look forward to hearing uplifting words that will confirm their own inner experience. There are the bored expressions: students who feel that the subject matter is all too familiar. They know it all already. And there are the anxious, and sometimes defensive, faces as well: students who dread the thought that the convictions with which they have been raised will once again be challenged or dismissed. One can sympathize with all of these attitudes. But the first step is to help the class become aware of them, and to ask why we seem to have such heightened or depressed expectations about studying a tradition which, at least in this academic context, is merely one among many.

Planning an introductory course or unit on Christianity presents a challenge regardless of whether one's training is in some aspect of Christian studies or in a different tradition. Good models are hard to find; the typical graduate school program exposes its PhD candidates to introductory courses in several of the world's religious traditions, but less often in Christianity *per se*. Moreover, the intellectual scruples instilled in us by long years of highly differentiated graduate education make us worry that unless we explain the details of historical criticism of the Bible, and the social and economic conditions that have shaped each succeeding wave of Christian reform and counter-reform, the result will be no more academically rigorous than a Sunday School lesson.

Because of such concerns, my own initial impulse was to collect what seemed to be the essential ingredients from introductory courses in New Testament, church history, theology, and philosophy of religion, mix them into a stew, and attempt to serve it up in a few short weeks. I soon discovered how discouraging such an approach can be for teachers and students alike.

If it won't work to piece together the specialized approaches and then subtract from them, it can be equally treacherous to attempt to present Christianity in its essence—that way lurks intellectual dogmatism, or worse, dogmatic intellectualism. Fortunately, an alternate approach is not difficult to discover; we need only look down the halls to see what our colleagues have been doing in their introductory courses on other traditions. The view is a bracing one, for it reminds us that Christianity is itself one of the world's religions and belongs to the global history of humankind. Although there is no formula for a history-of-religion approach to Christian studies, I would suggest that it entails paying attention to the following guidelines and aims.

1. *Helping students become more attentive to myth, ritual and symbol in the Christian world.*

One way to help overcome the "all-too-familiar" syndrome is to draw upon the increasing body of scholarly literature on the New Testament and the Christian tradition which makes use of history-of-religion categories such as sacred space and sacred time, sacrifice, purity and pollution, cosmogony and eschatology, death and rebirth, and so on. There is no need to burden students with exhaustive phenomenological typologies or comparisons; new vistas can be opened up simply by raising questions about the symbolic or mythic dimension of a Christian text or practice, or by making occasional reference to analogues in other traditions.[1]

2. Adopting a "beginner's mind" with respect to Christianity.

One never ceases to be a beginner with respect to the wisdom or the transcendent dimension of a religious tradition, and an introductory course is a good way to be reminded of this. As an experiment in acquiring the "beginner's mind," one might ask students to write a letter in which they explain a particular Christian institution or practice or doctrine to a friend from a different religious background and culture.

It is worth considering almost any device that will encourage students to ask their most basic questions; the naive questions often prove the most valuable. A medieval historian once told me of being astonished by a student who asked at the end of a lecture, "Was Jesus into meditation?" There are good reasons why this question should seem incongruous; but it could also make a wonderful jumping-off point for a class discussion about the historical Jesus, the different meanings of "meditation," or the difficulties that arise when we try to transfer religious terminology from one tradition or cultural setting to another.

3. Reading scripture through the eyes of tradition, rather than purely as an exercise in determining the historical facts of Christian origins.

For introduction to the formative elements in the Christian tradition, a natural choice would be to read one of the Gospels, accompanied perhaps by excerpts from St. Paul. Students will need some information about the methods of biblical scholarship; but excessive emphasis on modern historical criticism can detract from appreciating the Bible as a living tradition.

In order to help students discover the different ways in which the Bible has been heard by succeeding generations of Christians, I have sometimes tried to study scriptural passages in other settings. A slide-

---

[1]Initial reading of a general work in the phenomenology of religion can help make such categories intelligible. The standard choice in many introductory courses is Mircea Eliade, *The Sacred and the Profane*, tr. Willard R. Trask (New York: Harcourt, Brace, 1959). To focus on the relation between myth and history in the Christian tradition, one might choose instead to read Eliade's *Myth and Reality*, tr. Willard R. Trask (New York and Evanston: Harper & Row, 1963) or *The Myth of the Eternal Return*, tr. Willard R. Trask (Princeton, N.J.: Princeton University Press, 1954). The articles under "Myth" in *The Encyclopedia of Religion* would also be helpful, especially if students are being introduced to the "demythologizing" school of New Testament interpretation.

tour of a Gothic cathedral—reading the scriptural typologies expressed in stained glass and sculptured facade—can be a vivid way to introduce traditional Christian interpretation of the Bible.[2] To hear the Psalms chanted in a monastery chapel, or to catch echoes of the Gospels as they reverberate through the literature of hagiography and spiritual instruction (such as *The Life of Antony, The Confessions, The Little Flowers of Saint Francis,* or *Pilgrim's Progress*) is to discover the Bible as an inexhaustible source not only of Christian doctrine, but also of Christian culture.

4. Working towards a more genuinely historical perspective.

The unexamined time-line many students carry in their head goes something like this: Judaism is the religion of the "Old Testament"—it ceases to develop as soon as Christianity appears on the scene. Similarly, Eastern Christianity becomes frozen in the Western imagination after the schism of 1054, and Roman Catholicism, in Protestant eyes, belongs to the Middle Ages, having yielded all historical momentum to the Reformers. Modern Christian thought, according to this logic, falls into the hands of European and American mainstream Protestants. In reviewing basic historical texts on the Christian tradition, my first consideration is whether they will help to counteract such distorting assumptions. For the same reason, it is worth making a special effort to have the primary readings include a *modern* Catholic or Eastern Christian work (such as the nineteenth-century Russian narrative called *The Way of a Pilgrim,* a perennial favorite in my courses).

5. Working towards a more global perspective.

The historian of religion is just as interested in the Christianity of Appalachia or Ethiopia as in the Christianity of Riverside Church. Recent introductory texts (such as the ones I recommend below) tend to be more balanced in this respect, including material that represents folk as well as

---

[2]For an introduction to New Testament scholarship, see Norman Perrin and Dennis Duling, *The New Testament: An Introduction* (2nd. ed., New York: Harcourt Brace Jovanovich, 1982). On traditional methods of interpreting the Bible, see Sandra M. Schneiders, "Scripture and Spirituality," in *Christian Spirituality: Origins to the Twelfth Century,* ed. Bernard McGinn et al. (New York: Crossroad, 1985), pp. 1-20. Jean Leclercq's *The Love of Learning and the Desire for God,* tr. Catharine Misrahi (New York: Fordham University Press, 1961, 1974), is a wonderful resource for viewing the Christian Bible in the context of monastic culture. On the Gothic cathedral as a "Bible of the poor" see Otto von Simson, *The Gothic Cathedral,* (rev. ed., Princeton, N.J.: Princeton University Press, 1962), and Adolf Katzenellenbogen, *The Sculptural Programs of Chartres Cathedral* (New York: W. W. Norton, 1964).

elite traditions, women as well as men, and venturing beyond Europe to consider the Christian communities of Asia, Africa, the Americas, and the Pacific.

Introductory Texts

Corresponding to the scarcity of models for introductory teaching on the Christian tradition has been a scarcity of good short texts. Fortunately, the situation is improving; here are a few recommendations:

Jaroslav Pelikan's *Jesus through the Centuries* is the book which Pelikan says he always wanted to write.[3] A lively complement to Pelikan's magisterial five-volume doctrinal history of Christianity, the book is a cultural history of the changing face of Jesus in the Christian imagination. Pelikan draws generously from works of art, literature, and popular as well as high culture. Jesus appears as rabbi, prophet, sage, king, Cosmic Christ, Son of Man, martyr, monk, bridegroom, Universal Man, ethical teacher, liberator, and ecumenical symbol; and Pelikan shows how such images have shaped not only the inner experience but also the social and political life of each generation of Christians.

Ninian Smart's *In Search of Christianity*, now unfortunately out of print, is a good example of the history-of-religion approach to Christian studies.[4] He presents the Christian tradition as a "mighty river"—an image of unity in diversity. The reader is introduced to Orthodox Christians in Romania, Italian Catholics, Ethiopian Coptic Christians, Swedish Lutherans, Scottish Calvinists, missionaries and their converts in Africa, and so on. The emphasis is not on doctrines but on prayer and ritual life, mysticism and ascetic practices, myth and storytelling.

Christianity: A Cultural Perspective, by James B. Wiggins and Robert S. Ellwood, a recent offering of the Prentice-Hall Series in World Religions, is a brief, accessible, and empathetic entry into the variegated cultural expressions of Christian faith.[5] Treating Christianity as a "cultural system," the authors provide imaginative glimpses into the world of the first Christians, the drama of liturgical worship, the characteristic moods and themes of Christian art, the conflict and interdependence between

---

[3]Pelikan, *Jesus through the Centuries: His Place in the History of Culture* (New Haven: Yale University Press, 1985; paperback edition, New York: Harper & Row, 1987).

[4]Smart, *In Search of Christianity: Discovering the Diverse Vitality of Christian Life* (New York: Harper & Row, 1979); published in England as *The Phenomenon of Christianity* (London: Collins, 1979).

[5]Wiggins and Ellwood, *Christianity: A Cultural Perspective* (Englewood Cliffs, N.J.: Prentice Hall, 1988).

mainstream and "counterculture" movements, and the religious experience of ordinary churchgoers as well as famous mystics, heretics, reformers, poets, and sages.

A more unusual choice, with which I have had some success, is to use Mircea Eliade's discussion of the birth and development of Christianity in *A History of Religious Ideas*, vols. 2 and 3.[6] Students are intrigued, and sometimes troubled, by his emphasis on the archaic, mythic, and gnostic dimensions of the Christian tradition. It might be best to use this in a course in which students will also read a general work by Eliade such as *The Sacred and the Profane* or *The Myth of the Eternal Return*.

Stephen Reynolds's *The Christian Religious Tradition*, Sandra S. Frankiel's compact book, *Christianity: A Way of Salvation*, and *Christianity: An Introduction* by Denise Lardner Carmody and John Tully Carmody, are good basic historical texts which have made an effort to be inclusive.[7] Of the three, Reynolds is the most intellectually challenging, Frankiel is the most succinct, and the Carmodys' volume (which has a helpful annotated bibliography) is the most *au courant* with recent feminist, evangelical, and ecumenical trends in Christian thought.

Engaging Our Students

One of the benefits of studying religion in an academic setting is that it allows people from different religious backgrounds to examine their attitudes and assumptions in an atmosphere of mutual trust and respect. Whatever one may say about the sterility and false objectivity of the academic approach to religion (some of my favorite students can be quite obnoxious on this point), this activity of disciplined conversation between individuals of differing worldviews can yield insights that will be missed by the religious seeker who remains closed within a practicing community or tradition.

In recent years, however, I have found it increasingly challenging to elicit fruitful discussion where Christianity is concerned. There seems to

---

[6]Eliade, *A History of Religious Ideas*, vol. 2, *From Gautama Buddha to the Triumph of Christianity*, tr. Willard R. Trask (Chicago and London: The University of Chicago Press, 1982) and vol. 3, *From Muhammad to the Age of Reforms*, tr. Alf Hiltebeitel and Diane Apostolos-Cappadona (Chicago and London: The University of Chicago Press, 1985).

[7]Reynolds, *The Christian Religious Tradition* (Belmont, California: Wadsworth; originally published by Dickenson Publishing Company, 1977). Frankiel, *Christianity: A Way of Salvation* (San Francisco: Harper & Row, 1985). Carmody and Carmody, *Christianity: An Introduction* (Belmont, California: Wadsworth, 1983).

be greater polarization on religious questions; the student who is a conservative or evangelical Christian may feel particularly ill used and disenfranchised by the way we speak about Christianity in a world religions course. I see no easy solution to this problem, but it can be helpful to ask students to think from the start about the rationale for the course, and to do so in a creative and uninhibited way that allows them to relate their own questions to the concerns of the course.

In "Philosophers and Saints," I ask students during the second week of classes to submit a short ungraded statement on their view of the relation between religion and higher education. The responses show that students are indeed concerned about whether it is appropriate to study religion in a university; about what it means specifically to study Christianity in an academic setting; and about whether our current educational system is in fact providing a surrogate for the kind of moral and spiritual formation that was once seen as primarily a religious undertaking. Their statements then become part of the subject matter of the course, which approaches the Christian tradition through the theme of changing views of wisdom and holiness.

Another way to engage student interest, or at least to get the blood circulating, is to make "field trips" outside the classroom. Field trips are time-consuming and require careful planning and diplomacy; but they almost always build morale, and open students' eyes to the existence just beyond their doorsteps of countless different worlds of religious experience. In my own courses, group excursions have included a Quaker meeting, a visit to a monastery for Vespers, and a walking tour of Mt. Auburn Cemetery; I have also asked students to go individually to services at Catholic, Eastern Orthodox and Protestant churches in the area. As fascinating as such field trips can be, however, they backfire if students are put in situations where they feel obliged to pray or behave religiously in some way. This seems to be especially true when the setting is Christian. For any field trip, prior classroom discussion of what it means to be a tactful "participant-observer" is essential.

The above suggestions may help, but what matters most is to teach what one knows and loves. The effort to become more inclusive or up-to-date should not make us feel compelled to give up on the familiar and beloved "classics," nor to bury our particular talents. The problems peculiar to teaching about Christianity at an introductory level are potentially part of the solution; if we share our questions with our students, they will become engaged along with us in the process of answering them.

TEACHING AFRICAN-AMERICAN RELIGIONS

Karen McCarthy Brown

Teaching any of the world's religious traditions requires a certain amount of demythologizing. This process is more complicated in the teaching of African-American religions than it is in many other cases. Stereotypes and misinformation abound. The reasons are political, that is to say, they are about power. African religions came to the New World through chattel slavery. Those who brought them here did not come willingly. Racism, which is, among other things, the means by which this chapter in the history of the Western Hemisphere is justified, continues to distort the images of black religion in popular culture and to constrain the scholarly work which deals with these traditions.

Two recent popular films served to remind me that these distortions persist. "Mississippi Burning," a film about the 1964 murder of three civil rights workers, and the lesser known film, "The Serpent and the Rainbow," set in the political turmoil surrounding the overthrow of the Haitian dictator Jean-Claude Duvalier, both appropriated key events in black history and turned them into dramas centering on white characters. Both also stereotyped black religion and distorted its role in these historic events. The portrayal of Haitian Vodou in "The Serpent and the Rainbow" was especially offensive. Zombis, blood and snakes dominated. The religion of ninety percent of the Haitian people was reduced to sorcery.

During a period spanning four centuries, an estimated ten million Africans were brought in slave ships to the shores of North and South America, as well as to several islands in the Caribbean. Drawn mostly from West Africa—from an area which stretches from what is now Sierra Leone in the north, to the Kongo River basin in the south—the slaves carried with them a variety of rich and complex religious traditions. In the New World these cultural streams met and mingled, not only with one another, but also with those emanating from England, Spain, France,

Portugal, the Netherlands, aboriginal America and even, in the case of Trinidad, the Indian sub-continent. A leading scholar in the field, Albert J. Raboteau, is fond of pointing out that, in the Caribbean basin, diverse cultures mix on a scale similar to that of the ancient Mediterranean basin.

African worldviews have emerged in many new, syncretic forms on this side of the globe. Brazil, Surinam, Trinidad, Jamaica, Haiti, Cuba, Louisiana, the United States as a whole—all these places are centers for religious practices influenced, in varying degrees and strikingly different ways, by the ancient religions of West Africa.

African-based New World religions exhibit great variety yet they also have things in common. It is a mistake to speak about Africa as if it were one culture and a mistake to talk about African religion as if it were one thing. Yet, among the cultures from which the slaves were taken, there were also certain shared beliefs and attitudes. These undergird the African-based religions in the Western Hemisphere and make it possible for us to talk about them as members of a single family. The teacher of African-American religions faces a considerable challenge in the classroom. Yet it is a challenge well worth taking up since Africa has contributed so much to the wealth and variety of religion in the Western Hemisphere.

Most courses on African-American religions focus either on the Black Church in the United States or on the religions of the Caribbean and South America where African influence is more apparent. Few courses attempt to trace African influence throughout the hemisphere. Putting the two together is a little like mixing apples and oranges. This discontinuity, however, has more to do with the history of scholarship than it does with the religious traditions themselves. The Black Church in North America has been studied by historians, sociologists and theologians. In recent decades understanding and combatting the forces of racism has been a major motivating factor in this work. Furthermore, many of the most influential scholars in the field are blacks who come from the traditions which they study. Until quite recently, questions about Black Christianity, its particular forms and functions, have gotten much more attention than questions about African roots. By contrast, in the Caribbean and South America, most of the research on African-based religion has been done by anthropologists. With a few notable exceptions, the work has been a-historical and a-political. While many scholars have been quite sympathetic to these traditions, only a small handful of them are persons from the cultures they are studying. Furthermore, the current anthropological aversion to comparisons has led to one of the great ironies of the scholarship on religions in this part of the world. Although the overwhelming majority of the descendants of African slaves in the Caribbean and South America consider themselves Christians and practice a religion which has thoroughly blended African traditional forms with the brand of Christianity bequeathed to them by the slaveholders, their religions are rarely placed in conversation with worldwide Christianity or seen as types of it.

For all these reasons it is very difficult to teach a course which follows the full sweep of the influence of African religions in the New World. Nevertheless I continue to try to do just that. Applying anthropological insights and theories to the Black Church, on the one hand, and, on the other, emphasizing the historical questions raised by ethnographic descriptions of the religions of the Caribbean and Latin America is one way to get the apples closer to the oranges.

African-American Religions in North America

Until Melville Herskovits published *The Myth of the Negro Past* in 1941, it was the accepted wisdom that slavery had been such a traumatic event that it completely destroyed African culture in North America. It was believed that slaves encountered Christianity with no competing religious allegiances left over from the African homeland. Herskovits changed this perception by arguing strenuously for African survivals in a variety of areas of black life, including religion. Herskovits' view was not readily accepted by many scholars in the field, including some blacks. Years later, E. Franklin Frazier wrote in *The Negro Church in America* that "one must recognize from the beginning that because of the manner in which the Negroes were captured in Africa and enslaved, they were practically stripped of their social heritage."[1] A few pages later, he reiterated his point in an even more forceful manner: "It is impossible to establish any continuity between African religious practices and the Negro church in the United States."[2] This debate has continued for half a century and is not yet completely resolved. The weight of scholarly opinion, however, has shifted to Herskovits' camp.

Albert J. Raboteau's *Slave Religion: The "Invisible Institution" in the Antebellum South* has been available for more than a decade. Its appearance marked a change in the direction of scholarship on the origins

---

[1] E. Franklin Frazier, *The Negro Church in America* (New York: Schocken Books, 1974), p. 9.

[2] *Ibid.*, p. 13.

of the Black Church. Raboteau has a particular talent for appreciating the influence of Africa on the aesthetics as well as the theology of black religion in North America. This sensitivity, in part, allowed him to move beyond Herskovits' view of fragmentary African survivals to look at broad currents of African influence. Eugene Genovese's *Roll, Jordan, Roll: The World the Slaves Made* has added to the picture of the cultural mixing on the slave plantations. In *Trabelin' On*, Mechal Sobel, like Raboteau, makes good use of disciplines such as sociology and anthropology. Her focus is more narrow than that of either Raboteau or Genovese in that she is tracing the development of the black Baptist tradition. Her historical range, however, is longer. She begins her book with a chapter on "The West African Sacred Cosmos" and ends her story in the late 19th century.

Other historical works extend the picture provided by these three. Frazier's *The Negro Church in America* has been published in a single volume with C. Eric Lincoln's *The Black Church Since Frazier*. *Black Religion and Black Radicalism* by Gayraud Wilmore and Joseph Washington's controversial *Black Religion: The Negro and Christianity in the United States* have also been influential historical works. Books such as *Ain't I a Woman: Female Slaves in the Plantation South* by Deborah Gray White and the documentary history, *Black Women in White America* by Gerda Lerner make some significant additions to and reinterpretations of the existing historical picture.

The story of African-American religion in the United States is not complete, however, without consideration of new religious movements. The Black Jews, The Moorish Science Temple, The Nation of Islam and the Yoruba village located in Beaufort County, North Carolina are all examples of new religions with strong 'African' elements. But in these cases the influence of Africa has not come through the convoluted channels of memory. It has come through the self-conscious appropriation of African beliefs and customs—some real and some fanciful.

The bridge between the United States and the Caribbean can be seen more clearly in the new religious movements than in the Black Church. Rastafarianism, a neo-African movement which combines religion and politics, began in Jamaica but it has many followers in North America. (See Leonard Barrett's *The Rastafarians: Sounds of Cultural Dissonance*.) And I recently encountered a Black Muslim in a New York City subway station, selling incense and essential oils beneath a poster with pictures of "The Prophets". After Moses and Muhammad, came Malcolm X, Martin Luther King and Marcus Garvey. Garvey, the leader of the quasi-religious Universal Negro Improvement Association, galvanized blacks in North America during the 1920's. He came from Jamaica.

Figures such as Garvey were the vanguard of the more recent waves of Caribbean migration to the United States. A good number of North American blacks have been attracted to the religions which Cubans, Haitians, Jamaicans and Puerto Ricans have brought with them. These migrations keep the picture of African-American religion in the Western Hemisphere fluid and dynamic.

African-American Religions in the Caribbean And South America

In North America most slaveholders owned no more than a small handful of slaves, while on the enormous plantations typical of the Caribbean islands and of Brazil, the slave populations numbered in the hundreds. In these areas, urban centers, which played a key role in the preservation of African religious traditions, were also likely to have much larger numbers of blacks, slave and free than would be found in the North America. These are the main reasons why the religions of Caribbean and South America have a much stronger and more visible African dimension than do those of North America.

African-American religions in this part of the world exhibit an amazing variety. There are several variables which account for this and chief among them is the place or places in Africa from which the slave populations were drawn. Haiti, for example, has three clear lines of African input: the Fon peoples most of whom live in the area we now call Benin (formerly Dahomey); the Yoruba peoples (Nigeria) and the Kongo peoples (Angola and Bas-Zaire). By contrast the African influence in Cuba is much more purely Yoruba, as is that found in Bahia in northern Brazil; and the Akan of Ghana dominate in Jamaica. These quite distinctive traditions interacted with other variable factors, such as the nature of the slave system under which the first generations labored, including the brand of Christianity practiced by the slave masters. Geography was also an issue. In some countries, such as Jamaica and Brazil, with inaccessible interior regions, large maroon (runaway slave) communities developed. These were, no doubt, protected places for religious practice. The social, political and economic history of an area after the period of slavery was another important factor in determining how religions developed in New World settings. Haiti is a particularly striking example of the significance of post-slavery historical developments. After its successful slave revolution (1791-1804) a trade blockade was thrown up around the island and Rome refused to send Catholic priests even though Catholicism was the official religion there. Even after the revolution the slave population is likely to have contained a large percentage of people born in Africa. So in Haiti for more than half a century this group existed largely free of influence from the outside world. Needless to say, Haitian Vodou is among the most African of the New World black religions. By contrast, a group such as the Shakers of St. Vincent, a Christian splinter group with an African aesthetic, occupy a place near the opposite end on the spectrum.

Given the wide variety of these African-American religions, it is difficult to decide which ones to introduce in a course. Unfortunately such choices are often made for us by the incomplete scholarly record. Some areas have been intensely studied; others have one or two good monographs written about them; some have hardly been touched. Cuba, Haiti and Brazil have been studied most thoroughly. Lydia Cabrera's classic work on Cuban Santeria is, however, not yet available in English. Joseph Murphy's recent publication on Santeria as practiced by Cuban immigrant's in New York helps to fill this void, although under his hand this religion of dance, ritual and song becomes oddly theologized. The works of Alfred Metraux (*Voodoo in Haiti*) and Melville Herskovits (*Life in a Haitian Valley*) are classic ethnographies. Yet, to introduce Haitian Vodou to undergraduates I tend to prefer *Divine Horsemen: The Living Gods of Haiti* by the filmmaker and dancer, Maya Deren, because it is well-written and lively as well as being quite accurate. My articles in *Saints and Virtues*, edited by J. Hawley and *Shaping New Vision*, edited by Atkinson, Buchanan and Miles focus on the practice of Vodou in the immigrant communities, while my "Systematic Remembering, Systematic Forgetting," in Sandra Barnes *Africa's Ogun: Old World and New*, charts the influence of Haitian history on one particular Vodou spirit. My book, *Mama Lola: A Vodou Priestess in Brooklyn*, was written for a lay audience and could work well in the undergraduate classroom.

Roger Bastide's study, *The African Religions of Brazil* is the classic text on this area. It may be too dense for undergraduate readers yet it does provide an enormous amount of basic data on the history and development of various African-based religions throughout Brazil. Bastide's book also makes an important theoretical contribution. Subtitled "Toward a Sociology of the Interpenetration of Civilizations," this work provides a model which can be applied to the study of all African-American religions. Bastide argues that slavery split African culture from its social institutional moorings and only when dimensions of the African culture found New World institutional bases could they survive.

Once lodged in new institutional forms both culture contents and institutions changed. Bastide's theory is more successful than any other at explaining why, in the New World, some parts of African religions were totally forgotten and others took on more importance than they had ever known in Africa.

The Search for the Elusive Text

There is, alas, no single text which presents a reasonable survey of African-American religions. George Eaton Simpson's *Black Religions in the New World* comes closest to this ideal but it covers far too much territory, too superficially. The book which does a much better job of tying this diverse field together is Robert Farris Thompson's *Flash of the Spirit: African and Afro-American Art and Philosophy*. This wise and spirited book traces broad themes from Africa through the New World. Understandably it moves quite rapidly over the geographic and historical terrain. It is therefore best read in combination with works of a more specific nature.

BIBLIOGRAPHY

Barnes, Sandra. *Africa's Ogun: Old World and New*. Bloomington Indiana, 1989.

Barrett, Leonard. *The Rastafarians: The Sounds of Cultural Dissonance*. Boston, 1988.

Bastide, Roger. *The African Religions of Brazil: Toward A Sociology of the Interpenetration of Cultures*. Baltimore, 1978.

Brown, Karen McCarthy. *Mama Lola: A Vodou Priestess in Brooklyn*. Berkeley, 1991.

_____"The Power to Heal: Reflections on Women, Religion and Medicine," in *Shaping New Vision: Gender and Values in American Culture*. Edited by Atkinson, Buchanan and Miles. Ann Arbor, 1987.

_____"Alourdes: A Case Study of a Moral Exemplar in Haitian Vodou," in *Saints and Virtues*. Edited by J.S. Hawley. Berkeley, 1987.

Deren, Maya. *Divine Horsemen: The Living Gods of Haiti*. New York, 1983.

DuBois, W. E. B. *The Souls of Black Folk.*. New York, 1969.

Fauset, Arthur Huff. *Black Gods of the Metropolis: Negro Religious cults in the Urban North*. Philadelphia, 1944.

Frazier, E. Franklin, *The Negro Church in America*. New York, 1974

Genovese, Eugene D. *Roll, Jordan, Roll: The World the Slaves Made*. New York, 1972

Goodman, F. with Jeanette Henney and Esther Pressel. *Trance, Healing and Hallucination*. New York, 1974.

Herskovits, Melville J. *The Myth of the Negro Past*. New York, 1941.

_____*Life in a Haitian Valley*. Garden City, New York, 1971.

Lerner, Gerda. *Black Women in White America*. New York, 1972.

Lincoln, E. Eric. *The Black Church Since Frazier*. New York, 1974.

_____*The Black Muslims in America*. Boston, 1961.

_____*Race, Religion and the Continuing American Dilemma*. New York, 1984.

Metraux, Alfred. *Voodoo in Haiti.* New York, 1959.

Murphy, Joseph. *Santeria: An African Religion in America.* Boston, 1988.

Raboteau, Albert J. Slave Religion: *The "Invisible Instituion" in the Antebellum South.* New York, 1978.

Simpson, George E. *Black Religions in the New World.* New York, 1978.

Sobel, Mechal. *Trabelin' on: The Slave Journey to an Afro-Baptist Faith.* Westport, Connecticut, 1979.

Thompson, Robert Farris. *Flash of the Spirit: African and Afro-American Art and Philosophy.* New York, 1983.

Washington, Joseph R. *Black Religion: The Negro and Christianity in the United States.* Boston, 1972.

White, Deborah Gray. *Ain't I a Woman?: Female Slaves in the Plantation South.* New York, 1985.

Wilmore, Gayraud S. *Black Religion and Black Radicalism: An Interpretation of the Religious History of Afro-American People.* New York, 1983.

West, Cornel. *Prophesy Deliverance: An Afro-American Revolutionary Christianity.* Philadelphia, 1982.

Teaching About Religions Native to the Americas

Lawrence E. Sullivan

You may wish to include Native American traditions in your teaching on one or both of the following grounds: the first is necessity; the second is enrichment. After saying a word about these two quite different frames of reference, this note delineates some obstacles to beware of and some resources to turn to in composing a course or section on Native American religions.

A Necessary Component in the Curriculum

Can you teach the humanities in America without reflecting on the humanity native to America? No school fostering liberal education through critical reflection should dodge this pointed question. The absence of Native American ideas and history from the American curriculum risks reducing the educational enterprise to an ideology of conquest that aggrandizes the powerful and disvalues the vanquished.

Few tasks are more urgent in American education than teaching about cultures native to America. The scandal is not that math and science scores are lower than competitive international economy might require. When the Carnegie Foundation points to that kind of problem, it stirs concern, however momentary, and musters response. But it is truly scandalous that so few Americans are shocked by the lack of Native American history in our schools, even though the absence is glaring.

These assertions need not seem overblown in the face of woes that beset the nation's schools. Anyone would grant a possible connection between America's problems and its history. With respect to the native peoples exterminated and dislodged since the first moment of contact, American history begins with a very jagged edge. The sharp contours of that edge are made clear in tracing Native American history.

This craggy inequality thrusts up from recesses hidden in the historical foundations of American identity and pierces through every aspect of

American life, including education. With terrible symmetry , the beginnings of America as a nation threatened to end the life of Native Americans as cultural groups. The trail of tears and broken treaties is seldom to the fore in American historical consciousness. The slippery convenience of our cultural memory—the ability to screen from our history books the barbaric treatment of native peoples—is something we would find condemnable elsewhere. Blindness toward Native American traditions is built into the curriculum of many of America's schools and stands as paradigmatic testimony to the uneven evaluations of humanity that can constitute American experience.

Ironically, in the popular mind, ideas about Native Americans play a key role in constructing the image of America. In accounts of colonial and pioneer history, in tales of the Old West, and on the silver screen, Native American characters figure prominently. Michael Dorris, a professor at Dartmouth College and member of the Modoc tribe, points out that "flesh and blood Native Americans have rarely participated in or benefited from the creation of these imaginary Indians, whose recognition factor, as they say on Madison Avenue, outranks, on a world scale, that of Santa Claus, Mickey Mouse, and Coca-Cola combined . . . For five hundred years Indian people have been measured and have competed against a fantasy over which they have had no control. They are compared with beings who never really were, yet the stereotype is taken for the truth".[1]

By tracing the true fate of America's native peoples since the time of intrusion by immigrant groups, teachers expose cracks in the foundation of America—places where seismic plates of difference among the peoples of the Americas heave past one another and form fundamental misunderstandings. These formations pock our social landscape. The history of Native Americans is partly a tale of trouble, lies, and injustice—unquiet symptoms that haunt the hollows of America as a nation that defines itself as just and free. The study of native peoples will reveal contradictions that can become critical reflections central to a creative American education.

A serious reading of history can—perhaps must—begin here, with critical reflection and reflection on significant crises, just as can a bona fide search for truth, civic virtue, or values productive of well-being. The

---

[1]Michael Dorris, "Indians on the Shelf," pp. 99-100 in Calvin Martin, ed, *The American Indian and the Problem of History*. New York, 1987.

teaching of the humanities in America may be renewed by including an honest confrontation with the fate of humanity in America. Indeed, teachers of the human sciences may need to confront Native American history in order to shake themselves loose from the charge that their pursuits are an arcane and irrelevant escape from the American scene, where their teaching unfolds and their students live.

An Enrichment to the Curriculum

Most of what we know about Native Americans comes from times when they suffered great adversity. But misunderstanding is not the only reason to focus on Native American traditions. The fact is, they offer a wealth of human experience and they have proven to be wellsprings of human creativity for generations, even in the face of sustained difficulties. Native American traditions stand on their own as important resources for the humanities. Moreover, their philosophies, arts, architectural styles and technologies, music, poetry, ritual dramas, cosmologies, dance forms, and religious beliefs exist in extraordinary variety (for there is no single Native American "Way.") Their inclusion in our curricula should require no special pleading.

Religion is singularly important in examining Native American life, Ines Talamantez, Professor of Native American Religions at the University of California at Santa Barbara and a member of the Mescalero Apache community, goes so far as to say that in Native American communities, religion is culture and culture is religious through and through. Perhaps for this reason, the study of Native American traditions can enhance religious studies. There is much to ponder. Innumerable cases exist of complicated ritual and astronomic calendars, festival cycles, rites of passage, religiously significant dress, prayer or liturgical offering, and diverse patterns of religious authority.

Knowledge of Native American religions can change how one views the relationship of religion to political order, art, and social group. Religious life in native communities is not necessarily a private affair or set of doctrines, nor even a set of beliefs about a supernatural life apart from the concrete world. Religious life can consist in the practical recognition of the vitality and power filling the concrete world. Even an overview of Native American life conveys how religious life can flourish beyond the scriptural traditions of the "great world traditions" that are too often taken as norms in the study of religion.

There is nothing magical about teaching Native American traditions. In fact, the enterprise is fraught with pitfalls. Overly romantic visions can distort as much as woeful ignorance or negative bias. In preparation for teaching, it might help to become acquainted with the history of stereotypes that have plagued discussion of native traditions (Berkhofer: 1978).

A number of Native American intellectuals have addressed the problem of conceptualizing native traditions. Their pointed remarks are often direct and can serve as a baseline for attitudes to avoid as well as possible tracks to take. Vine Deloria, Jr. is a philosopher, lawyer, and member of the Standing Rock Sioux community. He argues that Indians and non-Indians "are speaking about two entirely different perceptions of the world" (Deloria, 1979, p.vii). Ward Churchill and M. Annette Jaimes warn teachers away from objectionable approaches and suggest several kinds of course offerings on Native American culture (Churchill and Jaimes, 1988).

It cannot be stressed too firmly that the Americas are home to myriad native cultures that range from small communities in the Amazon forest and the arctic circle to the dense populations of urban civilizations of the Aztec, Maya, Incas and others. There are thousands of distinct cultural-linguistic groups, each with its unique ecological setting, division of labor, calendar of religious feasts, and configuration of spiritual powers. The treatment of Native American religions can range from the study of hunting ceremonies recorded at the time of the first European contact to the 1989 seasonal festivals that allowed the Kayapo Indians of the Amazon to mobilize an international alliance of groups. Led by Payakan, the Kayapo succeeded in blocking loans from the World Bank and thus thwarting efforts to flood their lands for a massive hydroelectric power project.

I have developed full presentations of the above themes and others in two books. *Icanchu's Drum: An Orientation to Meaning in South American Religions* (New York, Macmillan,1988) is an argument about the nature of religion, using case materials from South American native cultures. *Native American Religions:North America* is a collection of 24 articles which portray different approaches to the study of Native American religions, ranging from general overview, to regional surveys, to specific cultural cases. Both works contain lengthy bibliographies.

The following works may be helpful in considering issues around which to construct courses or sections on Native American religions. Charles H. Long's *Significations* (Philadelphia: Fortress Press, 1986) may prove to be a helpful conceptual companion to these readings. Since more literature exists on peoples of North America, the following list includes a larger representative sample of recent works in that area.

Native Traditions of South America

Sullivan, Lawrence E., 1988 *Icanchu's Drum: An Orientation to Meaning in South American Religions.* New York: Macmillan. This book is an introduction to the religious life of native peoples in South America. It contains 42 pages of selected bibliography and many bibliographic annotations in the notes.

For bibliographic reviews of literature see also Juan Adolfo Vazquez, "The Religions of Mexico and of Central and South America." In *A Reader's Guide to the Great Religions* ed. Charles J. Adams, New York: Free Press, 1977; and J.A. Vazquez, "The Present State of Research in South American Mythology," *Numen* 25 (1978): 240-276. See also Susan A. Niles, *South American Indian Narrative: Theoretical and Analytical Approaches, An Annotated Bibliography*, New York: Garland Publishing, 1981.

The following works are a sample of some of the most engaging and teachable texts dealing with representative and important issues.

Urton, Gary, 1981. *At the Crossroads of the Earth and Sky: An Andean Cosmology.* Austin: University of Texas Press.

Urton, Gary, 1985. *Animal Myths and Metaphors in South America.* Salt Lake City: University of Utah Press.

Weiss, Gerald, 1975. *The World of a Forest Tribe in South America.* Anthropological Papers of the American Museum of Natural History, Vo. 52, Part 5. New York: American Museum of Natural History, 1975.

Wilbert, Johannes,1975. "Eschatology in a Participatory Universe: Destinies of the Soul Among the Warao Indians of Venezuela" In *Death and the Afterlife in Pre-Colombian America.*,ed. Elizabeth P.Benson, Washington D.C.: Dumbarton Oaks Research Library and Collections.

Wilbert, Johannes, 1987. *Tobacco and Shamanism in South America.* New Haven: Yale University Press. Wilbert has written a number of illuminating articles.

Taussig, Michael T., 1987. *Shamanism, Colonialism, and the Wild Man: A Study in Terror and Healing.* Chicago: University of Chicago Press.

Viveiros de Castro, Eduardo, 1986. *Awarete: Os deuses canibais.* Rio de Janeiro: Jorge Zahar, 1986. This will soon appear in English translation.

Wachtel, Nathan, 1977. *The Vision of the Vanquished: The Spanish Conquest of Peru Through Indian Eyes, 1530-1570.* New York: Barnes and Noble, 1977.

Reichel-Dolmatoff, Gerardo, 1978. "The Loom of Life: A Kogi Principle of Integration," *Journal of Latin American Lore*. 4. No 1: 5-27. Reichel-Dolmatoff has written a number of important works.

Urton ed. and Urton *Crossroads*.

Wright, Robin M., and Jose Barreiro, eds., 1982. *Native Peoples in Struggle: Russell Tribunal and Other International Forums*.

Zuidema, Reiner T., 1977. "The Inca Calendar." In *Native American Astronomy*. ed. Anthony F. Aveni. Austin: University of Texas Press, 1977.

Native Traditions of Mesoamerica

It is fortunate that Davíd Carrasco, *Religions of Mesoamerica: Cosmovision and Ceremonial Centers* (New York: Harper and Row) will be published soon. It provides a readable, focused introduction to religions in Mesoamerica. See also D. Carrasco, "City as Symbol in Aztec Religion: Clues from the Codex Mendoza," *History of Religions* Vol. 20, No.3 (1981). And also D. Carrasco, *Quetzalcoatl and the Irony of Empire: Myths and Prophecies in the Aztec Tradition*, Chicago: University of Chicago Press, 1982.

Austin, Alfredo López, 1988. *The Human Body and Ideology: Concepts Among the Ancient Nahuas*. 2 vols. Salt Lake City: University of Utah Press. This is an extraordinary work delineating Aztec cosmology.

Nicholson, Henry B., 1971. "Religion in Pre-Hispanic Central Mexico." in *Handbook of Middle American Indians*. edited by Robert Wauchope et al., Vol 10. Austin.

Todorov, Tzvetan, 1982. *The Conquest of America: The Question of the Other*. New York: Harper and Row.

Portilla, Miguel Leon, 1962. *The Broken Spears*. Boston: Beacon Press.

Portilla, Miguel Leon, 1980. *Native Mesoamerican Spirituality*. New York: Paulist Press.

Schele, Linda and Mary Ann Miller, 1986. *The Blood of Kings: Dynasty and Ritual in Maya Art*. Fort Worth: Kinbell Art Museum.

Edmonson, Munro s., 1971. *The Book of Cousel: The Popol Vuh of the Quiche Maya of Guatemala*. New Orleans: Middle American Research Institute of Tulane University.

Aveni, Anthony F., 1980 *Skywatchers of Ancient Mexico*. Austin: University of Texas Press.

Myerhoff, Barbara, 1974. *Peyote Hunt: The Sacred Journey of the Huichol Indians*. Ithaca: Cornell University Press.

Native Traditions of North America

Allen, Paula Gunn, 1986. *The Sacred Hoop: Recovering the Feminine in American Indian Traditions.* Boston: Beacon Press.

Axtell, James, 1974. "The Scholastic Philosophy of the Wilderness," in *The School upon a Hill: Education and Society in Colonial New England.* New Haven: Yale University Press.

Axtell, James, 1985. *The Invasion Within: The Contest of Cultures in Colonial North America.* New York: Oxford University Press.

Bataille, Gretchen M. and Charles C.P. Silet, eds., 1980. *The Pretend Indians: Images of Native Americans in the Movies.* Ames: Iowa State University Press. With a Forward on "American Fantasy" by Vine Deloria Jr.

Bataille, Gretchen M. and Kathleen Mullen Sands, 1984. *American Indian Women. Telling Their Lives.* Lincoln: University of Nebraska Press.

Berkhofer, Robert, *The White Man's Indian.* New York: Alfred A. Knopf, 1978.

Bolt, Christine, 1987. *American Indian Policy and American Reform: Case Studies of the Campaign to Assimilate The American Indians.* London: Allen & Unwin.

Churchill, Ward and M. Annete Jaimes, 1988. "American Indian Studies: A Positive Alternative," in *The Bloomsbury Review.* (September/October 1988), which suggests several thematic, inter-disciplinary courses and recommends bibliography.

Deloria, Vine Jr., 1973 *God is Red.* New York: Grosset and Dunlap.

Deloria, Vine Jr., *Behind the Trail of Broken Treaties: An Indian Declaration of Independence.* New York: Delecorte Press.

Deloria, Vine Jr., 1979. *The Metaphysics of Modern Existence.* San Francisco: Harper and Row.

Deloria, Vine Jr. and Clifford M. Lytle, 1984. *The Nations Within: The Past and Future of American Indian Sovereignty.* New York: Pantheon.

Deloria, Vine Jr. and Sandra L. Cadwalader, 1984. *The Aggressions of Civilization: Federal Indian Policy Since the 1880s.* Philadelphia: Temple University Press.

Deloria, Vine Jr,. 1984 *A Sender of Words: Essays in Memory of John G. Neihardt.* Salt Lake City: Howe Brothers.

Deloria, Vine Jr., ed., 1985 *American Indian Policy in the Twentieth Century.* Norman: University of Oklahoma Press.

Deloria, Vine Jr., 1987. "Revision and Reversion," pp. 84-90 in Martin, 1987.

DeMallie, Raymond J., and Douglas R. Parks, eds., 1987 *Sioux Indian Religion: Tradition and Innovation*. Norman: University of Oklahoma Press.

Dippie, Brian W., 1982 *The Vanishing American: White Attitudes and U.S. Indian policy*. Middletown, Conn., Wesleyan University Press.

Dorris, Michael, 1987. "Indians on the Shelf," pp. 98-105 in Martin, 1987.

Erdich, Louise, 1984. *Love Medicine: A Novel*. New York: Holt, Rinehart, and Winston.

Gill, Sam D., 1981. *Sacred Words: A Study of Navajo Religion and Prayer*. Westport, Conn.: Greenwood Press.

Hultkrantz, Åke. *The Religions of the American Indians*. (Berkeley, 1979) and Hultkrantz, *Belief and Worship in Native North America*. (Syracuse, N.Y., 1981).

Hurtado, Albert L., 1988. *Indian Survival on the California Frontier*. Yale Western Americana Series, No. 35. New Haven: Yale University Press.

Kupperman, Karen Ordahl, 1980. *Settling with the Indians: The Meeting of English and Indian Cultures in America 1589-1640*. London: Dent.

Lyman, Christopher, 1982. *The Vanishing Race and Other Illusions: Photographs of Indians by Edward S. Curtis*. New York: Pantheon/Smithsonian Institution Press.

Lyng v. Northwest Indian Cemetery, 1987. Brief of *Amici curiae*. (No. 86-1013) submitted in support of respondents by the National Congress of American Indians, Association on American Indian Affairs. The Karuk Tribe of California, The Tolowa Nation, The Hoopa Tribe of California. The Confederated Salish and Kootenai tribes of Montana, the Kootenai Tribe of Idaho and the Tunica-Biloxi Tibe of Louisiana for the case of Richard E. Lyng, Secretary of Agriculture, et al., Petitioners v. Northwest Indian Cemetery Protective Association, et al., Respondents, heard in the Supreme Court of the United States during its October Term, 1987. On Writ of Certiorari to the United States Court of Appeals for the Ninth Circuit. Obtainable from Steven C. Moore, Esq, Counsel of Record for Amici curiae, Native American Rights Fund, 1506 Broadway,Boulder, Colorado 80302.

Martin, Calvin ed., 1987. *The American Indian and the Problem of history*. New york: Oxford University Press.

Momaday, N. Scott, 1969, *House Made of Dawn*. New York: Harper and Row, 1968

Momaday, N. Scott *The Way to Rainy Mountain*. Albuquerque: University of New Mexico Press.

Morrison, Kenneth M., 1984. *The Embattled Northeast: The Elusive Ideal of Alliance in Abenaki-Euramerican Relations*. Berkeley: University of California Press.

Nabokov, Peter, 1986. "Unto These Mountains: Toward the Study of Sacred Geography," pp. 479-489 in Gordon Brotherston, ed., *Voices of the First America: Test and Context in the New World*. Special issue of *New Scholar*. Vol. 10 nos. 1 and 2.

Nabokov, Peter, and Robert Easton, 1989. *Dwellings at the Source: Native American Architecture*. New York: Oxford University Press.

Philip, Kenneth R., ed., 1986. *Indian Self-Rule First-Hand Accounts of Indian-White Relations from Roosevelt to Reagan*. Vol. 4 in the series Current Issues in the American West. Salt Lake City: Howe Brothers.

Powers, Marla N., 1986. *Oglala Women: Myth, Ritual, and Reality*. Chicago: University of Chicago Press.

Ridington, Robin, 1988. *Trail to Heaven: Knowledge and Narrative in a Northern Native Community*. Iowa City: University of Iowa Press.

Schlegel, Alice, ed. 1979. *Sexual Statification: A Cross-Cultural View*. New York: Columbia University Press.

Schlegel, Alice, 1984. "Hopi Gender Ideology of Female Superiority," *Quarterly Journal of Ideology*. vol. 8, no 4.

Talamantez, Ines, Apache Women's Initiation (forthcoming).

Vaughan, Alden T., 1965 *New England Frontier: Puitan and Indians. 1620-1675*. Boston, Mass.: Little, Brown.

Vecsey, Christopher, 1988. *Imagine ourselves Richly: Mythic Narratives of North American Indians*. New York: Crossroads.

Vizenor, Gerald, 1987. "Socioacupuncture: Mythic Reversals and the Striptease in Four Scenes," pp. 180-192 in Martin.

Walker, Deward E. Jr., 1987. "Protection of American Indian Sacred Geography: Toward a Functional Understanding of Indian Religion Focusing on a Protective Standard of Integrity," which appears as Appendix A to Lyng v. Northwest Indian Cemetery.

Whiteman, Henrietta, 1987. "White Buffalo Woman," pp. 162-170 in Martin. Zolla, Elémire, 1989. *I letterati e lo sciamano: L'Indiano nella letteratura americana dalle origini al 1988*. 2nd ed. Venice: Marsilio Editori.

AUSTRALIAN ABORIGINAL RELIGION
John Hilary Martin, O.P.

The religion of the Aboriginal people of Australia is a *secret* religion. While this may not be the most important thing to know about Aboriginal religion, it is the most important thing for any student or researcher to keep in mind. Some religions, like Christianity and Islam, avidly seek new members, Aboriginal religions do not. Even to discuss religious secrets with outsiders is regarded as an offense to be punished severely, with death if a major breach has occurred. This helps to explain the divergent and confusing views which have circulated about what Aboriginals believe. Researchers have sometimes jumped to conclusions on the basis of incomplete information or gotten their data second hand from informants who themselves only had peripheral knowledge. The reluctance of Aboriginals to share anything about their traditional beliefs led 19th century explorers and even some missionaries to conclude that the *natives* of Australia had no religion at all. Although this opinion was mistaken, it flourished because it fit in all too well with evolutionary theories prevalent at the time. Observers presumed that the hunter-gatherers recently contacted in Australia were *primitives*, a kind of collective living fossil that could be studied to provide insights into the life and culture of *all* prehistoric human beings. Since theory influenced scholarship, awareness of the changing perspectives of scholars who studied Aboriginal religion is indispensable for anyone teaching Aboriginal religions. T. Swain, *Interpreting Aboriginal Religion: An Historical Account* (1985) gives a brief, but useful survey of the changing views of scholars. The more general work by Eric J. Sharpe, *Comparative Religion: A History* will also be of help here.

An echo of evolutionary modes of thinking can be found in remarks that the simple Australian blacks had not yet developed true languages, but only babbled in syllables and incomplete sentences. Even a passing acquaintance with Aboriginal speech makes it clear that this view was quite wrong, but it has been perpetuated in a curious way by popular books which give bare lists of words taken out of context and drawn from many unrelated Aboriginal languages. Such books are to be avoided. A brief study by E. G. Vaszoli, *Aboriginal Australians Speak: An Introduction to Australian Aboriginal Linguistics* (1976) is a useful corrective. He shows the complexity and flexibility of Aboriginal languages, and outlines their present distribution throughout the Continent (about 40 separate *languages* now survive along with many dialects). Although Aboriginal languages are difficult for us to master, they are quite capable of communicating the subtleties of religious experience.

Observers in the first half of the 19th century could hardly fail to notice that Aboriginal communities carried out ceremonies and had elaborate customs and laws, often rigidly enforced, but they argued, again under the influence of evolutionary theory, that these primitive observances did not truly constitute a *religion*. This was the view of G. Grey in his *Polynesian Mythology* (1855) which influenced E.B. Tylor, H. Spencer and many later authors. Grey also felt that the Aboriginals of Australia could be directly compared with other primitives, such as the islanders of Polynesia, and Indians of North America. This is not to say that comparisons can never be drawn, but it should be made clear that Aboriginal religion has values of its own which must be treated separately. In an introductory course Aboriginal religions should not be lumped together *for convenience sake* with other religions of the Pacific area, still less allowed to be seen as just another example of the religion of the noble, or the ignoble savage. As the 19th century progressed more careful observation of Aboriginal myths and ceremonies began to be made by civil servants like A.W. Howitt (1854-83), *The Native Tribes of South-East Australia* (1904) and the team of W.B. Spencer and F.J Gillen, *The Native Tribes of Central Australia* (1899), *The Northern Tribes of Central Australia* (1904) and *The Arunta* (1927). These writings must still be used because they contain data no longer available to us (more than half the Aboriginal communities known in the late 1800's have either died out or been shattered after the incursions of Whites), but caution is required when using them since the *interpretations*, based on imperfect understanding of Aboriginal religion, often homogenize and generalize the material in the interests of presenting students with a systematic picture. At times they are also tainted with views which today would be regarded as racist and patronizing. Important data on spiritual authority and on healing was gathered by the trained antropologist, A.P. Elkin, *Aboriginal Men of High Degree* (1947, 2nd ed., 1977).

While all Aboriginal religions are secret, fortunately for outsiders not all secrets are at the same level. Elders will sometimes be happy to narrate stories in simple form and allow ceremonies to be performed before mixed audiences of children, friendly non-Aboriginal visitors, members of other Aboriginal communities and non-initiated adults. But even while this is done, the *inner meaning* of ceremony and story will be concealed in whole or in part from everyone who are not fully initiated. A given story or ceremony contains *many levels of meaning* which are progressively unveiled only over a period of time as their age, a particular occasion or the rank of the listener warrants. The *ultimate* level of inner meaning is never revealed to an outsider, but is reserved for the group of Elders who are its *owners*. The Elder/s learned the full inner meaning of the story or the ceremony from their forebearers who received it by an ancestral figure of the *Dreaming* and established their relation to it. While Aboriginal society was, and is, composed of small tribal units (*mobs* would be their word) each with its own particular traditions and stories which are believed to have come from the *Dreaming*, a number of beliefs and attitudes toward life were shared throughout the Continents. Some overview can be attempted if we are careful to avoid the trap of over-generalizing. The articles of R.M. and C.H. Berndt and of Stephen Wilde in the *Encyclopedia of Religion* are a good place to begin. *Australian Religions: An Introduction* by M. Eliade (1973) is another, although his interest in finding universal patterns of behavior may leave unwary readers with a impression of Aboriginal thinking which is more static and more dualistic than is warranted.

Any class lectures should probably begin with a discussion of the frequently misunderstood concept of the *Dreaming*—that time, unlike all others, when ancestral figures broke to the surface of the earth, roamed over the landscape to shape it and to populate it with all the flora and fauna we have today. At the end of their wanderings they returned again into the earth (or in some cases transformed themselves into birds or other beings which flew into the sky) to remain there. The places where they went into the ground were marked with significant land features, such as a water hole, perhaps a set of rocks, or even a particular tree. These places became a specific community's *sacred site*—sacred not simply in the sense of marking a spot where an important event had once occurred, but sacred because the power of the *Dreaming* ancestor still permeated the place and could be contacted if need be. An good introduction to the concept of the *Dreaming* and its consequences is W.E.H. Stanner,*White Man Got No Dreaming* (1979) derived from his lifelong experience among the Northern, Murrinh-patha people. His essays on the nature of myth and ritual in an Aboriginal context, including treatment of the important Aboriginal notion of Initiation, can be found in articles written between 1959-63 in *Oceania*, (later reprinted as *On Aboriginal Religion*, Oceania monograph 11, Univ. of Sydney, n.d.). *Oceania* has been, it should be noted, a major source for articles and book reviews on all aspects of Aboriginal culture. Another excellent discussion of the *Dreaming* together with consideration of the sacred character of land and personal identification through relation to one's own land is F.R. Myers, *Pintupi Country, Pintupi Self: Sentiment, Place, and Politics among Western Desert Aborigines*, (1986).

Even a brief unit on Aboriginal religions must take the time to look at specific Aboriginal stories and rituals, and not be reduced to a discussion of European theories *about* myth and ritual. There are many anthologies of Aboriginal stories on the market; choosing between them is not always easy. Some, such as A.W. Reed, *Aboriginal Fables and Legendary Tales*, (1965) are about physical phenomena and animal life and not particularly sacred stories as much as they are tales designed to amuse and inform. Some like R. Robinson,*The Man Who Sold His Dreaming* (1965), *Aboriginal Myths and Legends*, (1966) and *Legend and Dreaming*, (1967), while they can serve to introduce students to ideas quickly, do not connect the stories with specific geographical areas or tribal groups and fail to name narrators of the stories making authentication impossible. Since Aboriginal myths (and rituals) are *not* primarily accounts designed to explain universally observed phenomena (e.g., why does the sun set? why do birds build nests? etc.), but are narratives about the activity of specific ancestral figures of the *Dreaming* which form the history of a people and relate them to their sacred land sites, collections which tend to endow tales with an abstract and universal quality may mislead undirected students reading this material for the first time. Stories of the *Dreaming* need to be fleshed out and situated within their local contexts. This is done admirably by T.G.H. Strehlow, *Songs of Central Australia* (1971), who is careful to show the particular sacred site where the story has came from and that the story is the private property of an individual Elder or small group of them. C.P. Mountford, *Ayers Rock: its people their beliefs and their art,* (1977), shows the bonding of the people of the Uluru area (the Aboriginal designation for Ayer's Rock) with their land, but it must be noted that this work has been criticized for containing some factual errors and for violating the sensibilities of the local Pitjantjatjara community. Close association of religious ideas with the land is brilliantly illustrated by the account of a funeral in H. Morphy's *Journey to the Crocodile's Nest* (1984). Morphy's book, although an independent monograph which stands on its own, follows the film, *Madarrpa Funeral at Gurka'wuy* (N.T.), directed by Ian Dunlop (1979). *Journey* is unusual in that it describes in careful detail a lengthy ceremony which took place over many days. It is also well illustrated with stills from the movie.

Other important topics to be included in an introductory course would be the origin of human life (the spirit versus the semen child); death and continuing life after death; sacred objects seen as representative of the *Dreaming* ancestor (the *tjuringa* or *ranga*, in English, *bullroarer*); and the position of women. *Religion in Aboriginal Australia: An Anthology* edited by Max Charlesworth et al, (1984) has worthwhile articles on all these topics by recognized experts in their field along with a brief account of their training and expertise. In addition, on the topic of conception, death and reincarnation, we can mention T.G.H. Strehlow, *Central Australian Religion* (1964; reprint, Austr. Assn. for the Study of Religions, 1978); on the position of women, P.M. Karberry, *Aboriginal Woman Sacred and Profane*, (1939) and Jane Goodale,*Tiwi Wives* (1971). Much work has been done on descent relationships in family and tribe (the aboriginal phrase is to determine one's *skin color*). It is, admittedly, an important topic, yet its very complexity makes it difficult to treat adequately in an introductory course. M.J. Meggitt, *Desert People: A Study of the Walbiri Aborigines of Central Australia* (1974) is suggested for those who wish to pursue a study in depth in reference to a particular community.

One of the most striking features of Aboriginal culture is its art. This includes visual art, like ancient rock paintings which are to be found throughout Australia, bark paintings, body painting and ceremonial accoutrements, and an elaborate and subtle musical tradition. Artistic energy seems to have been directed entirely to religious ends, as distinct from decorative or commercial purposes. R.M. Berndt, *Australian Aboriginal Art* (1964) contains a good collection of articles which can serve as a general introduction to the whole field. An article in *Art and Australia,* "Australian Aboriginal Art," vol., 13.3., discusses various techniques which were traditionally used. The large and glossy, *Australian Dreaming: 40,000 Years of Aboriginal History,* J.Isaacs (1980), presents in a pleasant way much general information. While rock paintings can be dated only in very general terms, some are perhaps over 20,000 years old. They are regarded by Aboriginals as reflections of *Dreaming* events and in many locations (although by no means all) are in the hands of traditional owners. Their inner meaning would be kept private, of course, but some general understanding the iconography is known. I.M. Crawford, *The Art of the Wandjina: Aboriginal Cave Paintings in Kimberley, Western Australia,* (1968); S. Dacre, *Prehistoric Art of Australia,* (1974) and Godden and Malnic's series on *Rock Painting of Aboriginal Australia,* (1988) are valuable references here. Although N. D. Munn's *Walbiri Iconography: Graphic Representation and Cultural Symbolism in a Central Australian Society* (1973, 2nd ed., 1986), is not about rock painting, but about the sand drawing techniques used by Aboriginal women as they narrate stories for their audiences, it is helpful in providing a key to *some* of the conventional signs often employed in Aboriginal art. Paintings on bark were first mentioned by Europeans only in 1834, but an older tradition is suspected. The motifs found in rock painting were continued in bark painting, but they were developed stylistically in ways which show that Aboriginal art, as well as the religious thinking it expresses, were by no means static but open to development both in form and in content. Examples can be found in H.M. Groger-Wurm, *Australian Aboriginal Bark Painting and Their Mythological Interpretation* (1973) and *A Calendar of Dreaming* (16mm film) produced by G. Bardon, Aboriginal Arts Board of the Australia Council (1976). Aboriginal religious music is as important, if not more important, than its visual arts. A. Moyle is a pioneer in presenting this material both in books and on records. Her *Songs from the Northern Territory: an Ethno-musicological Study,* consisting of five discs with descriptive booklet (1964), was produced by Australian Institute of Aboriginal Studies (AIAS), Canberra. Chant and the music associated with religious ritual are well known to be powerful tools to aid memorization and to bond a community together, but for Aboriginals they are also a means of religious communication, perhaps the central repository of its religious knowledge and the main medium through which Aboriginal people conceptualize their world. An excellent and stimulating analysis of Aboriginal music is given by C. Ellis, *Aboriginal Music: Education for Living* (1985).

No treatment of Aboriginal religion should leave students with the impression that it is static phenomenon, incapable of development or change. We often hear about *40,000 years of Dreaming,* but this does not mean that during 40,000 years the *Dreaming* was incapable of responding to change or never underwent any internal development. The chapter "Healing Touch and Chant," in E. Roughsey, *An Aboriginal Mother:Tales of the Old and the New* (1984) can be taken as an example of a body of contemporary literature which graphically illustrates the rethinking of old ways in an urban context. The remarkably frank work of E. Kolig, *The Silent Revolution: The Effects of Modernization on Australian Aboriginal Religion* (1981), sets out to dispel the myth that traditional Aboriginal religion is doomed to an untimely end as Aboriginals become increasingly assimilated to western culture and younger generations lose interest. Kolig argues forcefully that nothing could be farther from the truth.

ABORIGINAL RELIGION: BIBLIOGRAPHY

Australian Aboriginal Mythology, ed. L.R. Hiatt, [Australian Aboriginal Studies no. 50] (Canberra: AIAS,* 1975)

Bell, Diane, *Daughters of the Dreaming*, (Sydney: McPhee Gribble/ G. Allen & Unwin, 1983)

Berndt, R.M., *Australian Aboriginal Religion*, (Leiden: E.J. Brill, 1974)

Berndt, R.M., *Love Songs from Arnhemland*, (Chicago: Chicago University Press, 1976

Black Australia, ed. M. Hill and A. Barlow, (Canberra: AIAS, 1978)

Eliade, M., *Australian Religions: An Introduction*, (Ithica: Cornell Univ. Press, 1973)

Ellis, C.J., *Aboriginal Music: Education for Living*, (St. Lucia: Univ. of Queensland Press, 1985).

Godden, E. and Malnic, J., *Rock Painting of Aboriginal Australia*, (Sydney: Reed Books Pty Ltd, 1988)

Goodale, J.C., *Tiwi Wives: A Study of the Women of Melville Island*, North Australia, (Seattle: Univ. of Washington Press: 1971)

Groger-Wurm, H.M., *Australian Aboriginal Bark Paintings and Their Mythological Interpretation*, (Canberra: AIAS, 1973)

Handbook of Australian Languages, ed. R.M.W. Dixon and B.J. Blake (Canberra: ANU Press, 1979)

Isaacs, J., *Australian Dreaming: 40,000 Years of Aboriginal History*, (Sydney: Lansdowne Press, 1980)

Kolig, Erich, *The Silent Revolution*, (Philadelphia: ISHI, 1981)

Morphy, H., *Journey to the Crocodile's Nest*, (Canberra: AIAS, 1984)

Munn, N., *Walbiri Iconography*, (Chicago: Univ. of Chicago Press, 1986)

Myers, F.R., *Pintupi Country, Pintupi Self*, (Washington: Smithsonian Institution Press, and Canberra: AIAS, 1986)

Religion in Aboriginal Australia: An Anthology, ed. Max Charlesworth, H. Morphy, D.Bell and K. Maddock, (St. Lucia: Univ. of Queensland Press, 1984)

Stanner, W.E.H., *On Aboriginal Religion*, (Oceania Monograph 11, Univ. of Sydney, 1964)

Stanner, W.E.H., *White Man Got No Dreaming: Essays 1938-73*, Canberra: ANU Press, 1979)

Strehlow, T.G.H., *Aranda Traditions*, (Melbourne: Melbourne Univ. Press, 1947)

Strehlow, T.G.H., *Central Australian Religion*, (Australian. Assn. for the Study of Religions: Special Studies in Religions 2, 1978).

Studies in Australian Linguistics, ed. A.P. Elkin, [Oceania Monographs 3] (Sydney: Australian Naitonal Research Council, [1938]).

Swain, T., *Interpreting Aboriginal Religion: An Historical Account*, (Australian. Assn for the Study of Religions: Special Studies in Religions 5, 1985)

TEACHING AFRICAN RELIGIONS

Karen McCarthy Brown

Teaching African religions at the undergraduate level is a wonderful challenge because it has the potential of changing the way we think about and teach almost everything else in religious studies. A teacher designing a course for North American students not only has to be familiar with African religions but also, because of the nature of these religions, he or she is inevitably led to critique the assumptions made in religious studies as to what constitutes the material of our field and how we present that material to students. In other words, what makes courses in African religions challenging is that they teach us about ourselves.

Religious instruction in Africa itself employs a pedagogy quite different from our own. Such things as music, visual imagery and ritual (including possession-performance) are key to indigenous religious instruction. Thus when we set out to teach African religions we are necessarily led to question our own emphasis on religious texts. Furthermore, because so much of the work on Africa has been done by anthropologists, African religions have become known to scholars primarily as dimensions of larger social and cultural systems. Thus African material also raises questions about our tendency to isolate religious institutions from other aspects of society such as economics, politics and social structure.

The end result of all this questioning may actually narrow the perceived gap between African religions and the others we deal with more routinely in religious studies departments. For example, we may come to appreciate that music and image have been powerful conveyors of meaning throughout Christian history and, furthermore, that the points of view they offer are not always consonant with those presented in texts from the same periods. Or, to take another example, we may decide that teaching about the religions of India through classical texts, while ignoring the social location of those whose lives are shaped by the religions, has produced an understanding of Hinduism, for example, which exists only in the academy and, in fact, is lived by no one. It is my belief that no religious studies program with a comparative dimension should pass up the opportunity to learn from integrating courses in traditional religions into their curriculums.

There is a prejudice among academics which also comes into play in the teaching of African religions. This is the conviction that traditional religions (unlike Judaism, Christianity and Islam) are ahistorical. Unfortunately this bias is shared by much of the material currently available on African religions. Historical work on the indigenous religions of Africa is just beginning to appear and some of it promises to add significant new understanding to the field.

Finding the Best Text on African Religions

There is no definitive text on African religions and, almost by definition, there cannot be such a book. Anyone writing a book or designing a course about African religions has to make hard choices. It is impossible to cover, in a single course or book, the richness and diversity of religious expression throughout the entire continent. It can be argued that there are thousands of distinct religious traditions represented in sub-Saharan Africa and, even by a more conservative measure of what constitutes a discrete tradition, the number still stands at several hundred.

Benjamin C. Ray's small book *African Religions: Symbol, Ritual, and Community* and E. Thomas Lawson's even slimmer *Religions of Africa: Traditions in Transformation* are both good basic texts and each can be used to advantage in structuring a course and setting its basic methodology. The strategies of these two books, however, are quite different. Lawson introduces the religions of Africa through two case studies, one of the Zulu and the other of the Yoruba. Ray's more satisfying text takes a phenomenological approach in which he illustrates standard categories such as myth, divinity, ritual and authority with specific examples drawn from a variety of African cultures. His book concludes with valuable chapters on "Religion and Rebellion," "African Islam" and "Independent Christianity." Ray draws his examples from the best scholarship in the field and he presents them carefully. There is some inevitable distortion deriving from his Eurocentric categories, but nevertheless, Ray's book is probably the best currently available and, when it is supplemented with other readings, it can be quite effective.

Another method of introducing African religions might be labeled the philosophical approach. This approach, urged by several texts in the field, ranges across the continent of Africa, looking for broad, common themes among its various religious traditions. These themes are usually conceptual ones. While it is true that there are certain basic attitudes, values and moods which run throughout the traditional religions of Africa, locating and naming them is a difficult enterprise, and it is one best undertaken only after particular traditions have been studied in some depth. Still this is a seductive approach for Western scholars because it appears to capture the richness of Africa in a relatively small number of ideas. Janheinz Jahn's *Muntu* is one book which attempts such sweeping generalizations and unfortunately it is frequently used as a text for African religions courses. John Mbiti's *African Religion and Philosophy*, an even more popular book, suffers from a similarly inauthentic pan-African tone of voice, which is further complicated by Mbiti's tendency to Catholicize things African. In this vein, Dominique Zahan's *The Religion, Spirituality, and Thought of Traditional Africa* is much more successful than either Jahn or Mbiti, but it still has a basically European mindset behind its categories. Robert Farris Thompson's *Flash of the Spirit: African and Afro-American Art and Philosophy* is the best choice for the 'philosophically' inclined. It is a lively, insightful and very readable book which uses indigenous categories of thought. The claims he makes are also more modest. Thompson works with specific African themes drawn from only four locales: Nigeria, Mali, Zaire and Cameroon. He traces these themes through the slave trade, into the Western Hemisphere. Thus Thompson's book has the great advantage of connecting Africa with dimensions of American culture which will be familiar to many students. I would also make one, more unusual suggestion for a text with a 'philosophical' bent. John Miller Chernoff opens much of the world of Africa, including its religions, through the channel of music. His *African Rhythm and African Sensibility: Aesthetics and Social Action in African Musical Idioms* is an inspired work which could be used quite effectively, perhaps along with actual music, to pull students into the African ethos. The major conclusion to be drawn from this discussion of introductory texts is that any text currently available will require the use of supplementary material.

Making Choices

By necessity, the choices about what will be covered in an African religions course are partly determined by the amount and quality of the scholarly work available on any given tradition. For example, the religions of Yorubaland (contemporary Nigeria) are almost always included in African courses because there is so much high quality work from this area. A recent publication by Henry Drewal, Roland Abiodun and John Pemberton, *Yoruba: Nine Centuries of African Art and Thought* provides an excellent example of the creativity in the field of Yoruba studies. Originally prepared as a catalogue for a major exhibition of Yoruba art, this substantial volume stands out for its commitment to the use of Yoruba linguistic and conceptual categories and for the methodological sophistication with which the authors approach the challenge of understanding Yoruba religion. *Yoruba* with its 250 photographs, many in color, would be an excellent resource for the teacher of a course in African religions but it is undoubtedly too expensive to be used as a class text. Although it could not be described as an engaging or provocative work, William Bascom's *The Yoruba of Southwestern Nigeria* remains the best text to introduce Yoruba religion within its social context and it is quite accessible to undergraduate students.

There is good material available, which is also appropriate for classroom use, on a variety of other religious traditions. I will name only a few books here. Marcel Griaule's *Conversations with Ogotemmeli: An Introduction to Dogon Religious Ideas* has become a standard and very successful ingredient in many courses on African religions. Its strength lies in the philosophical richness and complexity which it uncovers in Dogon religion and thus it is quite effective for use with students who assume there is no systematic or sophisticated thinking going on in traditional Africa. Victor Turner's *The Drums of Affliction: A Study of Religious Processes among the Ndembu of Zambia* can be used effectively and Wyatt MacGaffey's *Religion and Society in Central Africa* presents a careful and nuanced portrait of the BaKongo of lower Zaire. In addition, Daryll Forde's *African Worlds*, a collection of essays by different scholars on a variety of West and Central African religions, although older than these other books, is still a useful classroom resource. Any of these books, and many others as well (some of which have been included in the bibliography), would make good supplementary reading for students.

In discussing particular traditions, I must also mention James Fernandez's monumental work *Bwiti: An Ethnography of the Religious Imagination in Africa*. Its length (nearly 600 pages) probably militates against its use as a required reading for students in an introductory course, but this book could be an invaluable resource for a teacher and its methodological finesse places it among the most exciting recent works on African religion. Fernandez's book, about the Fang of Gabon, stands out for its commitment to indigenous thought forms, its recognition of the historical dimension of Fang religion and, most of all, for its awareness that religious people in Africa are not simply representatives of traditions, but individual human beings with powerful insights, strong feelings and well developed interior lives.

The Cross-Disciplinary Imperative

Openness to cross-disciplinary work is requisite for teaching about religious expression in Africa since, in most cases, art historians, ethnomusicologists and anthropologists have given us more information about Africa's traditional religions than religious studies scholars have.

The Problem of Course Design

Once we have in front of us a picture of the available scholarly resources, other constraints enter the process of course design. How much material and what sort of material should be chosen from each tradition? On the one hand we want to avoid a smorgasbord approach which takes, for example, a creation myth from the Dogon, a masking cult from the Yoruba and a healing ceremony from the Kongo peoples and then lets these small pieces stand for the wholes. On the other hand, concentrating too much on one particular tradition can also distort the view which students take away from a course on African religions. One of the things to be avoided is presenting a single group such as the Yoruba in such depth that we leave students with the impression that, if they know Yoruba religion, they know all the religions of Africa.

Another important question of course design concerns the inclusion of non-indigenous religious traditions. Islam has been in sub-Saharan Africa since the eleventh century and Christianity since the fifteenth. Christianity and Islam are indeed African religions and this should probably be taken into account when designing a course by that title. African Christianity and African Islam each presents its own challenge.

Beginning in the eleventh century, when Islam first crossed the Sahara via the trade routes, it has shown a propensity for blending rather easily with the religious and social customs of traditional Africa. Furthermore, Islam was not spread by missionaries but hand to hand, or more accurately, convert to convert. The result is that Islam in sub-Saharan Africa is a distinctive product of various cultural syntheses and cannot always be neatly distinguished from traditional religions. A good introduction to sub-Saharan African Islam is the short and clear survey by J. Spencer Trimingham, *The Influence of Islam upon Africa*. In the case of Islam, as in so many other dimensions of the study of religion in Africa, we academics are led to question our preoccupation with order, our desire for hard and fast boundaries among the world's religious traditions.

Christianity's entry into Africa south of the Sahara cannot be separated from the process of European commercial expansion and colonization. Furthermore, Christianity was spread through foreign missionaries and thus arrived in the form of a dramatic alternative to traditional values and commitments. Christian converts had to make choices of a sort not necessary for African Muslims. I have found Chinua Achebe's *Things Fall Apart,* and *Arrow of God,* both novels, as well as Wole Soyinka's *Ake: The Years of Childhood,* an autobiography, to be especially effective teaching tools in this general area. They present accurate and lively pictures of the conflict between traditional African values and those carried to Africa by Europeans and North Americans. And, of course, they have the added advantage of being stories told from an African perspective. Another less well-known, though equally potent African voice is that of the Zambian clergyman, E. Milingo in *The World in Between: Christian Healing and the Struggle for Survival.* In this book Milingo tells the story of his attempt to bring traditional healing practices into his Christian ministry and of the resistance which he subsequently encountered from his church. I imagine this book would be especially effective in a school with a strong Christian identification. It raises difficult and important questions about the Christian presence in Africa and, at the same time, it challenges our habit of removing political issues (or any kind of conflict for that matter) from the arena of religious studies. Acrimony, and even violence, have key roles on the stage of religious history and they should not be written out of the subject matter considered in the classroom.

African Christianity has also spawned independent churches and charismatic movements which make up an important part of the story of religious ferment in contemporary Africa. Karen E. Field's readable *Revival and Rebellion in Colonial Central Africa* is a good source for teachers interested in this dimension of African religion and perhaps for students as well. J. D. Y. Peel's *Aladura: A Religious Movement Among the Yoruba* and B. G. M. Sundkler's *Bantu Prophets in South Africa* are also respected texts which would be good resources for teachers. Considering new religious movements in Africa is one way to move African religions onto the stage of history where they ought to be.

In Conclusion

There are a few key points to remember in setting out to teach an introductory course on African religions: (1) The field is rich and diverse, both in subject matter and in methodology. No course can cover it all and no teacher can design a course which is truly representative of the whole. Choices are necessary. (2) There is no text which will give a ready-made course design. Any text will require supplemental sources for teachers and students alike. (3) African religions are danced and carved, sung and ritualized. They are pounded out on drums and woven in stories. Teasing out their meanings is a challenge in the academic world, where the company of books and ideas tends to be preferred. (4) African religions are also repositories of thought, insight and concept. Religious people in Africa think too, although they do not always choose to teach by lecturing. (5) Christianity and Islam, each in multiple forms, are also African religions. (6) African traditional religions participate in the flow of history. They are responsive to events in the world and they change. Furthermore religious differences in Africa, as in the rest of the world, have sometimes led to violence and even war. (7) African people are not simply representatives of their traditions. Religious individuals have made important contributions to their religious traditions and brought about changes within them. (8) Teaching a course on African religions in a college or university in the United States is not an easy task but it is a worthwhile one, if only for the insight it provides into the thought-patterns and behavior of the exotic tribe of scholars in religious studies.

BIBLIOGRAPHY

Achebe, Chinua. *Arrow of God*. New York: Doubleday, 1969.

_____ *Things Fall Apart*. New York: Fawcett, Ballentine, 1985.

Bascom, William. *The Yoruba of Southwestern Nigeria*. New York: Holt, Rinehart and Winston, 1969.

Chernoff, John Miller. *African Rhythm and African Sensibility: Aesthetics and Social Action in African Musical Idioms*. Chicago: The University of Chicago Press, 1979.

Drewal, Henry; Roland Abiodun, and John Pemberton. *Yoruba: Nine Centuries of African Art and Thought*. New York: Abrams and the Center for African Art, 1989.

Drewal, Margaret Thompson and Henry John. *Gelede: Art and Female Power Among the Yoruba*. Bloomington: Indiana University Press, 1983.

Fernandez, James W. *Bwiti: An Ethnography of the Religious Imagination in Africa*. Princeton: Princeton University Press, 1982.

Fields, Karen E. *Revival and Rebellion in Colonial Central Africa*. Princeton: Princeton University Press, 1985.

Ford, Daryll. *African Worlds: Studies in the Cosmological Ideas and Social Values of African Peoples*. New York: Oxford University Press, International African Institute, 1954.

Griaule, Marcel. *Conversations with Ogotemmeli: An Introduction to Dogon Religious Ideas*. New York: Oxford University Press, 1965.

Idowu, E. Bolaji. *Olodumare, God in Yoruba Belief*. New York: Praeger, 1963.

Jahn, Janheinz. *Muntu: The New African Culture*. New York: Grove Press, 1961.

Gleason, Judith. *Orisha, The Gods of Yorubaland*. New York: Atheneum, 1971.

Lawson, E. Thomas. *Religions of Africa: Religious Traditions of the World*. San Francisco: Harper and Row, 1984.

MacGaffey, Wyatt. *Religion and Society in Central Africa: The BaKongo of Lower Zaire*. Chicago: The University of Chicago Press, 1986.

Mbiti, John S. African Religions and Philosophy. Garden City, New York: Doubleday, 1969.

Milingo, E. *The World in Between: Christian Healing and the Struggle for Spiritual Survival.* New York: Orbis Press, 1988.

P'Bitek, Okot. *African Religions in Western Scholarship.* Nairobi: East African Publishing House, 1970.

Peel, J. D. Y. *Aladura: A Religious Movement Among the Yoruba.* London: Oxford University Press, 1968.

Ray, Benjamin C. *African Religions: Symbol, Ritual and Community.* Englewood Cliffs, New Jersey: Prentice-Hall, 1976.

Soyinka, Wole. *Ake: The Years of Childhood.* New York: Aventura, Vintage Books, 1983.

Sundkler, B. G. M. *Bantu Prophets in South Africa.* London: Oxford University Press, 1961.

Thompson, Robert Farris. *Flash of the Spirit : African and Afro-American Art and Philosophy.* New York: Random House, 1983.

Trimingham, J. Spencer. *The Influence of Islam Upon Africa.* London: Longmans, Green and Co., 1968.

Turner, Victor. *The Drums of Affliction: A Study of Religious Processes among the Ndembu of Zambia.* Ithaca, New York: Cornell University Press, 1968.

Zahan, Dominique. *The Religion, Spirituality, and thought of Traditional Africa.* Translated by Kate Ezra Martin and Lawrence M. Martin. Chicago: The University of Chicago Press, 1979.

TEACHING ABOUT RELIGION IN AMERICA

Howard Miller

"American religion" is, of course, not a "tradition" even in the sense of something as amorphous as, say "Hinduism." The United States is among the most heterogeneous of any religious culture that has ever existed and counts among its population adherents of virtually all the religious traditions discussed elsewhere in this book. And yet it seems right to include an essay on the subject in the book. American colleges and universities do, in fact, teach courses and award advanced degrees in "Religion in America." Moreover, observers from Tocqueville, to Lincoln, to G.K. Chesterton have suggested that religion is in some way at the center of the Americans' obsession with identifying themselves. If Americans are not Chesterton's "nation with the soul of a church," they nonetheless have been fascinated by the role religion has played in their development as a people. And religion has developed in the United States a cohort of characteristics that are recognizably "American." It is voluntaristic and denominational, activist and impatient with theological speculation, focused on morals and morality, centered on and dominated by the laity rather than the professional religionist and hostile to the forces of centralization and hierarchy.

There are obvious difficulties in trying to make sense of a religious culture made up of at least 200, and some would say more than 1,000, separate communities of believers. But the rewards of such an undertaking are considerable. Most obviously, those communities provide the student with a laboratory in which to test the theories social scientists have elaborated for understanding the development of religious structures and the social functions of religion. For instance, what better place to think about "church/sect" distinctions than in a culture in which both church and sect characteristically evolve into a religious category called the "denomination"?

Some of the religious denominations that emerged in the United States were born in America. The American laboratory, then, can tell us much about the circumstances under which and the processes whereby cultures produce religions and about the reasons why some of those new religious communities flourish and why others fail. In America those groups have ranged enormously in size and influence. Some, like the early nineteenth century followers of Jerimah Wilkinson, the "Publick Universal Friend," were never numerous and disappeared rather quickly after the death of their founder. But others survived and at least one of them has become a numerous and powerful religious force not only in America but throughout the world. Indeed, because of the recent publication of three superb books, the Church of Jesus Christ of Latter-Day Saints (the Mormons) provides an unusually profitable focus for teaching about American religion. Jan Shipps' *Mormonism: The Story of a New Religious Tradition*, with its sensitive anthropologically-informed inquiry, is a model of denominational history. Leonard J. Arrington's *Brigham Young: American Moses* is a first-rate biography of the man who gave substance to Joseph Smith's vision of a Western Zion. And Richard L. Bushman's *Joseph Smith and the Beginnings of Mormonism* is a sensitive, if not always successful, effort by a convinced Morman to deal as an historian with the miraculous origins of his faith. And, to remind students that not all "new" religions in America survive, there is always the doleful account by Leon Festinger and his colleagues of what happens "when prophecy fails," the story of a flying saucer cult in the Midwest of the 1950s and of its remarkable charismatic female leader.

There are, of course, an array of approaches to teaching about religion in America, and there are an impressive library of resources to assist in that task. The best way to encounter the sheer magnitude and variety of religious communities in America is in the four volume survey by the late Arthur Piepkorn, *Profiles In Belief: The Religious Bodies of the United States and Canada*. A briefer introduction can be found in the latest edition, edited by Samuel S. Hill, of Frank S. Mead's *Handbook of Denominations in the United States*. The field has also been very well-served by its historians. Among the best in print in the late eighties are Sydney E. Ahlstrom's magisterial *A Religious History of the American People*, which was written recently enough to have an inclusive understanding of what constitutes "the American people." A more recent survey is Martin Marty's *Pilgrims In Their Own Land: 500 Years of Religion in America*. The teacher should also be aware of Henry Warner Bowden's *Dictionary of American Religious Biography*, which was published late enough to include figures other than Great White Men. And there is an enormously helpful *Historical Atlas of Religion in America*, edited by Edwin Gaustad, the central feature of which is a spectacular color-coded map of the majority religion in each of the counties of the United States in 1976. Finally, the student who is intrigued by anything found in these surveys and reference tools can follow up on it in Nelson R. Burr's *A Critical Bibliography of Religion in America*, a model of an annotated bibliographical guide.

No matter if the teacher chooses an historical, topical or phenomenological approach to religion in America, there are problems. The most troublesome is that the study of religion in America is still primarily the study of Great White Men. One of the greatest challenges that has faced the students of American religion is to envision the field in such a way so as to allow the experience of red, brown, black and yellow people to become integral and organic parts of the mosaic that finally is the American whole. Catharine Albanese makes a largely successful effort to do that in her recent survey, *America: Religion and Religions*. Also very useful as an introduction to the issue of "otherness" and American religion is Laurence Moore's *Religious Outsiders and the Making of Americans*. In general, blacks have been better served in this endeavor than have other racial and ethnic minorities. Especially useful is Albert Raboteau, *Slave Religion: The "Invisible Instituition" in the Antebellum South*.

The issue of gender is equally challenging to students and teachers of religion in America. In a significant way, the imperative in thinking about the role of women and of racial and ethnic minorities in American religious culture is the same. In each instance religion—the sacred text and tradition of organized Christianity—was used to justify oppression and exploitation. But in both cases oppressed people also found within that tradition and in that text the source of effective resistance and of identity and communal solidarity. It is now well-known that women found in organized religion "space" within which to function and exercise power elsewhere unavailable to them. Teachers and students need now to rethink the entire development of religion in America in the lights of that achievement. The place to begin that crucial task is Rosemary R. Ruether and Rosemary Skinner Keller, eds., *Women and Religion in America*.

One of the most difficult problems in teaching about American religion is a function of the contrast between its remarkably homogeneous origins and its equally astounding hetreogeneous contemporary character. It is a real challenge to find ways to convey to students the over-whelmingly Protestant nature of American society before 1800 while finding ways at the same time to deal sensitively with the miniscule origins of the complexity that became normative as the nineteenth century developed.

Closely related to this problem is the current debate over the nature and future of what is called the "mainstream" or "mainline" of American culture. As late as the 1950s the liberal Protestant denominations, Methodist, Episcopal, Presbyterian, Disciples, Lutheran and the like, constituted a cultural force that was presumed, in some essential way, to represent the "mainline" of American Protestantism, the center by which groups to the left and right were placed in the spectrum of Protestant communities. That liberal cohort is no longer obviously the "mainstream" of American Protestantism. They are criticized from within and without as socially permissive, theologically naive and doctrinally undemanding. And as their numbers decline annually, a cohort of "religions of rigor" flourish on their right. Mormons, pentecostals and charismatics, and especially Southern Baptists have grown enormously in the past quarter-century and have attained an unaccustomed social respectability and political power by providing their members with doctrinal certitude, social direction and a strong sense of communal identity. Clearly none of these "religions of rigor" emerged overnight and the challenge is to find ways to "pick up" the origins of these communities and to reinterpret the development of American religion in ways that remain true to the historical realities of the nineteenth and early twentieth centuries even as they prepare us to recognize very different realities in contemporary society. The place to begin thinking about these concerns is in Wade Clark Roof and William McKinney's *American Mainline Religion: It's Changing Shape and Future* and Robert Wuthnow's *The Restructuring of American Religion: Society and Faith Since World War II.*

Another of the problems in thinking about American religious culture grows out of a paradox, one that involves a striking contrast between the perceived essential character of religion in Europe and in the United States and the differences in which those two areas are being studied currently. On the one hand, religion in Europe is supposed to be aristocratic, hierarchical and dominated by theological and philosophical speculation. Religion in the United States, by contrast, is said to be characterized by democratic ecclesiastical structures dominated by a laity impatient with theology and insistent on the centrality of religious experience. However, it is the students of religion in Europe who today are pioneering the study of what is called "popular religion" while the study of American religion remains focused on the thoughts and actions of Great White Men. We know much less about the religious experience of common people, those folk in the pews, than do the students of religion in Europe. There are, of course, important exceptions to that generalization. One thinks of John Demos' *Entertaining Satan*, which is much more than a study of the outbreak of witchcraft at Salem. It is, in fact, a model for the ways in which to think about the world of the occult that clearly co-existed well into the nineteenth century with the universe of organized religion in the United States. At the same time there has been the beginnings of efforts to get at the spiritual life of ordinary people, most especially in Charles Hambrick-Stowe's *The Practice of Piety: Puritan Devotional Disciplines in Seventeenth-Century New England*.

And then there is the problem of "secularization." Recent students of American religion, noting the undeniable increase in the number of "unchurched" Americans since the end of World War II, have had recourse to a wide range of interpretations of post war religious culture that focus to varying degress on the ineluctable progress of "secularism" in the United States. Those students, however, have paid too much attention, apparently, to the experience of those "mainline" Protestant denominations, have ignored the phenomenal growth of the "religions of rigor" and have not noticed the many ways in which religion and religious experience have retained their importance in the lives of an extraordinary number of Americans. And, even in the area of statistics, the number of Americans that report having attended an organized religious service within a month remains at an impressive percentage of the population, more than forty percent, a figure that marks one of the ways in which American society in the late twentieth century is most unlike European culture, which has entered what can only be called a "post-Christian" age. Clearly, what needs to be explained is the remarkable persistence of religion as a powerful societal force in contemporary American culture, not its retreat before whatever is meant by "secularism."

One problem in teaching about the development of religion in America seems to be getting more serious as American society becomes more conservative in the late twentieth century. It has to do with the history of religious freedom in American culture. The development of, first, religious toleration and, then, freedom of religion is one of the signal achievements of the American people. Religion was the first area in which Americans learned that the cost of toleration for their own ideas was their toleration of the ideas of others, even if convinced that those ideas would send their adherents straight to hell. But Americans accepted that necessity only very gradually, with enormous reluctance and with very little grace. Young Americans, however, are convinced that the first settlers established religious freedom for everyone here and that Americans have guarded it zealously ever after. They assume that there was some special "genius" at work in those first settlers that allowed them to see something that other Europeans could not see. The result is a complete inability to appreciate the way in which even noble achievements are historically and culturally conditioned and rarely, if ever, grow out of "national" characteristics.

Several problems in teaching about religion in American culture arise from the ways in which students themselves approach the subject. This is especially true when they study their own religious culture in the same course in which they are also exposed for the first time to world religions. That, of course, is the overwhelming problem of getting students to realize that American religious culture is much more complicated than their experience of it. Most students will gladly acknowledge the complexity and "otherness" of, say, Japanese Buddhism. But, when they get to their own culture, perhaps in relief, they assume that, after meeting Buddhists, Sikhs and Muslims, here is something that they, after all, have experienced and therefore understand. Even those students who insist that they are themselves no longer "religious" will assume that "American religion" is more available to them than Buddhism and that it must closely approximate their experience of it.

This problem is especially pronounced when dealing with the historical development of religion in America. Students are notoriously reluctant to grant what I have called the "differentness and irretrievability" of the past and condescend to it by assuming that they can enter into it and its sensibilities at will and without cost. For instance, evangelical Christians are often delighted to encounter the rigorous, demanding Puritans. They are sure that they can understand men and women who, like themselves, claim to live in "sacred" universes. They, of course, are then not available to the absolute differences between themselves and seventeenth century Calvinists. On the other hand, other students find just enough modernity in the Puritans to become convinced that they are just like they, essentially motivated by material considerations, for which their pious statements are but clever, cynical cover. Neither group of students is ready to learn just how difficult it is to let the past be the past, different and irretrievable. Learning that essential lesson from the study of history is one of the best ways to begin to appreciate the necessity for letting the "other" remain just that, even while we try to understand as much of it as we can.

A remarkable film is available that is useful in introducing to students an American religious experience that is absolutely different from any they will, almost certainly, have experienced themselves. And it takes place not in the exotic East but in Scrabble Creek, West Virginia. In the mid sixties a documentary, "The Holy Ghost People," was made about a group of snake-handling Christians in the poverty-stricken hills of Appalachia. It includes lengthy interviews with members of the congregation as well as a distillation of an evening-long worship service. Especially when read in conjunction with Weston La Barre's *They Shall Take Up Serpents,* or with the section on regional religion in Albanese's survey, the film is a tremendously effective teaching device and can elicit enthusiastic discussion from even the dullest of classes.

Another way to convey to students an immediate experience of the complexity and otherness of much of American religious culture is through its music. Effective libraries of the music of American religion can be collected only through extended and patient effort, but there is a single source that provides an excellent place to begin. During and after the Great Depression, the Music Division of the Library of Congress provided employment for musicians and anthropologists by sending them to record with primitive equipment the folk music of America. The result is a library of literally hundreds of long-playing phonodiscs. The student of religion will find among them the music of many Native American communities, of black Americans in slavery and in freedom, of white Southerners in Appalachia, of the Mormons, and so forth.

Finally, the teacher of religion in America can lead students to engage with the subject by leading them in researching and writing the religious story of the their own families. Students characteristically respond that their family has no religious history. But as they begin to interview and to rummage around, they find that that is far from the case. The assignment is as demanding for the teacher as it is for students. But it can be facilitated by Jim Watts's and Allen Davis' fine guide, *Generations.* Students respond very enthsiastically to the assignment, which has the final advantage of allowing those students to teach the teacher about the development of religion in America.

BIBLIOGRAPHY OF WORKS CITED

Texts, Surveys and Monographs

Sydney E. Ahlstrom, *A Religious History of the American People*. New Haven: Yale University Press, 1972.

Catherine L. Albanese, *America: Religions and Religion*. Belmont, CA: Wadsworth Publishing Company, 1981.

Leonard J. Arrington, *Brigham Young: American Moses*. New York: Alfred J. Knopf, 1985.

Henry W. Bowden, *Dictionary of American Religious Biography*. Westport, CT: Greenwood Press, 1979.

Nelson R. Burr, *A Critical Bibliography of Religion in America* (2 vols.). Princeton: Princton University Press, 1961.

Richard L. Bushman, *Joseph Smith and the Beginnings of Mormonism*. Urbana, IL: University of Illinois Press, 1984.

John Demos, *Entertaining Satan: Witchcraft and the Culture of Early New England*. New York: Oxford University Press, 1982.

Leon Festinger et al, *When Prophecy Fails*. Minneapolis: University of Minnesota Press, 1956.

Edwin S. Gaustad, *Historical Atlas of Religion in America* (rev. ed.). New York: Harper and Row, 1976.

Charles E. Hambrick-Stowe, *The Practice of Piety*. Chapel Hill: University of North Carolina Press, 1982.

Samuel S. Hill, ed., *Handbook of Denominations in the United States* (8th ed.). Nashville: Abingdon Press, 1985.

Weston LaBarre, *They Shall Take Up Serpents*. Minneapolis: University of Minnesota Press, 1962.

Marty Marty, *Pilgrims In Their Own Land*. Boston: Little, Brown, 1984.

R. Laurence Moore, *Religious Outsiders and the Making of Americans*. New York: Oxford University Press, 1986.

Arthur Piepkorn, *Profiles In Belief* (4 vols. in 3). New York: Harper and Row, 1977.

Albert J. Raboteau, *Slave Religion*. New York: Oxford University Press, 1978.

Wade Clark Roof and William McKinney, *American Mainline Religion*. New Brunswick, NJ: Rutgers University Press, 1987.

Rosemary R. Ruether and Rosemary Skinner Keller, eds., *Women and Religion in America* (3 vols.). San Francisco: Harper and Row, 1986.

Jim Watts and Allen Davis, *Generations: Your Family In Modern American History*. New York: Alfred J. Knopf, 1974.

Robert Wuthnow, *The Restructuring of American Religion*. Princeton: Princeton University Press, 1988.

Audio Visual Teaching Aids: Blair Boyd and Peter Adair, "The Holy Ghost People," (1968) CRM Films, 2233 Farraday Ave., Carlsbad, CA 92008.

Library of Congress, Music Division, "Folk Music of the United States," Vols. I and XV, "Religious Music" (1976).

SECULAR IDEOLOGIES: HOW DO THEY FIGURE IN RELIGIOUS STUDIES COURSES?

Ninian Smart

By secular ideologies or secular worldviews we mean such systems of belief and practice as Marxism, liberal democracy, Fascism, humanism and nationalism. All of these are in fact plural: there are differing forms of humanism, ranging from the scientific humanism of (say) Bertrand Russell, to the existentialism of J.P. Sartre. Not all these systems are by themselves complete worldviews—the liberal democrat may be a Christian, an atheist or a Buddhist, and so her total worldview will combine the ideas of liberal democracy with those of the religious traditions mentioned. Again, there are may forms of nationalism, according to the nation, and the way a nation may define its past can include a religious tradition—thus for most Romanians, Orthodox Christianity is irrevocably woven into the sense of the Romanian people's identity. So often a nationalism is a kind of religious nationalism.

In various ways, then, secular worldviews coalesce with religious ones; while others may adopt a hostile stance. Thus official Marxisms in East Europe, the U.S.S.R. and Asia often are or have been hostile to the traditional religions in society, such as Tibetan Buddhism.

On both counts it is important for the Religious Studies student to explore secular worldviews, either because they are often rivals to religions as traditionally defined or because they coalesce with religious traditions. In the first case, it is logical to treat all the rivals for human allegiance and commitment together. In the second case the blend is important for understanding modern developments in religion. For instance Khomeini's worldview includes both Islam and the ideology of the modern nation-State: it is not in this sense really so traditionalist, but has an innovatory side to it. Again, the modern Hindu ideology of such people as Vivekananda and Radhakrishna combines themes from classical Hindu theology, modern nationalism and democratic humanism. It is thus a complex blend, which proved very potent in the modern Indian struggle for identity-creation and for Indian national independence.

The ideologies we need to consider in the modern world have their birth in the Enlightenment (18th - 19th centuries), and consist in three main forms: liberal humanism, stressing the open society, the use of reason in resolving problems and utilitarianism (i.e. the doctrine that what is right and wrong is determined by what conduces to or hinders the greatest happiness of the greatest number, and the least suffering of the least number); socialism and particularly Marxism (emphasizing the importance of economic forces, and ultimately communism, and the role of religion as inimical to social liberation); and nationalism (the doctrine that each national group should have its own territory and State, and the incarnation of this doctrine in various particular nationalisms). These strands can cross over: socialism and liberal democracy combine in the social democratic tradition; liberalism and Christianity combine in liberal Protestantism, and in a more limited way in evangelical Christianity; Marxism and religion combine in Christian liberation theology; Marxism and nationalism in Vietnamese Marxism, Albanian Marxism and so on. Fascism existed as a variety of hyper-nationalist ideologies, e.g. in German Nazism.

Apart from the fact that secular worldviews both rival and coalesce with religious traditions, in fact they often resemble religions. Tillich called them quasi-religions; while I think that we should treat worldviews together, as worldview analysis, covering both secular and traditionally-religious worldviews. These then become two species of the genus worldviews. The similarity between such secular worldviews and religious traditions can be seen through a dimensional analysis. Thus nationalism has its myths or sacred narratives (the history of a nation as taught in schools, celebrated in national holidays, etc.); its experience or sentiments (feelings of glory at the nation's achievements, etc.); ritual (marchpasts, memorial days, the flag, the anthem and so on); and institutions (the President or monarchy, the army, teachers, etc.). It may add doctrines either of religion (England as a 'Christian nation') or ideology ('the new China'). It is true that there is no necessary belief in the Transcendent. If it is belief in the Transcendent that distinguishes traditional religions from secular worldviews, then secular worldviews differ from religions in point of reference, but not profoundly in form. It is these formal, dimensional elements which might justify us in applying Religious Studies analyses to them. Also of course, it is reasonable to think that had the comparative study of religion arisen in traditional China rather than in the West it would have been easy to include secular world-views in the general treatment, for it would not perhaps have consisted in the comparative study of *religion* as it has been understood in the West. The separation of Church and State also conduces to a sharper definition of religion (for tax purposes and all sorts of other legal purposes) than would otherwise perhaps have been the case.

It may then be that the distinction between religion and secular ideology is itself an ideological or a religious distinction which we do not need to accept. But even without this consideration, there seem to be good reasons why the student of religions needs to take secular ideologies as part of her field. We of course begin from the midst of the religions, and we use insights gained in their study to illuminate the analysis or secular beliefs and practices. The weight of concerns in the study of religion is still religion: all that we have need to notice is that our explorations are open and sometimes lead us into the secular.

Incidentally it is important to notice that there are two rather different meaning of the word 'secular'. In one sense—the one we use here—the secular concerns itself with what lies in this world, it does not look to the Transcendent, it is not involved with ancient rituals or overtly mythological symbolism. The secular society in this sense is one in which little attention is paid to religion and older forms of worship. This does not imply, as we have already indicated, that the ideologies and way of the secular society do not contain religious-type elements (history as myth, for instance) but it rather more importantly is turned towards material, cultural and educational goals, rather than towards traditional eschatological hopes and fears. The second sense of the term 'secular' refers to the secular State, that is a system of government and politics in which there is no required religion. It once was the case that in England, for instance, Catholics, Nonconformists and Jews were disadvantaged in higher education and the professions (for university education itself meant that the person being admitted to the university had to affirm the Thirty-Nine Articles of the Church of England); and such societies (which had been the norm in Europe for three centuries) were not 'secular'. But the United States Constitution and analogues which later evolved are 'secular' in that there is a division between church and State, and in theory no citizen is disadvantaged because of her religion. The successor to the older establishmentarian states are those of the Marxist world, except that a secular (first sense) creed becomes the requisite for advancement in such nations. Marxism rather than religion becomes the officially approved worldview. Conversely India, a notoriously religious country and so not secular (first sense) has a secular (second sense) constitution. The second sense might best be called "pluralistic". Secular ideologies can be pluralistic or not—Fascism and Marxism tend not to be; but social democracy and humanism tend to be.

We have noted the importance of the Enlightenment in creating the ideological forces which have been so important in the modern world; important too was radical Protestantism which tended to take an individualistic stance. This was implied in the notion of adult baptism. In the 19th century liberalism was often in conflict with established churches, and the combination of liberal ideals and the struggles for national liberation could lead to tensions between some nationalists and the churches, e.g. in Italy. One can observe like tensions in Asian and other countries. There are also tensions between Marxism and traditional religions because of Marxism's overtly anti-religious, atheistic stance.

Though modern secular (i.e. non-transcendental) worldviews are the most important, they did have some forebears in the West and in other cultures—Greek skepticism, Lucretius and Epicureanism, for example; and the Lokayate tradition of ancient India. But modern secular worldviews are much strengthened not only by the drift away from traditional religion that has occurred in a number of urbanized, industrial societies, but much more by the success and prestige of modern science. So it is not possible to explore modern ideologies without attempting to grapple with ways in which they are, or claim to be scientific. Many versions of liberal humanism, Marxism and psychoanalysis claim to be scientific.

As with their religious counterparts, secular ideologies exist in a variety of subtraditions, so it is best to think of Marxism, humanism, existentialisms and so on. Thus, the doctrines of Soviet Marxism diverge from those of Maoist China or Albania; the humanism of Julian Huxley (with its emphasis on evolution) differs from the more 'literary', symbol-oriented outlook of Jungian psychoanalysis; the existentialism of Heidegger is very different from the more socially activist version of Sartre. The technically presented and sometimes aggressive positivism of philosophers such as A.J Ayer after World War II was one ingredient in a process in which often in English-speaking philosophy departments the dominant worldview expressed has been a kind of scientistic humanism. This, by the way, sometimes leads to an unhealthy unease between students of philosophy and students of religion, as pushing institutionally different kinds of worldviews (whereas it is not the task of the university or the public school to take a stance, but to study more impartially the varieties of human worldview).

Because we are typically in cultures especially of the Western world, immersed in values of a secular (non-religious) kind, it often happens that we take for granted features of our culture, and thus are blind to the ritual and symbolic aspects of secular life. Thus part of the advantage of taking secular worldviews alongside traditionally religious outlooks is that it will encourage symbolic analysis—the deciphering of the deeper values implicit in the arrangements of everyday life. Thus it is worth getting students to reflect on the ceremonial attributes of television, e.g. on occasions of national importance; the symbolisms and rituals of science (e.g. the way experts are treated; the garb of surgeons and nurses; the attempt to spread scientific ideas and methods to every sphere of life); the use of games to inculcate certain values; the hidden messages of differing styles of architecture, etc. There are also implicit worldview-themes in much that is said and written is some areas of public debate, e.g. on economics, the development of "Third World" countries, etc. Also among various more secular groups and activities there are some which verge more obviously on the religious—psychotherapy, est, Essalin, etc.

Such analysis would begin to make us see how it is that worldviews carry enough symbolic power to grip people; they are not just intellectual formulations about the universe and about human nature. It is not scientific knowledge *per se* which carries such power, but the mystique and authority that leads inevitably to an outlook which is scientistic (that is, which sees scientific inquiry as the exclusive source of knowledge).

Of the various worldviews the most important rivals to religions are scientific humanism and Marxism. The most important ideas to combine with traditional religions are nationalism and a liberal democratic ethos. The combination of religious tradition and nationalist sentiment can be seen in Northern Ireland, Sri Lanka (Buddhism and Sinhala nationalism), Poland (among members of the Solidarity movement), Romania (Orthodoxy and Romanian nationalism), Iran (Shia Republicanism), India (Hindu pluralism, democracy and Indian patriotism), Afrikaner nationalism in South Africa (Dutch Reformed Church and nationalism), Black theology in the U.S. (Black nation and Christianity, alternatively Black Muslim movement), etc. Liberalism combines with religion in liberal Protestantism especially (Bultmann's combination of liberal existentialism and the Gospel), in Catholic modernism, in liberal Hindu neo-Vedanta, etc. United States "civil religion" which has been much debated over the last twenty years combines Enlightenment democratic values and some elements of Christian theism.

One of the main debates in recent decades has been about the supposed growth of secularism and the decay of traditional religions. But the period has also seen the flourishing of new religious movements, religious revival in parts of Eastern Europe, Africa and parts of Asia. But it is obvious that secularism is the dominant motif in many European countries, and is a large force in North America; and has increased significance in a number of other previously religious countries. This is another reason why we cannot afford to ignore it in Religious Studies courses, and so the secular ideologies have a place in surveys of world religions and in other wide-ranging courses, especially about Western religion.

Some Books on Modern Atheisms

Blackham, H.J.:*Six Existentialist Thinkers* (London: Routledge & Kegan Paul, 1961; reprinted 1978). A clear introduction to six main existentialists, Kierkegaard, Nietzsche, Jaspers, Manel, Heidegger and Sartre, of whom the last two and Nietzsche are especially important for the history of modern atheism and humanism.

Kolakowski, Leszek:*Positivist Philosophy* (New York: Doubleday,1972) pp 263. A history of the positivist strand in modern thinking mainly since Hume.

Ling, Trevor: *Marxism and Religion in Europe and India* (London: Macmillan, 1982) 168 pages. This is a good, though fairly advanced introduction to Marx's attitudes to religion—not just official or State religion, but also Boehme's mysticism, and the nature of Indian religion. It includes essays on Weber, the persistence of religion in the Soviet Union and a discussion of whether Marxism can be treated itself as a religion.

Macquarrie, John: *Twentieth Century Religious Thought*, 2nd edition (New York: Scribners 1981) 429 pages. A good encyclopaedic mine of brief accounts of religious and antireligious thinkers of the late 19th and 20th century.

Russell, Bertrand: *Wisdom of the West* (London: Macdonald 319) ed. Paul Foulkes. A lively and sometimes simple-minded history of Western philosophy, which could make a stimulating elementary introduction.

Smart, Ninian: *Worldviews: Crosscultural Explorations of Human Beliefs*, New York: Scribner's 1983. This book surveys the present state of worldviews in the world, and explores ways of understanding them. Though the approach begins with religions, it includes a lot of examples from secular ideologies. It concludes with tips on how to continue exploring on your own.

Stace, W.T: *Religion & the Modern Mind* (London: Macmillan, 1953). A good history, clearly written, of the relations between religion and science in the post-medieval period.

Viking/Fontana Modern Masters series. This well known series of small paperbacks has a number of volumes expounding and criticising various secular worldviews, notably the following titles: Richard Wollheim: *Freud;* Anthony Storr: *Jung;* Bryan Magee: *Popper;* Robert Conquest: *Lenin.*

❧III❧
"How I Teach the Introductory Course": A Symposium

THE INTRODUCTORY COURSE: THE MOST IMPORTANT COURSE

Wilfred Cantwell Smith

What I shall do here is to sketch something that I taught first and that was subsequently designated as the foundational course in the religion programme at Harvard. The title was "Introduction to the History of Religion". I had to struggle with my gradual recognition that in this country that title made it sound like, and the course description confirmed in students' minds the conception of, a "survey course"—in bad odour. In wrestling with the resistance or opprobrium that this aroused I became slowly aware of at least part of what is at issue here; and this reflecting contributed to certain more recent discernments that I have been enabled to develop on modern Western academic and secular orientations generally.

The concept "survey" has in modern times come inherently to embody several of the things that are wrong with the current academic outlook. '*Sur*' means "on" or "over", which fits with the notion that the student or the teacher is above the material that is being studied; as in concepts like 'mastering' and 'controlling', concepts that always disquiet me not a little in the humanities. The '*-vey*'of "survey" relates to "view" and is ultimately from *video*, 'to see', suggesting the distance that the modern intellect puts between itself and what it investigates. The whole nowadays corroborates a notion of the mind's looking out over, and to some extent down upon, an array of data that are to some degree being made available to it for use, that are at our service—the objectivity mood of the natural sciences and of the humanities. Also needed is that fundamental respect before any fellow human being that it is not merely a delinquency but an intellectual error not to have; and especially of course respect before the great minds and hearts that the humanities primarily study and cherish, and before the human multitudes that the social sciences observe and try to understand. In both, one is encountering what is greater than we. Especially of course in certain aspects of the study of human religious life, we are introduced to what those involved report that they have found to be supremely great; so that it makes sense to listen carefully to what they say.

Superficially, however, my version of the course does indeed seem to resemble the sort of survey course that is increasingly thought of as exactly what one would *not* do as an introduction in our field. This is so especially in coverage. It is a full year's course; and of the forty-some lectures in all, the majority are allotted in equal batches to the major traditions and communities. There are six each to Hindus; Buddhists; China & Japan other than Buddhist; Christians; and Muslims. There are three for the Jews; two each for the Greek heritage in the West, which I call "philosophia"; for "the Near East from Alexander to Muhammad" or "the Hellenistic-Manichaean age," an era that I find tantalizing; and for Modern Western Secularism. And there is one each for Paleolithic, for modern "extra-civilizational societies" or "little traditions", for Ancient Egypt, for Zarathustra and the Parsis, and for Ancient Israel. Doesn't that sound dreadful? To clarify a little why, nonetheless, I contend that this is not a survey, in a pejorative sense, but is something else, let me contrast with the interpretation of "survey" as 'looking down upon', or anyway 'looking out over', what for me at least lies implicit in the apparently innocently yet in fact significantly different title, "Introduction to the History of Religion".

There was an erstwhile trite remark, that "introducing" has to do with leading into something. *'Intro'* indeed means 'within', 'inside'. Certainly I conceive my course as endeavouring to lead the students, as gently yet firmly as may be, to inside the religious experience of their fellow human beings around the world and across the centuries. One uses the data of the traditions as a means for enabling oneself to understand the persons and groups for whom these have been, often supremely, significant.

"History" is the next term in my course-title, and this too deserves a little unfolding. By it I do not mean historiography, nor an awareness of the past. Also, certainly for me it is emphatically not the name of a discipline. By "history" I mean rather the process through time in which human beings have been and of course still are involved; that mysterious continuous transforming movement whereby one situation *becomes* another situation.

Fundamental is a strong awareness that history is not the past, but is a process that has indeed been under way for a long time yet still continues: it is that movement within which we ourselves are to-day and every day caught up. We participate in it—in its contemporary phase, as heirs of all its preceding phases and in some degree as active shapers of its later ones. Certainly one of the objectives of the course is to enhance the students' awareness of themselves as such participants in world history; just as one of its massive benefits has been to enhance year by year my ever more detailed, ever more realistic such awareness for myself.

The final term is "Religion". I reject, of course, the plural "religions"; and by "religion" mean religiousness, or in it include, as you might expect, both tradition and faith. It is a couple of decades now since my *Meaning and End of Religion* and its advocating of the pair 'tradition' and 'faith' as more scholarly terms than 'a religion' or 'religions'; and I have noticed that in that time the former word—'tradition'—has become quite widely used in our field, especially in historical studies, whereas 'faith' gets drastically less attention. In my course, in contrast, I try to induce the students via a comprehension of the data to develop an apprehension of the *engagement* of the persons and communities concerned, an appreciation of the human involvement that is of course the reason for a tradition's having arisen and having continued, as well as the reason for our taking notice of it.

Part of the point of all humanities study, of course—and of humane social science study—is to broaden the students' (and the teacher's) sense of humanity, of what it means, and has meant, to be a human being, of sharing in a common human enterprise that turns out as one studies to be wider than one had previously imagined, and deeper, stranger, longer; as well as more terrifying and more entrancing; and more worth coming to intellectual grips with.

Some students, of course, think of themselves as "secular", and begin, at least, with a sense of religion as something in which they personally are not involved, even though their signing up for the course indicates that they are for some reason interested in finding out more about it. That is fine: as might be inferred from the list of topics, I stress the point that secular is one of the positions that human beings have dreamed up and adopted, a position also to be taken seriously and to be considered alongside a number of other positions; that they are not outside the human realm looking in.

Whatever such differences among members of the class, I hope that they will come jointly to see the past of the variegated religious history of humankind as constituting our common heritage to-day; its present as our common context; and will come to see its future phases as still to be worked out, in part by us—and as both I and they grow older, increasingly by them.

The opening sentence of my opening lecture in the course has for some years now run as follows:

> We human beings on earth have been religious now for a very long time, and in a great variety of ways.

The first word, "We", is significant. Any study of religion limps that has not moved beyond thinking of it as an "it". In Buberian fashion we might operate in those terms with the data of the tradition, but not with the persons for whom (and because of whom) those data are meaningful. Yet neither will it do to think of religion as "they", if one but means "those other people, over there" (or: "way back then"). Thus my phrasing: "We human beings"; and I certainly aim at getting across the realization that all of us are involved.

So far as the rest of that opening sentence is concerned, I may report that in that first lecture I go on to remark that during the course of the year we shall be looking at some of the major and at one or two of the minor ways; and that at the end of our time we shall be considering briefly the current phase of the long story; but we begin with that matter of the "very long time". I then proceed to devote the remainder of that opening lecture to the Palaeolithic era, trying to make come alive certain aspects of that; particularly the cave art, and the introduction of burial of the dead as hominids were turning into *homo sapiens*. In any case, on the burial issue, for instance, I challenge the standard view that burial signifies a belief in immortality, which seems to me a ridiculous *non sequitur*, and I challenge the students to reflect rather on our common mortality, theirs and mine: also on our feelings when a leader dies, citing Martin Luther King's assassination.

My lectures, as I tell the students from the start, are designed to interpret the data to them, not to present those data, which on the whole they can get from reading. I see no point in my presenting in class material that they can find in books; and I suggest that if the class hour arrives and they have not read in preparation for it, they would probably do better to spend that hour in the library rather than to come to my lecture. The lectures followed to some degree the style of my book *The Faith of Other Men*. That is, these various lectures presented some aspect of the religious tradition under discussion, as illustrative both of that tradition and of a human orientation to life and to the universe, in which I invited the students to recognize that they themselves might, conceivably, be involved, or at least in which it was reasonable or anyway under-standable for millions of people to have been involved.

For example, my three lectures on the religious life of Jews dealt re-spectively with three topics—peoplehood, law, and the Sabbath. On the Sabbath it is a joy to have fifty minutes to set forth its power and signifi-cance, which my own upbringing contributed something to enabling me sympathetically to attempt. I presented it partly as an instance of Law, largely as an instance of sacred time (there is one in my Buddhist group on sacred space), and chiefly as an instance of the vivid sense of tran-scendence within human life experienced in, or shall we say through, a particular shape.

Since I illustrate law at this Jewish stage of our total study, I point out to the class when we come to the Islamic case that for Muslims also law is a fundamental religious category—in a way that is formally com-parable, even if substantially different. This sort of point clarifies why I insist that the year's course is an integral whole, not a sequence of dis-parate parts.

At Harvard a course of this sort and with this title had previously been taught by Arthur Darby Nock, that great classics scholar, but he had done it as a composite venture, himself teaching the Greek sector and having a panel of other faculty members doing each a sector: the professor of Sanskrit the Hindu part, and so on. I remark to the students that it is obvious to me, and presumably to them, that there are members of the Harvard faculty who know more about this or that segment of the whole than do I, except perhaps in the Islamic case, but that nonetheless I am attempting the whole thing rather than having it done piecemeal in the fashion sometimes known as a "parade course", because another basic element in the course is to get across the realization that it is pos-sible to come to contemplate the seemingly overwhelming variety of world history's human religious scene without, in fact, being over-whelmed by it, without being bewildered; that on the contrary, coming to know that variety is enriching, and indeed can be exhilarating.

In addition, I point out to the class that the alternative pattern, of a galaxy of teachers for this course, would seem to indicate that a member of the Harvard faculty is not competent to comprehend the material, but that the students are somehow expected to do so.

To return to the content of the lectures. As I have said, I tend to select a specific item for each tradition, and for the forms of faith that on the whole each inculcates and expresses. I have mentioned the Jewish case. Let me proffer also the Buddhist. Of the six lectures allotted to the Buddhist, three are respectively on Borobudur, on the historical sweep and variety of the whole movement, and on the four-word statement (three, in Pali) "All life is *dukkha*". With the second of these, attempted in various ways, I was not happy; it never became a really good lecture.

I have been less dissatisfied with my presentation of the First Noble Truth: "All life is *dukkha*". This lecture I proffer as a drama in three acts. The first opens with a scene in Paris just after the French Revolution when the leader Saint-Juste declares *"Le bonheur est une ide neuve en Europe"*. This relates to the translation of *dukkha* as "suffering," and I spend some time on the American proclamation of the pursuit of happiness as a suggested human goal, with some comment on the historicity of that development and its current implications, and on suffering as a reality in human life, for instance for non-Westerners and for Harvard students now while they are young and perhaps more poignantly and personally in the future. The second act switches to an alternative interpretation of *dukkha*, wherein I suggest "All life is awry". The final part of that lecture presents and analyses the observable fact that Buddhists individually and a Buddhist country like Burma, I have noticed, are often in fact remarkably cheerful folk—more so than their neighbors; and it asks the students to toy with a thesis that all religious Weltanschauungen (and various secular ones too, not only Marxist but turn-of-our century progress optimism currents, for example) tend to speak of what life would be like without their particular outlook; as with the Christian notion of sin as that from which Christians feel themselves forgiven. Thus I end with a presentation of the Buddhist movement as a proclamation not of sorrow and suffering but of triumphant good news, counterbalancing the first fifteen or twenty minutes during which I have made what I trust is a fairly effective apologetic for the "all life is suffering" motif, which the morning news normally helped, alas, to make cogent.

The Borobudur lecture is illustrated with slides. It is a monument that I have seen two or three times and been deeply impressed with. It serves to exemplify the matter of sacred space, as mentioned above. It also serves well to illustrate both the issue of religious art, and its potentially powerful impact, and the motif of pilgrimage. Students can readily be enabled to envisage the ascent of the visitor up the various levels of the massive pyramidal structure, from the everyday world of turmoil and strife, mightily portrayed in the magnificent and entrancing carved reliefs, on the first balcony, through successive stages of higher storeys and spiritual attainment to, ultimately, the formless at the top, pointing still further upward; and then the pilgrim's return down and back again into the everyday world to some lesser or greater degree transformed by the experience. This provides a superb occasion for introducing (to return to that word) them to one facet of one particular sector of the specific Buddhist movement, on the one hand, and one facet of general human potentiality and vision, on the other.

The other three Buddhist lectures usually have dealt respectively with *dharma* and the question "Was the Buddha an atheist?"; with an introduction to Mahayana; and with *mudras*, the position of the hands in Buddhist statuary. I published the first of these in my *Questions of Religious Truth*; and a small part of the third in my introduction to religion in the new Encyclopedia Britannica.

Obviously I am not going to go here through all the topics treated in the course. Let me just mention my opening lecture on the Christians, however. As I have indicated, I try to use each lecture to present, and to engage the class with, some item that seems representative both of the specific tradition under discussion, and of our common humanity. Thus I have an Islamic one of scripture, a Hindu one on the recognition of diversity, and so on. In the Christian case, I begin by pointing out that in most sectors of the course thus far I have tried to be appreciative. There is a danger, however, I now confess, that this approach may fail to acknowledge another fundamental fact of the religious scene: namely, the amount of disastrous mischief that it has perpetrated, the havoc that at times it has wrought, and continues to wreak. I therefore now give a lecture on Religious Wickedness; and obviously I can wax quite eloquent on that subject. As ever, I base the argument on strict historical facts; but there is no lack of these, of course. I explain that my choosing this topic as an illustrative and inescapable one within the entire sweep of our subject is surely requisite and proper; and that my placing it here has two grounds. One is that I myself am a Christian; and human history is far too replete already with instances of human beings' pointing out the vices of other communities' involvements while attending to the virtues of their own, whereas in fact every human movement has some of both, and it seems to me proper that, since I giving the course am a Christian, I place this important matter of religious wickedness within my own sector of the whole, even though it has its counterparts everywhere else also (including the secular!).

The second ground for my locating the consideration of Religious Wickedness within the Christian sector of the course is that Christians in fact have a distinctive doctrine of sin ("original sin is the only Christian doctrine for which there is indisputable empirical evidence", it has been quipped), and at their best they feel, in *Imitatio Christi*, that they should bear the sins of the world. It is appropriate specifically to the Christian, therefore, I suggest—to us Christians—to locate this topic here.

My other five lectures on the Christians, however, are more positive. One, for instance, is on the idea of God. My treatment attempts various other things, such as the role of ideas in religious life and of doctrine in Christian; but *inter alia* presents the theistic movement as one of the most consequential movements in human history—a movement in which the Church has participated, and whose rise, spread, development, and current phase are impressive, are rewarding to study.

The final lecture in the course begins by recalling the opening sentence of the opening lecture: "We human beings have been religious now for a very long time, and in a great variety of ways". What I have hoped to do is in significant part to get across the ubiquity, the variety, the persistence, of human religiousness; of (our!) human involvement in this mighty matter. As I have stated in that final lecture, religion does not raise people above the human level, only to it. I usually conclude that hour by a quotation from each of Hindu, Buddhist, Muslim, and Christian authorities suggesting that each aims at enabling us to be human properly. I also aver that from world religious history, as we have been studying it, we may infer a culminating principle. To be religious is not necessarily to live well; it is to take the question of living well, seriously.

THE INTRODUCTORY COURSE: LESS IS BETTER

Jonathan Z. Smith

"Better fewer but better."

-V.I. Lenin

In a sense, I prefer the topic I was first invited to speak on: "The Role of Courses in Religion in the Liberal Arts Curriculum... Including an Assessment of the Current State of the Liberal Arts" to the topic I discovered I was expected to speak on when the program arrived in the mail: "How I would Teach an Introductory Course in Religion." But, no matter. You cannot think about the one without the other. The second topic presupposes the first. That is to say, to think about an introductory course—any introductory course—is to think about the nature of liberal education. The least interesting term in the title is "religion."

I am delighted that such a topic has been proposed. If taken seriously, it marks the beginning of our potential for maturity as a part of the profession of education. Because of this, I note with sadness that this conference is the result of independent entrepreneurship (as was Claude Welch's pioneering work) rather than being a major focus of our putative professional society, the American Academy of Religion. Note the contrast to a mature discipline such as history which, as early as 1899, had a committee of the American Historical Association reporting to a national meeting in plenary session on the teaching of history in secondary schools. In 1905, the same was established for the first year of college work in history. (Both reports, published by the Association, still merit reading). In 1967, an important refereed journal, *History Teacher*, was founded. In 1976, the Association sponsored a major national conference on "The Introductory Course," hotly debated at subsequent annual meetings. In June, 1982, the Association devoted the bulk of its scholarly journal, *The American Historical Review*, to a "Forum" on the Western Civilization course. A rapid reading of the Association's *Annual Reports* reveals that a significant proportion of presidential addresses have been devoted to issues of education.[1]

I report these matters not entirely by way of invidious comparison, but rather to suggest, on the one hand, how far we have to go as a profession, and, on the other, to signal my delight that you have gathered to take this initial step.

There is nothing necessarily sinister in our lack of an articulate consensus on such matters. We are, after all, in many ways in our infancy. Until the 60's, it would have been almost impossible for anyone doing doctoral work in religious studies to be trained by graduate professors who, themselves, regularly taught undergraduates. I suspect that the majority of present members of the AAR were so trained. In influential fields, such as biblical studies, the pattern persists to this day. That is to say, if graduate education as a whole is notorious for its irresponsible lack of interest in educational issues, in religious studies this is compounded by sheer ignorance. Perhaps this is why our conveners phrased the topic for these evening sessions in the diplomatic subjunctive, "How I would teach..." rather that the reportorial indicative, "How I do teach introductory courses." In my case, I do. It is an activity which is not just indicative but imperative. For almost a decade I have taught nothing but introductory courses in my college. Most are designed for first and second year students, no course is designed specifically for majors or, for that matter, for potential majors. In a typical year I teach in the Social Sciences Core, I teach a year long sequence in Western Civilization, and I teach some sort of introduction to religion. My remarks will be based in part on this experience, in part on my other career. Since 1973, I have worked, spoken and written as much on liberal education as I have on religion, serving in a variety of administrative roles in the college at Chicago and on national commissions on undergraduate education.

I take as my starting point the proposition that *an introductory course serves the primary function of introducing the student to college level work*, to work in the liberal arts. Its particular subject matter is of secondary inter-

---

[1]I have taken the next four paragraphs, with minor alterations, from J.Z. Smith, "No Need to Travel to the Indies: Judaism and the Study of Religion," in J. Neusner, ed., *Take Judaism, For Example* (Chicago, 1983); 216-7. For another version, see J.Z. Smith, "Why the College Major? Questioning the Great Unexplained Aspect of Undergraduate Education," *Change* (July-August, 1983): 14-15.

est (indeed, I suspect it is irrelevant). All of my remarks this evening aim at unpacking this proposition from several vantage points.

First, it is necessary to step back and reflect, briefly, on the nature of the liberal arts curriculum. As I have written elsewhere, as one surveys the more than three thousand institutions of higher leaning who, together, offer 534 different kinds of bachelor degrees, it becomes apparent that there are a multitude of spatial arrangements, the ways in which the blocks of courses are organized: general requirements, major requirements, prerequisites, and the like. Each is appropriate to the peculiar institutions. What remains more or less constant are the temporal arrangements. Whatever we do we must do it in the equivalent of four years. Regardless of the academic calendar, there is almost always less that four full days of teaching time in a *year-long* course, less than one hundred hours of class meetings. And, there is no reason to presume that any student who takes one course on a given subject will necessarily take another one. Less than one hundred hours may represent, for a significant number of students, at best, their sole course of study in a particular subject matter. It is at this point—with the introductory course—and not with the major that curricular thought must begin. For within such a context, no course can do everything, no course can be complete. The notion of a survey, of 'covering,' becomes ludicrous under such circumstances. Rather, each course is required to be incomplete, to be self-consciously and articulately selective. We do not celebrate often enough the delicious yet terrifying freedom undergraduate liberal arts education affords the faculty by its rigid temporal constraints. As long as we do not allow ourselves to be misled by that sad heresy that the bacehelor's degree is but a preparation for graduate studies (a notion that is becoming pragmatically unjustified; it has never been educationally justifiable), then *there is nothing that must be taught*, there is nothing that cannot be left out. A curriculum, whether represented by a particular course, a program, or a four-year course of study becomes an occasion for deliberate, collegial, institutionalized choice.

I take as a corollary to these observations that each thing taught is taught not because it is 'there,' but because it connects in some interesting way with something else, because it is an example, an "e.g." of something that is fundamental, something that may serve as a precedent for further acts of interpretation and understanding by providing an arsenal of instances, of paradigmatic events and expressions as resources from which to reason, from which to extend the possibility of intelligibility to that which first appears to be novel or strange. Whether this be perceived as some descriptive notion of the "characteristic," or some more normative notion of the "classical," or some point in-between, matters little. These are issues on which academicians of good will can responsibly disagree.

What ought not to be at controversy is the purpose for which we labor, that long-standing and deeply felt perception of the relationship between liberal learning and citizenship.

I would articulate the grounds of this relationship as follows. From the point of view of the academy, I take it that it is by an act of human will, through language and history, through words and memory, that we are able to fabricate a meaningful world and give place to ourselves. Education comes to life at the moment of tension generated by the double sense of 'fabrication,' for it means both to build and to lie. For, although we have no other means than language for treating with the world, words are not after all the same as that which they name and describe. Although we have no other recourse but to memory, to precedent, if the world is not forever to be perceived as novel and, hence, remain forever unintelligible, the fit is never exact, nothing is ever quite the same. What is required at this point of tension is the trained capacity for judgment, for appreciating and criticizing the relative adequacy and insufficiency of any proposal of language and memory. What we seek to train in college are individuals who know not only that the world is more complex than it first appears, but also that, therefore, interpretative decisions must be made, decisions of judgment which entail real consequences for which one must take responsibility, from which one may not flee by the dodge of disclaiming expertise. This ultimately political quest for fundamentals, for the acquisition of the powers of informed judgment, for the dual capacities of appreciation and criticism must be the explicit goal of every level of the liberal arts curriculum. The difficult task of making *interpretative decisions* must inform each and every course.

If I were asked to define liberal education while standing on one leg, my answer would be that it is *training in argument about interpretations*. An introductory course, then, is a first step in this training. Arguments and interpretations are what we introduce, our particular subject matter serves merely as the excuse, the occasion, the "e.g."

This may seem a bit airy-fairy to you, so I shall begin again. An introductory course is not best conceived as a first step for future professionals, nor is it best conceived as an occasion for "literacy," for initial acquaintance with some aspects of the "stuff." *An introductory course is concerned primarily with developing the students' capacities for reading, writing and speaking*—put another way, for interpreting and arguing. This is what they are paying for. This is what we are paid for. We are not as college teachers called upon to display, obsessively, those thorny disciplinary problems internal to the rhetoric of professionals (e.g. in our field, the autonomy and integrity of religious studies). Our trade is educational problems, common (although refracted differently) to all human sciences. So, there are formal tests for an introductory course: it must feature a good deal of *self-conscious* activity in reading, writing, and speaking, because it is not enough that there be required occasions for such activities. In my own courses this means weekly writing assignments on a set theme which requires argumentation. Each piece of writing must be rewritten at least once regardless of grade. Please note: this requires that every piece of writing be returned to the student with useful comments no later than the next class period. In addition, there should be written homework. (Examples: Take pages 21-25 of Durkheim's *Elementary Forms* and reduce his argument to a single paragraph using no words not in Durkheim; or, Here is a list of 33 sentences from Louis Dumont, state the point of each in your own words). At least once a quarter, I call in all students' notebooks and texts. After reading them through, I have individual conferences with each student to go over what they've written and underlined and what this implies as to how they are reading. But this is insufficient. It is not enough that there be all this activity. Both the students and we need help. We need to provide our students with models of good writing. Wherever possible, beyond its intrinsic interest, each text read should be exemplary of good writing and effective argument. We also need to make available to our students the sort of help others provide. For example, in my introductory courses I regularly have the students buy Jack Meiland's little book *College Thinking: How to Get the Most out of College* and discuss portions of it with them.

Even more, we need help. At the most minimal level, most of us do not know how to write a proper writing assignment so as to make clear to the student what is expected of them. Most of us can recognize mistakes in writing and poor argument, we can circle them or write a marginal comment, but most of us do not know how to correct the mistake. We do not know how to help our students improve in the future, how to prevent the problems from recurring. These are not matters where sheer good will or pious wishes help. For example, circling spelling or grammatical errors has been shown, from a pedagogical point of view, to be a waste of time. We need to go to competent professionals and be taught how to teach writing. This is the *basic requirement* for a teacher of introductory courses.

This raises a larger question: the professional responsibilities of college teachers. Bluntly put, *we have as solemn an obligation to 'keep up' with the literature and research in education and learning as we do in our particular fields of research.* Even more bluntly, no one should be permitted to teach an introductory course who is not conversant, among other matters, with the literature on the cognitive development of college age individuals, with issues of critical reasoning and informal logic, and with techniques of writing instruction. While there is some art in teaching, it is, above all, a skilled profession.

To move to the particular question, "How I Teach Introductory Courses in Religion?" I have taught introductory courses in all three modes described by this project: the survey, the comparative, and the disciplinary. From a pedagogical standpoint, there is no difference between them. They all require explicit attention to matters of reading, writing and speaking, to issues of interpretation and argument—to that most fundamental social goal of liberal education, the bringing of private adherence to the pedagogical rule that "less is better." For example, my year-long survey, "Religion in Western Civilization," is organized around a single issue: "What is a tradition? How are traditions maintained through acts of reinterpretation?, and three pairs of topics: kingship/cosmology; purity-impurity/wisdom; voluntary associations/salvation. Note that the first member of each pair is preeminently social; the second, ideological. This allows a modest introduction of theoretical issues into a course which consists, essentially, of reading "classic" primary texts.

All three modes require explicit recognition of the educational dilemma of breadth and depth. Each of my introductory courses divides each topic into two parts. The first, usually entitled "the vocabulary of x" features the rapid reading of a wide variety of little snippets simply to get a sense of the semantic range of the topic and to experiment with what clusters of relationships can be discerned within the vocabulary. The second part features the slow and careful reading of a few exemplary documents. Each section of each introductory course is preceded by a lecture in which the topic is introduced; but, of more importance, in which the syllabus is "unpacked." The students need to know what decisions I have made, and why? What have I included? What have I excluded? They also need to hear some cost accounting of these decisions.

That is to say, I want my students to use the syllabus as an occasion for reflection on judgement and consequences, to be conscious of the fact that a syllabus is not self-evident, but (hopefully) a carefully constructed argument.

Beyond these generalities, I have two, and only two, criteria which govern the selection of the example and the organization of the syllabi: one has more to do with the form, the other with content.

Each of my introductory courses is organized around the notion of argument and the insistence that the building blocks of argument remain constant: definitions, classifications, data, and explanations. If we are reading second-order texts together, we have to learn to recognize these in others; if we are reading primary religious documents, we may have to construct them for ourselves. In some of my introductory courses, we devote the first week to explicit attention to these matters, thereby building a vocabulary by which we can identify and discuss these elements in subsequent readings. In other introductory courses, the courses themselves are organized around these rubrics and we spend the entire term exploring them. For example, any introductory course must begin with the question of definition ("What is civilization?" "What is western?"—I have my students take out a piece of paper and write their answers to these questions within the first five minutes of the first day of the course. We spend the rest of the period classifying their answers, discussing them, and discussing what makes a good definition); or a unit of a course might be designed to display the question of definition (in one introduction, I use as readings: Penner and Yonan, W.C. Smith, R. Otto, P.Berger, M.Spiro and R.B. Edwards).

The second rule is more central: *nothing must stand alone*. That is to say, every item studied in an introductory course must have a conversation partner. Items must have, or be made to have, arguments with each other. The possibilities are manifold; the only requirement is that the juxtaposition be interesting. For example, in what you have termed disciplinary courses, I search very hard for readings which contain two representative scholars who employ identical data (e.g. Piddocks vs. Orans; the Kronenfelds vs. Levi-Strauss); or for a striking juxtaposition which reveals hidden implications in a given position (e.g. showing Leni Riefenstahl's "Triumph of the Will" after reading Durkheim's *Elementary Forms*; reading the classic pornographic novel, *The Story of O* after reading Eliade and others on initiation).

Congruent with a concern for the relationship between the enterprise of liberal education and citizenship and with the observation that critical inquiry as often taught ("there's always another point of view") too frequently results in cynicism, the students must not be left with mere juxtaposition. There must be explicit attention to the possibilities and problems of translating, of reducing, one item in terms of the other. And, there must be explicit attention to consequences and entailments. What if the world really is as so-and-so describes it? What would it mean to live in such a world? What acts of translation must I perform? What would be gained? What would be lost?

Finally, if possible, there should be a "laboratory" component in an introductory course. The students should have to do something which fosters reflection on all of the above. It can be based on observation (for example, in the unit on purity/impurity I have my students describe an actual mean, determine the rules which governed it, and attempt to reduce them to a system. This is in no way the same as the ancient rules; but, it provokes thought). It can be based on a real research, for example, in my Bible and Western Civilization sequence, each student chooses a Bible printed before 1750 from our rare book collection and attempts to determine the significance of the format. The text is in each case the same; but the Bibles look very different. Why? It can be explicitly argumentative (for example, I have my students write a "tenth" opinion, employing some particular perspective, on some recent Supreme court decision involving religion after reading the transcript—e.g. What would Durkheim have ruled in the Rhode Island creche case?).

In sum, there in nothing distinctive to the issue of introducing religion. Its problems are indigenous to the genre of introductory courses. The issues are not inherently disciplinary. They are primarily pedagogical. This is as it should be. For our task, in the long run, is not to introduce or teach our field for its own sake, but to use our field in the service of the broader and more fundamental enterprise of liberal learning.

HOW I TEACH THE INTRODUCTORY COURSE

Robert N.Bellah

I thought this was going to be a very easy assignment—"How I Teach The Introductory Course"—and then when I thought about how in fact I teach my introductory course it became more problematic. The course is not an introduction to Religious Studies or Comparative Religion, but to the Sociology of Religion. Yet over the years I have turned it into a course that deals with what I see as the major theoretical and historical issues of the religion of humankind. Sociology of Religion indeed turns out to be one part of this course, but I think it really is an introductory course to Religious Studies. I must say that I come by this notion partly out of my own professional socialization, if I can speak sociologically. Talcott Parsons was my teacher and he believed that there was nothing that could not be included in what he called the general theory of action. For good or for ill, he included it all.

In teaching the introductory course in religious studies, which is for me the Sociology of Religion course, I try to weave several things together. I try to develop what might be called a general phenomenology of religious consciousness that is rooted in social scientific work and social psychology in particular. Simultaneously, I try to develop the scheme of religious evolution about which I have written some years ago. Then I try to build into the course detailed examples in which we deal with primary data and get a sense of the tangible concreteness of religion in a particular context. I always try to do two quite different examples to help the student see the contrast between some of the major world religions.

The last time I gave the course, the two examples I used were early Christianity and early Confucianism. I used Wayne Meek's book, *The First Urban Christians*, and selected readings from Mark, Acts, Matthew and several of the Pauline Letters that Meeks uses, particularly in his discussion of the nature and structure of the Pauline communities. For

Confucianism I used a D.C. Lau translation of *The Analects* and *Mencius* and Fingerette's *Confucius*. This was followed by a history of Christianity up to the American experience using such works as Max Weber's *Protestant Ethic* and William McLoughlin's *Revivals, Awakenings, and Reform*.

I find the students don't read very much and so I can't assign too many pages a week. I also find an incredible range of capacities to read and write. The best students I have at Berkeley are as good as the best students I ever had at Harvard. The worst students are illiterate—not in the sense that they can't identify individual words, but they cannot tell you what a sentence means, nor can they write an intelligible sentence. And that is a real challenge—one that, after nearly twenty years at Berkeley, I haven't ever really been able to cope with. Not too many years ago when I handed out my reading list, one of the students came up and said, "Do you mean we should read all these books?" I said, "Yes." And he said, "I'm not into reading." I suggested if he wasn't into reading, this wasn't the course for him. So, I struggle.

In reflecting on my organization of the course, I am reminded of a quote from Foucault:

> Truly to escape Hegel involves an exact appreciation of the price we have to pay to detach ourselves from him ...We have to determine the extent to which our anti-Hegelianism is possibly one of his tricks directed against us, at the end of which he stands, motionless, waiting for us.

I guess I have to accept the fact that I am hopelessly Hegelian. The religious evolution schema is of course fundamentally Hegelian, and the whole Parsonian project is in many ways Hegelian. The notion of development and the notion of moving from one stage to another through conflict and through overcoming certain antinomies is fairly basic to the way I think. Such a development might be seen in the movement from religious orthodoxy to enlightenment orthodoxy to symbolic realism. And now we're at a new stage: a reassertion of religious orthodoxy at a higher level.

A primary task of my course is to lure students into the notion that religion is to be taken seriously. For some of them that's no problem. But for many students religion is simply one of those things that the simple-minded believe. They feel the task is simply to understand why anybody would believe such strange things. The ethos of what I have called "enlightenment fundamentalism" is as prevalent at Berkeley as it was at Harvard, and it does not lend itself to serious attention to religion. The other "prejudice"—which as a student of Gadamer I understand is not necessarily a negative word—that the students bring to the class is the notion that the most important thing in the world is what has occurred most recently. In the Fall of 1984, for instance, we had to talk about the moral majority and the religious significance of the Dallas Convention that nominated Ronald Reagan; lately it has been other things. I have to pull them into seeing that Australian aborigines and ancient Egyptians are at least as interesting as Jerry Falwell, and that is not always so easy to do. Yet, I think that trying to develop a phenomenology of consciousness can be useful, since it ties into that aspect of middle class culture which we describe at length in *Habits of the Heart* as the powerful therapeutic orientation, and serves as a way of getting students to pay attention and perhaps become personally involved in the study of religion.

In this regard, I would disagree somewhat with what George Lindbeck says in his impressive *The Nature of Doctrine*. Lindbeck distinguishes quite sharply between an experiential-expressive theory of religion and a cultural-linguistic theory of religion, and includes almost everybody from Schleiermacher to the present, including Wilfred Cantwell Smith and myself, as espousing the experiential-expressive approach. This approach is, coincidentally, from Lindbeck's point of view, quite wrong, and instead he would have us adopting a cultural-linguistic theory. Lindbeck does have the courtesy to recognize that one can find, in the New Testament, warrant for the experiential-expressive: Paul's speech at the Areopagus, for instance, is a typical example of the experiential-expressive point of view.

Although Lindbeck's book is extraordinarily fruitful and what he calls the cultural-linguistic approach is critically important, I would reply to his critique of what he calls the experiential-expressive theory by observing that it is not just a theory: it is itself a modern tradition. It is rooted in modern experience and it has its own integrity which we have to deal with as seriously as we would any religious tradition.

In developing a phenomenology of consciousness, to study modern religion, we have to deal with the experiential-expressive forms of it and to do so I start with a good bit of psychology, including Abraham Maslow, which although verging on pop psychology is worth some attention. Part of Maslow's theoretical approach to human experience is his distinction between those experiences in which we are trying to make up for a lack, or a deficiency, and those where we are simply in a state of "being experience" or "being cognition", experiencing immediate fulfillment. The latter has a different phenomenological quality to it, and to the extent that we integrate that into our personality we become a different sort of person than one dominated by the deficiency kinds of motives.

I link these ideas up with Alfred Schutz's notions of multiple reality. Schutz, a student of Husserl, was deeply influenced by Max Weber and very much influenced by William James, and attempted to develop a notion of multiple worlds, or multiple realities, based on different modes of experiencing the world. Schutz takes as his methodological reference point the world of "working", the world of everyday, a realm of motives very close to what Maslow calls "deficiency cognition". But then he deals with a whole range of other kinds of experiencing reality such as art, dreaming, religion, and so forth, and develops a fairly rich phenomenology of experience.

The purpose in all this is to get students to see that the pragmatic world of everyday is not the only world. For instance, when they are attending a football game or watching it on TV they are in a different state of reality from the world of working. This seems to reinforce the Eliadean notions of sacred time and space which operate with different principles than that of everyday time and space.

The fundamental conceptual structure of phenomenology of consciousness that I try to develop comes from Jerome Bruner's *Studies in Cognitive Growth*. Bruner's "levels of consciousness" include the "enactive," "symbolic," and "conceptual," but I have prefaced these, on the basis of the phenomenology of religion, with "unitive consciousness" as well. The interesting thing here is that there is a correlation between these modes of consciousness and the process of maturation in the individual human being.

"Unitive consciousness," that of the child in the womb, should perhaps therefore be bracketed, for we don't have ways of interviewing such a child. "Enactive consciousness"—what Bruner, following Piaget, suggests is the way the child in the first months relates to the world—involves the use of the body in interaction with the world without any symbolic element at all. The child learns what a ball is or what a pencil is by feeling it and seeing what happens to it when it drops it. In other words, it has a bodily or embodied experience of objects, including significant human objects. "Symbolic consciousness" develops only gradually toward the end of the first year and into the second year with the rudimentary use of language and with a variety of modes of expression which have been studied in, for instance, the art of very young children. What we call art is to them a rather direct expression of their own volatile moods. It is only with the acquisition of the grammatical use of language by the age of four or five that "conceptual consciousness" begins to develop. Indeed, as we know from Piaget, there is a long process that probably isn't completed until adolescence, when the capacities for rational manipulation of the object world without the immediate involvement of the sense of self is achieved. A fully mature person operates with all levels. We never really lose any of them, and no one could possibly live at the level of conceptual consciousness alone.

There is a lovely example of this layering of consciousness in the writings of Descartes. He complains that for twenty years he was "impressed confusedly" by objects he was "unable to understand." Descartes goes on to write:

> Instead of having my brain a clean slate at twenty, I found innumerable false ideas engraved upon it. What a pity that man is unable to think clearly from the date of his birth.

In other words, Descartes grieves that he wasn't born at the age of twenty. Had he been, I think, he would be without art, religion, and a great deal that makes life worth living.

There are numerous examples of linkages between this phenomenology of individual development and cultural/religious development. Richardson recounts Jonathan Edwards reflecting on what I call "unitive consciousness":

> There came into my soul and was, as it were, diffused through it a sense of the glory of the divine being. A new sense quite different from anything I ever experienced before. I thought to myself how excellent a being that was and how happy I should be if I might enjoy that God and be rapt up to him in Heaven and be, as it were, swallowed up in Him forever.

Richardson goes on to say that Edward's feeling of union with "the all encompassing whole" was accompanied by two other feelings: the general rightness of all things; and well-being.

The feeling of union, then, is not identical with the sense of judgment and rightness, nor with the sense of personal salvation and well-being; though it is accompanied by those two feelings.

In thinking about enactive consciousness, there is a passage in Yeats that I like to have students read. Yeats, six days before his death, said, "I know for certain that my time will not be long. I am happy and I think full of an energy I had despaired of. It seemed to me that I had found what I wanted. When I try to pull it all into a phrase, I say, 'Man can embody truth but he cannot know it.' I must embody it in the completion of my life."

There's a certain sense in which one might take that statement as an extraordinary expression of the truth of the doctrine of incarnation. But fundamentalist students, among others, want to *know* truth, not embody it, and therefore they are threatened by a notion of truth that isn't out there: specifiable, logically clear, and able to be made a "truth claim."

In discussing ritual and sacrament, I explain how religious life does involve embodiment. At this point I tie into the religious evolution scheme and spend much time on Australian aboriginal ritual with the wonderful insights of W.E.H. Stanner. His structural analysis of the phases of the initiation ritual in northern Australia, and Dom Gregory Dix's analysis of the structure of the Eucharist, are, formally at least, the same.

I try to become graphic in my examples when we get into the symbolic level. There are marvelous examples from children in this regard. Children between the ages of one and two come out with things which are not really pictures at all. They are direct extensions of the body of the child. The pencil is part of the body, and its markings are the result of motion that is very natural at that age. Jackson Pollack is a very sophisticated version of this so-called action painting. And yet, even in the child's actions, we see something more than sheer chaos. There are circles that begin to have shape and form.

This brings to light a cross-cultural matter of boundedness. Children have an interest and sheer delight in boundaries, making a form that is definable. Unfortunately, adults come along and say, "What is that a picture of?" and of course it isn't a picture of anything because there isn't any distinction between the child's self and the world. The adult's issue of epistemology is not really relevant. The child is experimenting with the notion of form—as much the child's form as the world's form. Both these things are going on simultaneously. Before too long in the child's maturation we begin to get things that are recognizably relatable to the classic form of the mandala, the circle and the square that is crossed. And though I am certainly no Jungian, this leads naturally to a discussion of humans and their symbols. Without conceding anything to archetypes, one can see that the problem of form, of unity, of coherence, of order, simultaneously, in self and world is going on in a great deal of religious art and in the efforts of children to make sense of the world. There is much in common between the cathedral's rose window—the circle suffused with light—and the sunflower drawn by a child: the sun, the flower, and often in it, a smiling radiant face.

We crush the creativity of children by our relentless literalism in stressing representational accuracy. There is a point at which that marvelous, natural creativity is blotted out and we get scribbled houses, cows and stick people. The extraordinary richness of the creative expression is over because our particular society has idolized literal accuracy.

At this point in the course I talk about what is going on in poetry and narrative writing, and point out again that here the sharp distinctions between subject and object are irrelevant. In a story that works, we are all the characters. In the passion narrative, for instance, if one doesn't know that one is Judas, Pilate, and Peter as well as, in some sense, Jesus, then one doesn't know what's really going on. It is not the purpose of narrative to hold sharp distinctions in the way that scientific analysis or even the world of everyday work does, but to open us up to the extraordinary connections that tie us to all the characters in the story and reveal different aspects of ourselves.

Then I like to hit the students over the head with my favorite poet, the alleged atheist, Wallace Stevens. Some of them are enthralled; some of them say, "I don't understand poetry". A passage in one of Stevens' poems that isn't very well known speaks of the process of secularization:

> The heaven of Europe is empty, like a Schloss
> Abandoned because of taxes...It was enough:
> It made up for everything, it was all selves
> Become rude robes among white candle lights,
> Motions of air, robes moving in torrents of air,
> And through the torrents a jutting, jagged tower,
> A broken wall—and it ceased to exist, became
> A Schloss, an empty Schlossbibliothek, the books
> For sale in Vienna, and Zurich to people in Maine,
> Ontario, Canton. It was the way
> Things jutted up, the way the jagged stacks,
> The foul immovables, came through the clouds,
> Callosal blacks that leaped across the points
> Of Boucher pink, the sheens of Venetian gray.
> That's what did it. Everything did it at last...

And then Stevens' evocation of what it was like before: "There was a heaven once..."

In this context we also deal with aspects of archaic religion and the ancient Near East. We also deal with historic religion, its use of myth and the criticism of myth. I talk about myth in Plato and why Plato uses myth and yet also is an opponent of poetry. I also talk about why historic religion always is in an uneasy relationship to symbolic and enactive consciousness: because it insists on the tension between the new understanding of conceptual consciousness and older modes of expression, adopting the former without abandoning the latter.

In the middle of the course, we stop all this nonsense and start reading the *New Testament* or *Confucius* and *Mencius*. In Lindbeckian terms we shift from a theory which is experiential-expressive to a cultural-linguistic approach: attempting to see what the texts are telling us not only about thought, but about action, ritual, ethics, and how the world makes sense.

The final section of the course is a bit more conventional. I call on Ernst Troeltsch and look through the phases of the relationship between church and world, in the history of Christianity, especially the meaning of the Protestant Reformation, particularly for North America. This leads into a concluding week or so on the contemporary situation in the United States.

In a course of this nature, the effect on students is often quite extraordinary. Of course, there are those who simply are not able to see what's going on and are pretty mad at me by the end of the term; others regard this as the most important course they've had in college. It opens up connections that were never made in their education. It links what they've been learning about the world to what they are also, to some degree, learning about themselves. It's a revelation to them that any teacher would care to do that.

When I first started to teach this course I used to uniformly generate four of five cases of crises of faith in which students would come to me and say, "but what you say means that religion is not true," and I would sometimes try to shore them up and tell them maybe I didn't say what I meant to say. Recently, I'm more apt to get people coming up to me at the end asking "What church should I join?" I'm not prepared to help them with that problem either.

That religion should seem real is certainly one of the things that I'm trying to get across in an introductory course. It should seem serious, a central dimension of experience. I try to express what I deeply believe, that as a descriptive phenomenology of human culture, religion is the central integrating mechanism that links culture, personality, and society. Far from being the peripheral and irrelevant thing that the ethos of the University usually declares it to be, it is not in itself the most important thing—that would be idolatry—but it is about the most important thing.

The Introductory Course: A Balanced Approach

Ninian Smart

In brief, an introductory course should have four kinds of balance: dimensional balance; ancient-modern balance; East-West balance; and large-small balance. Of course I do not intend such prescriptions to be taken too woodenly, for if one thing is certain it is that we need to be selective in devising introductory courses. We may also want to mix in a treatment of various theories of religion—such as those of Durkheim, Freud and Levi-Strauss. It might be useful if theories could illustrate some of the diverse disciplines in religious studies. Thus Otto might illustrate something about phenomenology; Durkheim about anthropology; Weber about sociology; John Hick about philosophy (and indeed phenomenology); Marx about history; and so on.

The trouble about many of my suggestions about objectives and balance, however, is that we seem to be overloading the syllabus. How could it be at all possible to deal, even selectively, with all these topics in ten or fourteen weeks? Let me try to sketch a means which combines some of my suggestions. I cite it merely as an example. It follows a pattern I have sometimes used, either by myself or sharing teaching with a colleague.

The idea is to center an introductory course on various figures in the history of the traditions. These figures would be matched to dimensions. Some would be ancient and some modern, some East and some West, and some individuals and other types. We would thus select seven figures to match the dimensions, and given a teaching program of ten weeks devote seven weeks to them. The first two weeks could be devoted to laying the basis of the later work—explaining dimensions, the multidisciplinary approach, the uses of empathy and so on. The final week could be used for final reflections. Let us assume three sessions a week. One would deal with the figure; another with the general context which makes sense of her or him, and another with theoretical issues. An example of the kind of list I mean is as follows, with matching dimensions, approaches, backgrounds and figures of theory.

Figures	Dimensions	Approaches	Backgrounds	Figures of Theory
Jesus and the Last Supper	Ritual	Anthropology	Christian Origins	Turner and Douglas
Siva	Mythic	Psychology	Hindu myths	Freud and Jung
The Buddha and impermanence	Philosophical	Philosophy	Buddhist origins	Vivekananda, Hick and the unity of all religions
Gandhi and nationalism	Ethical	Ethics	Nationalism in the world and in India	Aquinas: just war theory
The Shaman	Experiential	Phenomenology	Shamans, prophets mystics	Otto, Eliade
U.S. Presidents	Social	Sociology	American civil religion	Bellah
Hildegard of Bingen	Artistic	Iconography	Religious	Gombrich

The last is a figure who will remind us of the need for adequate representation of the female in religious history: one should add Women's Studies to the sources of insight, which tends to crosscut the other disciplines (as do area studies such as African Studies, Asian Studies and so on).

One could mention other potent lists: let me just give two examples. These are arranged in the same order of dimensions as the list given above.

Confucius and the importance of li	Moshe and the Torah
Mao: a modern myth	Dying and rising gods
Augustine and original sin	Vivekananda and Advaita
Prophets and ethics	Martin Luther King and non-violence
Isaiah Shembe and a new religion	Ramakrishna and religious experience
Monks and otherworldliness	Gandhi and caste
Michelangelo and the Sistine Chapel	The Buddha in statues

In addition to the questions of course-construction there are of course issues of method in teaching. Since people are individuals, I leave matters of style to the personalities of those who have to perform. This, by the way, should remind us that lecturing is one of the performing arts. An individual therefore has to exploit the strengths of her or his personality and mannerisms. But there are some policy issues of some importance. One relates to the interface between professional life and personal life and personal commitments. It is unfortunate if a professor uses Religious Studies (or any other subject) as a kind of pulpit. But it is natural enough for students to guess as to your commitment, if any. It is natural first because of natural curiosity: it is all part of gossip. And it is natural too because often the student is exploring her own values and so may seek guidance from the instructor. It is also natural in order to estimate any slant in presentations. The second of these reasons for enquiry as to a professor's religion or ideology is a bit dangerous. We are not typically paid a salary to bring the young into a particular faith, but to make them informed and sensitive about matters of world views: to make them religiate in short. But the question, if asked, is not easily dodged. It is best simply to say. However, there is an important tip which I can give—a little technique which is a way of distinguishing between public presentation and private opinion.

It is this. If there is a table or overhead projector before me, I stand on one side (the right, usually) in giving out what I take to be the case from an academic point of view, including estimates of the probability or otherwise of some of the claims made. If I am asked something which calls for a private opinion, I stand to the left. I sometimes do this in the midst of lectures without having been stimulated to do so by a question. For instance, if I am discussing Gandhi and non-violence, I may interrupt to stand on the left to express my own view, which is a theory of the minimization of violence (not of the absence of violence). I would do so because of the interest and importance of having an opinion on such a topic. This method of using a visible sign of the importance of distinguishing between value-judgments and matters of opinion on the one hand, and more "objective" claims on the other, is rough and ready. In ethical, philosophical and so-called theological matters one is dealing more with the left-hand side: with history and descriptive studies more with the right. Naturally, the distinction between the two is not clear cut. But it is worth driving home the need for students to know what they are trying to do when they are engaged in such trying. It may get them to think about the relation between values and facts, even "deep facts", where we enter into others' experience.

It is perhaps important to introduce a fieldwork element into introductory courses. This is especially so for Cook's Tours and introductions to Asian religions and to Western religions. It is especially easy on the two coasts, and is not difficult in many places in between. This is because in many regions in the U.S.A. there are substantial numbers of Asian migrants, and such phenomena as Chinatown, Koreatown and Little Tokyo. Los Angeles and New York and many other cities have large Jewish concentrations; and these cities have substantial Moslem communities. There is thus no difficulty in such areas in finding synagogues, mosques, Buddhist temples, gurdwaras, Hindu temples and Chinese and other East Asian temples to visit. The rich variegation of California society has caused us in Santa Barbara to launch a program called "Religious Contours of California" in which high school teachers have been given help and encouragement in incorporating world religions material in their social studies, history, literature, economics and other classes, and using home-based Californian communities as a jumping-off point for understanding the wider world. A similar scheme has been launched in Illinois, and the pattern is suitable to many parts of North America.

Because Religious Studies is multidisciplinary there are many overlaps with other departmental offerings in the college or university. Therefore, in encouraging students to pursue Religious Studies further after they have completed an introductory course, it is worthwhile mentioning not only religion courses but other cognate offerings in history, art, literature, anthropology, philosophy and so on. Cooperation with other departments is, after all, highly desirable.

Sometimes the study of religion is merged administratively with another subject. The most common combination is philosophy and religious studies. It is worth reflecting therefore on whether some special introductory offering should be devised for such combinations. The first thing to note is oblique to the question, but important. It is that the philosophy of religion should be encouraged to learn something from the milticultural nature of the modern study of religion. Too often the philosophy of religion is confined essentially to the Western tradition and to the agenda set by Kant. It is vital to meld in ingredients from Eastern philosophy—particularly Indian and Buddhist philosophy, which often has powerful affinities to Western philosophy, as well as differences. The fact that the ultimate in Eastern religions is often delineated in a quite non-theistic way is important, and creates a new perspective on the traditional arguments for the existence of God.

While a merger with philosophy should not discourage the presentation of the modern study of religion in an integral manner, it should not denature the more descriptive and analytic elements of religious exploration. Nevertheless, there could be greater emphasis on the reflective issues than I have tended to allow in my previous examples. There could be greater time given, for instance, to comparative religious ethics and to comparative "theology". One might for instance select out two traditions—say Christianity and Buddhism—and after surveying some of their characteristic features devote four or five weeks to reflection on their doctrines, philosophical commitments and ethical insights. One might, for example, deal with differing interpretations of mysticism (or meditation) and their philosophical basis; and the reasons for the divergent analyses of the human condition (original sin versus original ignorance). More practically, one could examine Buddhist and Christian attitudes to the virtues.

In the foregoing I have outlined possible approaches to the introduction to Religious Studies in the undergraduate curriculum. I regard the main introductory courses as important. I follow the old Scottish custom in which the senior member of faculty characteristically teaches, among other things, the most basic course. I typically teach such a course at least once a year in the University of California. The way I have sketched possibilities here corresponds to my understanding of the general nature of the modern study of religion. But since that understanding tends to emphasize the descriptive and analytic side of the subject, rather than more value-laden areas of the inquiry, some may feel that insufficient attention is paid to "spiritual" and ethical values. I would like to say a word on this.

First, our job on the descriptive side is to hold up a mirror to traditions, including to religion on the ground. If a tradition has its beauties— and which one does not?—it may be that the student (we ourselves?) may fall in love with it, or even with a melange of traditions. We are middle-persons, in this way. It may be that our phenomenological approach better brings out beauties than any amount of hectoring or furrow-browed intellectual wrestling with proofs.

Second, we have to offer some important virtues, which arise out of our very mode of operating in the field. We stress imaginative empathy for others. We emphasize the plural character of the world, and the implication that toleration is a major outcome. Empathetic imagination and toleration are not negligible—they form the chief basis of interpersonal relations. At a deeper level we hold that we should take seriously what our fellow humans take seriously, and go a step towards loving what others love, because they love it. This is part of the basis of actual love of others. So even without discussing issues like abortion, non-violence, business ethics and so forth, we are already spreading some virtues, just by our very operation. We represent the deeper side of liberalism, which is the presupposition of the university's or college's mode of behaving. I in particular feel the vital importance of fairness and empathy in dealing with others folks' values. So the ethos of Religious Studies is something which I hope would also come across in an introduction to the field.

ANOTHER WORLD TO LIVE IN: TEACHING THE INTRODUCTORY COURSE PHILOSOPHICALLY

Huston Smith

Ninian Smart's preceding article on this topic presents, I am sure, an eminently viable way to teach the Introductory Course. At the same time it provides me with an ideal foil, for our two apologias, juxtaposed, highlight how differently the course can be approached. Ninian wants to apprise students of religion's power—it's truth is secondary. He wants his students to see that it is impossible to understand social movements and history generally if religion is left out of account. I naturally agree,[1] but my priority is the opposite—for me religion's truth is uppermost. The difference between us is in part personal, but it is also disciplinary. Ninian approaches religion from the angle of phenomenology and the social sciences, whereas I, a philosopher, find phenomenology confining. Ontology is too central to be bracketed.

Of the three questions Ninian proposed that we ask about the Introductory Course—What is our subject? What is our objective? Who are our students?—I find the second most important and I shall devote almost half of my statement to it. After indicating the goal I set for myself, I shall say how I try to reach it.[2]

I. My Objective

More clearly in retrospect than while I was regularly teaching the Introductory Course I see that my central object was to offer my students another world to live in. Offer it to them, not herd them into in, but I shall defer that point—for now the other world itself is at issue. T.S.

---

[1]The past tense would be more accurate, for I am formally retired. But as I continue to teach occasionally on call, I shall conform to the tense of this series.

[2]See my "Does Spirit Matter? The Worldwide Impact of Religion on Contemporary Politics," Introduction to Richard Rubenstein (ed.), *Spirit Matters* (New York: Paragon House, 1987).

Eliot's admission that good poets borrow while great poets steal encourages me to confess that I lifted the phrase "another world to live in" from Evelyn Underhill. Once before I used it in something I wrote, and I shall quote the passage because it points to the aspect of religion I most want my students to notice.

> The Lord appearing high and lifted up to Isaiah; the heavens opening to Christ at his baptism; the universe turning into a bouquet of flowers called Patmos, and I was in a trance." Saul struck blind on the Damascus road. For Augustine it was the voice of a child saying, "Take, read"; for Saint Francis a voice which seemed to come from the crucifix. It was while Saint Ignatius sat by a stream and watched the running water, and that curious old cobbler Jacob Boehme was looking at a pewter dish that there came to each that news of another world which it is always religion's business to convey.[3]

What is this "other world" that religion announces?—invariably announces, I would say, when it is alive. We can call it the Transcendent World if we keep in mind that it is also fully (though hiddenly) immanent, and I see nothing in education more important than making it available to students who want it.

They do not have a fair chance at that world today, for almost everything in their culture, their education emphatically included,[4] works to throw it into doubt. "If anything characterizes 'modernity,'" The Chronicle of Higher Education tells us, "it is a loss of faith in transcendence, in a reality that encompasses but surpasses our quotidian affairs."[5] Our students inherit that loss. I consider the loss to be serious, and also (ironically) unnecessary, for it results from a conceptual mistake. Because that mistake encroaches on my subject—religion—I take it as part of my responsibility to correct it, which is why I set reclamation-of-the-lost as my foremost course objective.

I mentioned in passing that a good part of this statement will be devoted to that objective, which means that I shall not get to course content until my last section. This may seem disproportionate, but I think the priority is justified. Peter Drucker says the most common mistake corpo-

---

[3]"The Incredible Assumption," in my Beyond the Post-Modern Mind, (Wheaton, IL: Theosophical Publishing House, 1982), p. 190.

[4]"While 94 percent of Americans believe in a supreme being only 73 percent of Harvard and Stanford alumni so believe. Whereas 63 percent of Americans generally hold that religion is a very important part of their lives, only 24 percent of the Harvard and Stanford alumni responded affirmatively" (Harold Lindsell, *The New Paganism*, [New York: Harper and Row, 1987], p. 137).

[5]January 9, 1978, p. 18.

rations make is to pour time and energy into devising brilliant answers to wrong questions, and his point applies here as well. If we select a second-rate objective for our course, its most brilliant execution will not redeem it from being less than it might have been. What justifies an objective is the precision with which it identifies the foremost need of our students in the area of our responsibility. It is because that is not a simple task that I give it major billing in what I have to say.

I said that our loss of the Transcendent World has resulted from a mistake, and the mistake it this: We assume that the modern world has discovered something that throws the transcendent world into question, but that is not the case. It is not that we have discovered something. Rather, we have lost sight of something. For reasons that are completely understandable but nonetheless regrettable, we have unwittingly allowed ourselves to be drawn into an enveloping epistemology that cannot handle transcendence.

In various ways perspective observers have been saying this for a century or so, but with something of the rush of discovery I recently hit on a way to strip the mistake to its bare bones, reducing it to virtually a syllogism as follows.

1. Science has become our sacral mode of knowing. As court of ultimate appeal for what is true, it occupies today almost exactly the place that Revelation enjoyed in the Middle Ages. An intellectual historian has pointed out that already a hundred years ago Westerners had come to have more confidence in the periodic table of chemical elements than in anything the Bible asserts.

2. The crux of science is the controlled experiment. I am speaking of course of modern science. Generic science (old as art and religion) relies on reasoning from careful observations, but what distinguishes modern science is its introduction of the controlled experiment and reliance on it as decisive. It is this addition that has caused modern science to take off from generic science and remake our material and conceptual worlds. It explains our confidence in science as well, for the controlled experiment delivers proof, winnowing hypotheses and retiring those that fail its test.

3. We can control only what is inferior to us. Intentionally control, that is, for chains can fetter my movement without being my superior. Also, this principle holds only between orders of existence, for within the same species variables can skew the picture: the Nazis controlled the Jews without being superior to them. By superior/inferior I mean by every criterion of worth we know and probably some we know not. Many things are superior to us in size (the moon) and brute power (an

earthquake), but neither are superior to us in all respects, including intelligence and freedom. Human beings controlled the American buffalo more than vice versa—it's that kind of correlation between intended power and orders of existence that this third point flags.

4. The conclusion follows inexorably. Science can disclose only what is inferior to us. Have we ever in any science course or textbook encountered anything that exceeds us in every positive attribute we possess? The question is rhetorical—the answer is no. What might beings that are superior to us be? Discarnates? Angels? God? The point is, if such beings exist, science will never disclose them for the sufficient reason that it is they who dance circles around us, not we they. Because they possess perimeters we are not even aware of, let alone able to control, it is impossible for us to reduce the variables that pertain to them to the point where experiments could produce on/off, clear-cut proofs.

Nothing in this "syllogism" proves that there is anything superior to us, but it does prove that if there is, science cannot bring it to light. It proves that conclusively, I would think, save to those whose enthusiasm for science leads them to associate that word with truth in its entirety rather than with truths that are discovered by a particular method. This confuses things no end. It also does science the disservice of rendering it amorphous and forcing it into the impossible position of trying to be all things to all people, eventually where it falls short of that goal now.

Absence of evidence is not evidence of absence—it might help students break through the metaphysical muddle of our time if we taught them to chant this as a modern mantrum. Because the science of acoustics has nothing to say about beauty, it doesn't follow that Brahms isn't beautiful. It is easy to see this in restricted domains, but expanding the point to worldviews is difficult; hence J.C. Smart's report that positivism is dead except in religion. So to drive home the expose of our modern mistake which I have been circling, I want to return to my syllogism and run through it again by way of an analogy.

If we liken the scientific method to a flashlight, when we point it downward, towards the path we are walking on, say, its beam is clear and bright. Suppose, though, we hear footsteps. Someone is approaching, and to see who it is we raise the beam to horizontal level. (This represents the social sciences and the light they cast on our species.) What happens? The light starts to flicker; a loose connection has developed. The social sciences can tell us some things about ourselves—the physiological substrates of experience and how people behave on average. The complete person as an individual, though, eludes its clutches. Replete with idiosyncrasies, freedom, and commitments, to say nothing of soul and spirit if such components exist, she/he slips through the meshes of science as sea slips through the nets of fishermen. To tie this directly to our syllogism's conclusion—that science can disclose only what is inferior to us—it is axiomatic in the social sciences that in investigating areas where freedom figures, subjects must be kept in the dark about experimental design. This places them in a tilt relation to scientists who know more about what is going on than they do. Finally (to complete the analogy), if we tilt our flashlight skyward—towards the heavens may we say in present context—its light gives out completely. Its batteries drop to the bottom of the casing leaving us completely in the dark. Once again this does not prove that the heavens are populated. It argues that it they are, science cannot apprise us of that fact, much less introduce their denizens.

And science is what now provides us with our sense of reality—we are back to where our syllogism took off. And back to why I want to offer my students an other-than-flashlight world to live in, to bring to full circle this section on course objective. Unaware of what has happened—blind to the way method has vectored metaphysics and epistemology constricted worldview—modernity with a stroke of its methodological pen has all but written off the region of reality that religion up to the last century or so has been riveted to. As E.F. Schumacher reflected toward the close of his life; most of the things that most of humanity has most believed in did not appear on the map of reality his Oxford education handed him as it launched him on life's adventure.

Are we to think that his is a minor thing that has happened—one which we and oncoming generations, powered by the gusto of new-burgeoning life, can take in stride? I think not. Take it perhaps we can, but I do not think our species can take it in stride. We were meant for better things: complete worlds, not the half-world of modernity. And since the shrinkage is unnecessary, resulting (as I have noted) from a mistake, who is to spring students from their metaphysical cage if not we? I do not see other departments of the university rushing forward, arms outstretched and waving, to volunteer, which is not surprising, given that the university is itself "rooted in the scientific method" as Steven Muller, President of the John Hopkins University, points out.[6] For the way that method cramps the social sciences one can consult Robert Bellah's essay in the National Institute of Campus Ministries Journal, Summer 1981; for

---

[6]*U.S. News and World Report*, November 10, 1980.

the way it has skewed philosophy in our century, we have Richard Rorty's address to the Eleventh Inter-American Congress of Philosophy;[7] and I have, myself, taken a run at its effects on the humanities at large in the essay "Excluded Knowledge," in my *Beyond the Post-Modern Mind*.

But enough of polemics. I am not saying that enlarging our students' ontology should be the only aim of religious studies. I am, though, arguing that that object should be one of our aims, and as I do not see it mentioned elsewhere in this series, let me say why the other course objectives I find presented need to be supplemented.

II. Alternative Objectives

We all know that Robert Bellah is not Ninian Smart, and that neither of them is Wilfred Cantwell Smith. Still, as sociologist, phenomenologist, and historian respectively, all three represent "the human sciences," as the social sciences are now frequently called. So with apologies for seeming to make clones of them, I shall lump them together as representing the social/phenomenological approach which holds that teaching should center on the features of religion that can be grasped objectively.

Having already endorsed this as a legitimate approach if it is supplemented, I shall let John Updike note what happens if the supplement is dropped. In his latest novel, Roger's Version, a young computer hack who is also a Jesus freak, corners a professor at the Harvard Divinity School to solicit his help in getting a grant to prove God's existence via the New Physics. In the course of his pitch he lets drop what he thinks of the Divinity School's approach to religion.

> What you call religion around here is what other people would call sociology. That's how you teach it, right? Everything from the Gospels to The Golden Bough, Martin Luther to Martin Luther King, it all happened, it's historical fact, it's anthropology, it's ancient texts, it's humanly interesting, right? But that's so safe. How can you go wrong? Not even the worst atheist in the world denies that people have been religious. They built temples, followed these taboos, created these traditions, et cetera. So what? Your average normal cheerful nonbeliever says it was all poetic, pathetic foolishness, like a lot of other aspects of human history. I looked over your catalogue before I came, and studying all that stuff doesn't say anything, doesn't commit you to anything, except some perfectly harmless, humane cultural history. What I'm coming to talk to you about is God as a fact, a fact about to burst upon us, right up out of Nature. (p. 19).

---

[7]Proceedings of the American Philosophical Association, Vol. 59 (July 1986).

Updike burlesques, of course, but his point about what happens when religion is relentlessly objectivized has a point.

The alternative to social science objectivity that gets billing in this institute is the Chicago school's hermeneutical approach. Frank Reynolds admits that religious studies has a normative agenda, but simply "one that it shares with all other interpretative enterprises that are fostered within the academy." Frank wants above all to make students aware of the different way religion can figure linguistically. He wants them to see the aims and strategies the various ways employ, together with their underlying motives and assumptions. Somewhere in this religious wordplay philosophico-theological claims enter the picture, but no more than Smart is Reynolds concerned to grapple with those claims, wrestling to assess their truth. His focus is on providing students "with critical strategies for unearthing motives and assumptions, laying them bare to criticism."

Here again I agree that teaching these critical strategies should be part of the agenda of religious studies, but only if it doesn't sidetrack (by deferring indefinitely) the issue of truth claims. For the dark truth here is that if the strategies Reynolds teaches were turned reflexively on the hermeneutic emphasis in religious studies itself—used to excavate its motives and assumptions—the exaggerated attention hermeneutics now enjoys would recede, restoring the endeavor to its normal, unbloted place. For there are no neutral methods. Every method stipulates what it will accept as evidence and stakes out a domain within which acceptable answers must fall (see again my "Excluded Knowledge" referred to above). Consequently, to privilege method—in this case hermeneutic strategies—over truth is to conceal rather than disclose what's going on. This is a heavy charge, but something fundamental, not just to religious studies but to the dynamics of our whole current intellectual scene, is a work here. It is too big to go into here, but something that Wilfred Smith, that most useful of living historians, picked up while he was at Harvard can be taken as its telltale trace. In the report on liberal education that was hammered out while Wilfred was there, the word "truth" doesn't even appear.

I am growing concerned about the way I keep putting off the content of my course, but one more preliminary must be touched on. There are teachers who grant that ontological objectives are logically appropriate for religious studies but are not sure that they belong in the academy.

III. Academic Propriety

We are a skittish lot, we teachers of religion. Newcomers to the academy, we see bugbears and bogeymen where colleagues in more established departments do not. Because we teach about people who can get so possessed by something—so en-theos-iastic, to use what is etymologically the exactly right word here—that they preach, and proselytize, and yes (as the shadow side of all this) go on at times to persecute, we fear that we may be tarred with those self-same traits. If the law doesn't come at us with "separation of church and state" clauses, an academic review board may, charging that we have hidden theological agendas and are not objective. So best to teach religion social scientifically, as sociology, psychology, anthropology, and history. Or phenomenologically, bracketing the truth-issues of theology and metaphysics. Distance ourselves from our subject. Think critically, but not religiously. Teach about religion, but not religion per se.

These distinctions have never seemed quite real to me, perhaps because I have somehow been exempt from the nervousness that attends them. For as long as I have been teaching, this whole matter of academic propriety has been for me one big non-issue. One can, of course, manufacture an issue by imagining egregious cases, but I have never encountered a case that was real. Not once have I felt, or sensed that my students or colleagues have felt, the slightest discomfort with my pedagogical style. (Content, vis a vis my colleagues, is another matter.) And the reason seemed clear. I don't want to strongarm anyone. It's the pedagogical instantiation of Augustine's "love God and do what you please." Because pedagogically my heart is pure, I can relax and teach spontaneously. A key component of this spontaneity is, of course, witnessing to the truth as I see it and giving it every assist I can manage, but that lies on a different continuum from strongarming and indoctrination. If as teachers we are debarred from witnessing to the truth that we see—and giving thereby an ounce of direction to our time, are we allowed to hope—what are we up to? As for review boards, I would love to have one come my way charging that I load the dice in favor of transcendence. It could give me a "bully pulpit" pointing out a thing or two to the university about the way its prevailing assumptions and procedures condition student's minds in the opposite direction.

Mention of pulpits, though, does lead me to make one retraction. I said that academic propriety has not been an issue for me, but I do wonder from time to time if I sound preachy or like a public scold. I think of something Charles Lamb once said to Charles Kingsley. Kinglsey asked Lamb if he would like to hear him preach sometime, to which Lamb responded, "I don't think I have ever heard you do anything else."

The tone in which I teach is not different from the tone of this present statement. Am I preaching?

IV. Course Content

I have spent more than half of my paper arguing the objective for my course because it seems to differ in kind from the others in this series. In outline and content, on the other hand, the course is only routinely distinctive.

I begin with the big picture, which again betrays my metaphysical bent. I find meaning descending from the whole to the part as much as it rises from part to whole—I like to know where I am in the world at large before I start poking around in my backyard. So I begin my Introductory Course with a gimmick which I call "Slicing the Religious Pie." A pie serves well, not only because it (like the world) is round, but also because we slice pies in the way we draw distinctions in thought.

I begin with the pie uncut. This represents (to invoke the title of a bygone book) "our believing world"—human history in its entirety as it testifies to woman/man as homo religious. What are we to say of religion as this generic component of human nature? In short, how should religion be defined? There is no single way, of course, so I propose a working definition for the course. Religion is the human outreach for— its tropism towards—the one, the more, and the mystery.

The one. The dream of unity, of wholeness, of integrity and integration draws us irresistibly. Split personalities are tragic, and we all need to get our acts together. Moreover, this drive for unity reaches beyond ourselves. We seek at-one-ment with the ground of our existence, or whatever we label the final context in which we live and move and have our being.

The more. We are transitional creatures. We live always on the verge—on the threshold of something that exceeds all that we have thus far laid hold of or experienced. In Nietzsche's aphorism, man is a bridge, not a destination.

The mystery. Detective stories have debased this luminous word. In its traditional, numinous sense, a mystery differs from both a puzzle and a problem. A puzzle has a trick to it. With a problem there's no trick, but it does have a solution. A mystery is that distinctive kind of problem where the more we understand, the more acutely we perceive how much we do not understand. The larger the island of knowledge, the longer the shoreline of wonder.

Wherever religion surfaces authentically, we find it powered by these three lures. That's the pie uncut. (Unauthentic religion is religion pressed into the service of worldly ends—the desires of the unregenerate ego. Folk religion contains a lot of it, and of course to some extent it creeps in everywhere. I come down hard on this distinction between authentic and inauthentic religion, but then I pretty much drop the point, mine not being a course on religious pathology or even anthropology.)

As, now, we ready ourselves to cut the pie, where should we begin? This is a way of asking, What is the most important initial distinction to draw in cutting our pie in half, so I draw a horizontal line through my blackboard circle and write above the line "historical" and below it "tribal." Historical religions have sacred tests and a cumulative tradition; they are also more differentiated in the sense that Robert Bellah effectively elucidates in his essay "Religious Evolution."[8] By contrast, tribal religions are typically oral. Eliade called them archaic, and "primitive" is another acceptable designation if the word is not used pejoratively; civilization and writing bring gains, but losses as well. I use the Native Americans as my opportunity to speak well of tribal religion before leaving it to attend for the rest of the course to the historical ones.

Dividing those religions into their Eastern and Western families produces the second cut in the pie. The Western families include Judaism, Christianity, and Islam, and the Eastern one Hinduism, Buddhism, Confucianism and Taoism. (I point out that this overview uses broad strokes and omits smaller religions such as Jainism and Shinto.) Naming the religions on each side of the divide produces ostensive definitions, but that is only my starting point; I go on to suggest theoretical points on which Eastern and Western religions differ. The differences are in emphasis only; each feature that one family highlights turns up in the other family as well, but subdued. On the subject of God, the Western religions stress his personal nature while the Eastern one pay more due (than has the West) to his/her/its transpersonal reaches. Regarding the soul, Western religions emphasize the individual soul while Eastern religions introduce the universal soul (Atman, anatta, Buddha-nature, and the like). In faith, the West emphasizes what Tillich called prophetic faith (the holiness of the ought) while the East highlights ontological faith (the holiness of the is).

---

[8]Chapter 2 in his *Beyond Belief* (New York: Harper and Row, 1970).

This is rich terrain. The distinction between the personal and transpersonal regions of the divine comes as a revelation to most students. It suggests something that had never before occurred to them; namely, that if the personal God that has been pressed on them seems unbelievable and uninspiringly anthropomorphic, this need not be the end of the religious road. Beyond that personal God, even in the West, stands Eckhart's Godhead and Tillich's "God above God," muted counterparts of nirvana, nirguna Brahman, and the Tao that cannot be spoken. The entire apophatic, mystical, negative theology lies in wait. The notion of a universal soul—what the New England Transcendentalists called the Oversoul—is equally liberating to many. Emerging as they are from adolescence, college students have begun to sense the limitations of "the skin-encapsulated ego," as Alan Watts called it, and are ready for an alternative. As for the two kinds of faith, with the near collapse of modernity's hopes for historical progress, students are ready to think seriously about alternatives or complements.

A semester allows time for one more cut. From a distance the East can look like one homogenous mass, but as we draw closer to it—come to understand it better—we find it dividing into South Asian (India for short, but including Sri Lanka, Tibet, and aspects of Southeast Asia); and East Asia (China for short, but including Japan, Korea, and again aspects of Tibet and Southeast Asia). India and China are as different from each other as either is from the West. Nothing in China is as "Indian" as our Middle Ages, while the Chinese have a practicality and down-to-earthness that modern Westerners resonate to more readily than do Indians.

Having geographically separated the East Asian, South Asian, and Western families of religions, I again plunge for substantive issues—issues that have importance for student's lives—by proposing that the groupings present interesting and important philosophical differences. To be human is to interface on three fronts: with nature, with other people, and with ourselves. These confrontations present us with natural, social, and psychological problems. In their great formative periods, the three families of religions have deployed their energies differently on these problems. Specifically, the West has attended more to nature than have the other two traditions. China, for her part, specialized in the social problem, while India concentrated on psychology."[9] Each made dis-

---

[9]See my "Accents of the World's Philosophies," *Philosophy East and West* VII, 1 & 2 (1957); and its companion piece, "The Accents of the World's Religions," in John Bowman (ed.), Comparative Religion (Leiden Brill, 1972).

coveries in its area of specialization that continue to be important, while by the same token each can usefully learn from the other two if it has the wit and will to do so.

Having opened my course with the embracing framework of my religious pie, I devote its remainder to filling it with content. Throughout, my intent is to carry students as far as possible into the existential outlook of the religious subjects whose tradition is on deck. To sign off with the point with which I opened this statement, my indirect intent (but foremost hope) in all this is to use these empathetic, quasi-shamanic journeys into the faith—worlds of living peoples to enlarge my student's sense of reality—the ontological options they perceive as available to them. (Flannery O'Connor described this indirect method well when she wrote in one of her plain-spoken letters: "You can't clobber any reader while he is looking. You divert his attention, then you clobber him, and he never knows what hit him.") I invoke a bit of history to get a tradition on stage, and I gesture towards its rituals and art. Its embracing view of the self and its world, though, is always stage center. This reflects my personal interests as well as the fact that my course have always been listed or cross-listed in philosophy.[10]

---

[10]A version of this address, credited to the NEH Institute to which it was delivered, was prepublished in *Religious Studies and Theology*, 7:1 (January 1987).

RELIGION AS LANGUAGE

Karen McCarthy Brown

I was trained in the social sciences and this has shaped my approach to the religion courses I have taught. Without wishing to make the social scientific approach normative, I offer here a description of one such model which has proven valuable to me in introducing students to the cross-cultural study of religions. It views religion from a social perspective, but I believe it is useful in designing syllabi for introductory courses in the religions of the world.

The principal gains from focusing on the social character of religions are two. First, such an approach may justifiably set aside questions of ultimate truth, meaning and value without denying the ground or legitimacy of those questions for adherents of particular religious traditions and, perhaps more importantly, for students and teachers who seek to study them. Such bracketing may be, quite simply, the most realistic approach at the introductory level given the difficulty of the subject matter. Second, by focusing on the social embodiment of a religion, we scholars have a built-in check against the temptation of reducing a religion to that which the academy recognizes most readily and handles most easily: words, concepts and texts.

This social emphasis may bother those who think of the purest form of the religious as intense and private experience. Yet it is good to remember that the Buddha did not encounter Yahweh under the Bodhi tree nor did Jesus come back from 40 days in the desert with intimate knowledge of the Tao. So it appears that even the most private religious moments also have a socially or culturally specific character. By contrast, this broad interpretation of the social to include the inner world of vision and imagination may confuse and irritate those who think a proper social analysis should confine itself to the study of religious institutions and to the questions of authority, structure and change that are appropriate to such a study. To the latter group I can offer no easy comfort for it is undoubtedly true that the task of teaching about religions from a social perspective becomes infinitely more complicated if we declare in advance that the subject matter includes the full range from the personal to the institutional. Yet it seems to me that the potential gains make the extra effort well worthwhile. Perhaps the major reason why it is so very difficult to design any good introductory religion course in precisely this: in one way or another religion deals with the whole of life and not some neat and separable portion of it.

I have often used a communications model in my cross-cultural religion courses. Although I recognize that the test of such a model is not one of truth but only of relative usefulness, it is nevertheless difficult to discuss the issues involved in introductory religion courses without first forming an image of what religions are. The basic analogy (and I do not claim that it is more than that) is one between a religious system and a language. Through this particular analogy the study of the world's religions gains several things.

The first gain lies in increased awareness of the culture specificity of religious systems. Religions like languages arise out of the collective experiences of particular peoples. Like languages, they create worlds, which do not determine what we think and feel and do, so much as describe the range of what is thinkable, feelable and doable.

The second gain lies in enhanced appreciation of the difficulty of translation from one religion to another. Understanding anything that is other than us requires that, at some point in the process, we draw connections between us and them, knowledge of the obvious difficulties of translating precisely from one language to another and awareness of the intimate connection between a people's language and the physical and social conditions of their lives, provide a helpful brake on comparing one religion with another too quickly or in too facile a manner.

Preparation for the innate untidiness of the subject matter is the third gain. There is no ideal form of language: there are only the forms that are spoken now or were spoken in the past. For example, Castilian Spanish is not the only Spanish that is spoken. Although some would claim it to be the standard for the language, we have reason to question whether this is not a linguistic form of class elitism, a filter we have to be on the alert for in any description of "true" Sufism or "real" Sioux religion. Languages that arise between other major language systems—pidgins and creoles— also have analogies in the religious sphere and further complicate our efforts at locating and describing discrete religions. Here we have to watch that it is not only these in between traditions that are labeled syncretistic, as if the other traditions were pure and *sui generis*. All religions, like all languages, have family trees that connect systems which may appear quite separate from the contemporary viewpoint. Furthermore, all religions like all languages routinely borrow from others in contact situations.

The fourth gain of the communications model is that it eases us away from the expectation that religions will be internally consistent. If an analogy is drawn between a language and a religion, the former refers to a language system and not to an individual instance of speaking or writing in that language. It would not occur to us to ask if the English language, in and of itself, is consistent. The same attitude is a healthy one to cultivate toward religious traditions. To borrow a phrase Edmund Leach used in relation to myths, religions are "good to think with"[1], and I would add, it is possible to "think" all sorts of things within the same religious system. Without this caution students of a religious tradition may be fooled by its claims to consistency and immutability and thus fail to appreciate the way in which religions like languages are historical accretions, subject to change in form and content.

Finally, the communications model increases our ability to pay attention to the nonverbal dimensions of religious expression. Strange as it may seem to cite this as a benefit of an analogy between religion and language, I have found it to be one. We often do not know what to do with the dances, ritual gestures, sacred foods, and plastic arts that are part of religions. Frequently we succumb to the temptation to reduce them to illustrations of creed or text, thereby limiting our access to the forms of religious expression which are central for many people. The language analogy enables us to look at these non-verbal dimensions of religion as communication systems in which it is understood that the individual units (the smell of frankincense, the roll of a hip, the taste of ghee, the letting of blood), like the individual units of sound in a language, are not meaningful in themselves but only in systems of relations. Once we begin to explore these non-verbal elements in a variety of systemic relations new meanings open up. For example, one could explore the composition and mode of production of ghee, its valence as an animal product in Hindu culture, its place in the economy and diet of India and so forth. Such an exploration of the semantics of ghee would make its use as a ritual offering more meaningful.

---

[1] Edmund Leach, *Claude Levi-Strauss*, (New York: The Viking Press, 1970), p. 31.

I have found the language analogy a helpful device in teaching about religion cross-culturally. It seems to foster open-mindedness and to help in making the study of the religions of the world a challenge both to empathy and intellect. However, I have not found it helpful at the introductory level to bore and confuse students with the technical discussion of linguistics that underlies this model. The rich subject matter of world religions already crowds the syllabus. Therefore, unless a course is specifically focused on questions of methodology, it may be useful to let carefully chosen images carry the methodological weight and provide the focus and consistency that is necessary for a successful course. Consequently I will often open a course with a series of images of religion that capture the more important aspects of the communications model without belaboring its intellectual ancestry. The comments below are similar to those that I might make in the first lecture in an introduction to world religions.

Introducing the Model of Religion

Whatever else religion is, it is a very special sort of communication that a people make about themselves, one whose symbolic language can be at one and the same time vast enough to encompass the Whole and particular enough to give meaning and direction to a moment in individual and/or collective human life. Indeed the genius of religion often appears to lie precisely in this ability to make connections between the Whole and the moment. A Mexican peasant woman lighting a candle in front of an image of Mater Salvatoris may be simultaneously addressing a problem with her ne'er-do-well son, giving meaning to the endless drudgery of her life, placing herself in line with her ancestors who not so far back addressed a related Zapotecan goddess and putting herself in touch with her Lord and Savior Jesus Christ through the mediation of his Holy Mother, Mary. In the same way a group of Muslim or Jewish men may, through reference to the promise to Abraham, reinforce the solidarity of the group by giving meaning to the sacrifices required of individual members, solidify their political position with the populace, place themselves in line with a venerable tradition of holy men and surrender their will to Allah, or their lives to Yahweh's purpose. In neither of these examples should we assume that one level of expression or meaning is reducible to another or that one is a cover for what is "really" going on.

What enables religious language—I obviously intend more by that term than words alone—to speak at once of the cosmic and the particular is its peculiarly condensed character. Religious utterances are like water flowers, those like paper pellets from Chinese markets that, when dropped into water unfold into complex many-layered bouquets.

As Clifford Geerts and others have pointed out, we human beings come into the world more vulnerable and less well-equipped for life than any other species. We have very little genetically programmed, instinctive behavior to guide us. Fairy tales, maxims and proverbs—and more to the point, religious stories, prayers, acts and images—help to fill this gap.[2] They pass on the wisdom of those who have gone before us in a condensed form that is easily retained and yet is rich enough to function in a myriad of circumstances and address us on as many different levels. As children we are fed highly condensed religious images that expand within us to give us a rich inner world more or less consonant with the outer world, that is with the world of "our people". Developing such a model of the Whole, like learning a particular language, not only gives shape and meaning to the inner drama but also makes connection with the group possible. It is this which alleviates the terror of isolation, frees the individual from the herculean task of constructing his or her own world, and finally enables us to say "we".

So it seems appropriate to think of religions as models of the Whole of the sort described above and held more or less in common by any social group that would speak of itself as "we." This of course does not make them neat phenomena for the "we" shifts and changes according to circumstances.

Sharing a common history is one of the things that makes people likely to say "we," yet this is not a sufficient guarantee. The Jews, the Christians and the Muslims interpret some of the same history in quite different ways. Geographic proximity is another prod toward the "we", but the Jews say "we" of a group that is spread across several continents. Furthermore scholars debate whether there really is a unified religion known as Hinduism on the Indian subcontinent or whether this is a wishful projection of scholarly order on something more diverse than unified. To give yet another example of the difficulty of identifying discrete religions: In 18th-century Africa, there was very little if any occasion for the Yoruba peoples of what we now call Nigeria and the kongo peoples of Angola and Bas Zaire to say "we". Yet, because of a shared (and traumatic) historical experience and because of their resulting

---

[2]See for example, Clifford Geertz, "The Growth of Culture and the Evolution of Mind," in *The Interpretation of Culture: Selected Essays by Clifford Geertz*, (NewYork: Basic Books, 1973).

proximity on the slave plantations of Haiti, their descendants now say "we" within a religious tradition that combines significant elements from both regions. These same people, whose religion has been dubbed "Voodoo" by outsiders, think of themselves as Catholics (a heritage of the French Catholics who ran the great sugar plantations), who not inconsistently also "serve the spirits", spirits who can equally well be invoked by Africa names or the names of Catholic saints. What complicates this picture further is that a significant percentage of the world's Roman Catholics would probably deny these several million Haitians the right to call themselves Catholic. So one group may be willing to include another in its "we" but the feeling is not always mutual.

Thus, teaching about the religions of the world does not lend itself to neat lists on the blackboard or precise color-coded maps. It is always a question of perspective. Looking at religion globally is a little like trying to describe a complexly figured tapestry in which one figure's foreground is the background of another, and one scene casually borrows the curve of an eyelash in someone else's picture to serve as the horizon line in its own composition. Such a tapestry could never be seen all at once. In a real sense, it would exist only in the constantly shifting focus of the viewer. I imagine it would be something like weaving that tapestry if we scholars were ever to construct a full picture of the religious life of humankind. But of course we cannot and the greater wisdom tells us that we should not even try.

There may be many good reasons in this troubled and dangerous would of ours to try to find a way for people around the globe to say "we" at a more inclusive level. Furthermore, there is a convincing argument to be made that the cross-cultural study of religion has a genuine, if limited, contribution to make toward the saying of this larger "we." Yet it seems important to suggest that such an admirable goal, when adopted as the reason for beginning the study of another religion, may end up undermining more than supporting that goal. Premature resolution of differences between world views somehow always ends up being a resolution on our terms. I have found it more productive to tempt students to try to solve the puzzle of understanding another on the other's terms, to 'play' with the possibility of putting the world together in a way quite different from the one to which we are accustomed and, occasionally to feel the fresh air that blows through the cracks between the worlds.

A BRIEF ARGUMENT OF AN ENDANGERED SPECIES: THE WORLD RELIGION SURVEY COURSE

Mark Juergensmeyer

The one course that we have all learned to hate is the World Religions Survey. Its seemingly endless parade of introductions to now this religion, now that one, has become a caricature of the worst of liberal arts education: a superficial overview that routinely and mindlessly imposes a Western model of human culture on the rest of the world. If that were not bad enough, the course is humiliating to teach. No one knows everything, or even enough of everything to presume to be an expert on Shi'ite, Yoruba and Jodo Shinshu beliefs simultaneously. Worse, the teacher knows that the student knows that, so classroom performances become exercises in public humiliation. No wonder that this course is often dumped on the youngest members of the faculty (who, by virtue of their recent status as graduate students, are presumably accustomed to humiliation already) and no wonder also that the course is often simply dropped. "We have no one who can teach it," the exasperated department chair will say, as if there actually were a category of teachers who were trained in "World Religions" and somehow the department was not able to afford one.

Even if teachers do not like to teach them, students and administrators expect that such a course be taught, and the course in World Religion survives, mostly by popular demand. It is quite possibly the one course in Religious Studies that easily comes to the mind of an outsider to the field, and it is quite possibly the only course that many non-Religious Studies students—especially those in the sciences and technical fields—find sufficiently interesting and understandable to take.

I would like to endorse the interests of these students and affirm that colleges should indeed have such courses, and that teachers—especially senior faculty—should indeed be encouraged to teach them. I would go so for as to claim that if a department or program in Religious Studies has no other course in its curriculum, it should have this one. In saying this, I should point out that I have nothing against the kinds of courses that introduce religion thematically or phenomenologically—I have taught such courses myself, and find them rewarding. Nor do I think that the World Religion courses are necessarily the best introduction for the student who is going to make Religious Studies his or her field. The issues about the field that such a course presents, and the general knowledge that it provides, will likely be found elsewhere in the Religious Studies curriculum. My concern is rather with the general student, and with the service that the World Religion course provides for the whole of the liberal arts curriculum. I feel that it is so important for the broader purposes of the liberal arts that a college or university should arrange to have someone teach this course even if it offers no other Religious Studies courses at all.

My reasons for supporting such a course are not, however, utilitarian. I do not think that we should offer courses only if they are popular, or only if their sole reason for being is that they pander to a certain low level of intellectual curiosity. Departments of Astronomy should not be asked to teach the history of astrological signs, nor should teachers of Religious Studies be asked to teach something intellectually disrespectable just because others find the subject matter interesting. Rather, my reasons for endorsing the World Religion survey is because I find it to be immensely rewarding intellectually, and at the heart of what Religious Studies as a field is about. It need not be taught in the parade fashion, and it need not be predictable.

What excites me about the course is that it is one of the few opportunities in the liberal arts curriculum to discuss the whole shape of world culture: how it developed, and where our present experience stands in relation to the whole. To my mind, such a course is ultimately about the present social and spiritual condition of modern urban Westerners, even if it appears as if most of the course—or even all of it—is about the way other people, at other times and places, have viewed the world. By understanding the world views of others, we are nudged towards an understanding of our own.

If one takes seriously the notion that the World Religion course should be as essay on the history of world culture and our location in it, then several guidelines for structuring the course follow:

- it should move in a roughly chronological order through historical periods;

• it should be attentive to cultural outlooks characteristic of large geographical regions at particular times (such as Mediterranean or ancient Chinese culture);

• it should stress changes in traditions and interactions among them as well as their continuities;

• it should present the various religious expressions of a people's world view, and not just their doctrinal positions. Or to put it another way, when doctrinal positions are discussed, they should be put into the wider social and intellectual context of the historical period in which they appear.

It also follows that such a course must be done all in one sitting, so to speak. The course should contain everything—no religious culture of any size should be left out—and the course should not be divided into two as it sometimes is done. Such division works against the main point: that the world history of religion is a single, interactive event. And when the course is split into "Religions of the East" and "Religions of the West" the division suggests that the two are not related, which is erroneous, and that religious traditions are primarily distinguished by geography, a point that is also false. The largest Islamic countries are in South and Southeast Asia, for instance, and the Philippines is as interesting an example of Christian culture as is England or the United States.

In saying that the course should contain everything I mean a selective everything, of course. Although its scope should be historically and geographically inclusive, the images and facts that are selected to portray this diversity should be limited. I like to focus on a few examples— reading selections from the Gilgamesh epic, for instance, to convey the world view of ancient Mesopotamian culture.

My course begins with a discussion of the common sense notions of religion and religious traditions, and I explain why the course will not present the "religions" in as familiar a form as the student might expect. The readings for the course are introduced: these are selected readings, mostly from original sources, that appear in a xeroxed Reader, and one or two books to cover a subtheme that will run throughout the course. I usually choose a different subtheme each time—such as gender roles, saints, or the concept of tradition—to portray how particular religious cultures differ from one another in dealing with such matters. These subthemes serve as a counterpoint to the major theme of the course, the singular history of world religion.

In the next lecture I begin the story of religion at the beginning, or as close to the beginning as we can find it. We look at the attempts of various scholars, from Frazer to Freud, to think about the origins of religion, and then look at the earliest evidence of human culture: cave drawings and burial objects. We even look beyond our species, and ask whether in the ritual behavior described by animal ethology there are forms of what might be called a proto-religion.

Religious culture as we know it, however, begins with the great river civilizations located near the Nile, the Tigris and Euphrates, the Indus and the Yangtze. We focus on two of these—the ancient Egyptian and ancient Mesopotamian—and explore how the characteristics of settled, riverbank societies are expressed through mythic and ritual formulations. In comparing the mythology of the Gilgamesh and Enuma Elish epics with later variants of the same myths portrayed in Genesis, we see in the next lecture how the religious consciousness of ancient Israel develops out of this Middle Eastern terrain and differs from it. The biblical history of ancient Israel is briefly charted, with emphasis on the differences between its tribal beginnings, its united kingship, and its continued existence in diaspora. The rise of prophets and the rise of messianic and revolutionary cults at the end of the biblical period set the stage for the emergence of what I call at this point the Jesus cult. The question of who Jesus was consumes a lecture in itself, a conversation that has been stimulated in recent years by the controversy over the film "The Last Temptation of Christ." The question of Jesus is discussed not only as a problem for present-day scholars, however, but for members of the early Church, as they tried to understand the implications of his role for themselves and for the nature of their community.

The scene in the next lecture shifts slightly (or rather, we let the travels of Paul do the shifting for us), and we find ourselves in the ancient Mediterranean world. This gives us the opportunity of seeing how elements of Egyptian and Persian religion (especially Zoroastrianism) exerted an influence on that world, and of seeing how early Christianity up to the time of Constantine was one of several religious cults and strands that met the needs of a cosmopolitan urban civilization. A separate lecture, often held in a synagogue near campus, discusses the rise of Rabbinic Judaism during this same period. The following lecture returns to the expansion of Christianity post-Constantine, and in shifting the geographical scene to Europe, we are able to discuss European tribal religion and how tribal religions in general are able to influence the universal religious ideologies such as Christianity that supposedly replace them. European Christianity displays the pattern of cultural syncretism that is found in Christianity in other parts of the world, including the ancient varieties that developed in India and Africa. These forms of Christianity are briefly mentioned, but the main emphasis of this lecture and the next is on the magisterial theology, architecture and organization of medieval Christianity. One of the lectures takes place in a Roman Catholic monastery near campus, and a demonstration of the progression of Church music from chants to hymnody indicates the changing character of Christendom during this period.

Another shift in scene returns us to the Middle East, where we see, in the context of tribal Arabian religion and pockets of diaspora Judaism and Nestorian Christianity, the emergence of Islam. The revelation of the Qur'an to Muhammad is of course the focal event, and in the next lecture the description of Islamic civilization as it became elaborated in the great empires brings us back to a consideration of the grand religious civilizations of the medieval period. The lecture on European religious mysticism is able to draw on Christian, Jewish and Islamic formulations of mystical experience during this period, and to show, to some extent, their similarities and awareness of one another. A demonstration of sufi practices and readings from the Zohar help to make the differences and similarities clearer. The end of this segment of the course points east, for Islamic mysticism (and the great Islamic Empires) had a significant Asian context as well as a Middle Eastern and European one.

In turning east, however, the course turns back in time, all the way back to the river cultures discussed at the beginning of the semester: this time the river is the Indus, however, rather than the Nile or the Tigris. Much of what we know of Indus valley civilization is similar to the other great river cultures of the day, but some of it is distinctive to the South Asian context, and when these elements are fused with the religion of the tribal Aryans from the West, in the middle of the second millenium B.C.E., the resulting Vedic religion inaugurates what we know as Hindu culture in South Asia. Aryan culture in the West evolves into Zoroastrianism; in India it develops speculative teachings that reflect on the nature of the self and these are the subject of the next lecture, which views the teachings of the Upanishads, the Buddha and early Jainism as three variations on a similar theme. The lectures immediately following trace the growth of the Hindu strand as the great epics of the Mahabharata and Ramayana portray a personal God, a God that the later bhakti strand of Hindu faith understands as loving, and in some forms, as love itself. The form of bhakti preached by Guru Nanak, the first teacher in the Sikh tradition, places love above God, at least any form of God that can be envisioned by human imagination. These lectures are enhanced by presentations of stories from the epics and by a visit to a Hindu temple or a Sikh gurudwara.

The development of a devotional Buddhism parallels this development in Hindu culture, although in the case of Buddhism it is coupled with the transmission of the faith to other parts of Asia. The expansion of Buddhism through the endeavors of missionaries and by merchants travelling over the silk route to China gives us the opportunity to compare the similarities and differences between Buddhism and the other two religious traditions that have an expansive, multi-cultural character: Christianity and Islam. The Chinese setting is the major area of Buddhist expansion, and to understand it we have to spend some time considering the early Chinese religious context and its Taoist and Confucian sensibilities. The insertion of Buddhism into this context changes both the context and Buddhism, and new forms of faith evolve. It is a pattern that is replicated in Korea and Japan, as subsequent lectures discuss. The lecture on Japan leads naturally to a consideration of the contemporary explosion of new religious movements in that country, and this in turn leads to the broader topic of the role of religion in modern urban cultures. Modern forms of Hinduism and Islam in Asia are also explored.

Perhaps it may not seem proper to begin this final section of the course—the discussion of religion and modernity—with Asia, but it illustrates that this is not exclusively a Western topic, nor one peculiar to Christianity and Judaism. We do turn to those traditions, however, in looking at the forms that modern religion has taken in Europe, beginning with the Enlightenment and the Protestant Reformation. We trace these developments through European denominationalism to early American religion, and note the competition between communalism of the Puritans and the individualism of the Deists that continues to some extent in American culture today. The American setting also allows for a discussion of cultural domination, syncretism and annihilation; using Native American religion, Polynesian religion and African slave religion as examples. The lecture on the latter takes place, ideally, in a Black church. The final lecture is on the role of religion in modern secular society, with the campus as a case study. Here many of the great cultures of the past are represented, although often in a trivialized way—as a personalized, supermarket form of religiosity—while ideologies of nationalism and Marxism contend with secular humanism as champions of the modern world view for large masses of Western society. The rejection of these ideologies and the assertion of a more traditional and religious form of nationalism has led to a great deal of political tension in areas such as the Middle East, Iran and Sri Lanka, and to a revival of religion of a fundamentalist sort in the West—even on campuses such as Berkeley. The story of religion in the world and throughout the world's history has come home.

❧IV❧
The Classroom Experience

THE CLASSROOM SCENE: TEACHING, MATERIAL CULTURE AND RELIGION

Richard M. Carp

Teaching displays the phenomenological structures and requires the practical skills that define the medium of performance, taking place in the extended face-to-face relationship between a performer (the teacher) and an audience (the students).[1] Above all, teaching/learning is an event, or better a sequence of events, shaped primarily by the performer and powerfully but secondarily by the audience.[2] A course is a dynamic pattern with a beginning, a middle and an end: each session is an event (a "class"), and the whole sequence of sessions is an event (a "course"). Despite the importance of the syllabus, readings, and other literary activities, the unity of a course is a temporal unity, defined by rhythm, pulse, climax and resolution.

A course needs organization not only as a syllabus (a spatial thought-form of topics and readings) but also as an event (a temporal thought-form of tempi, rhythms and themes); classes both "build upon" and "follow upon" one another, like the sequence of scenes in a play. They generate a pattern, partly through recall and foreshadowing, that evinces a coherent and experienceable whole. This is not a literary wholeness, like that created by the sequence of locations and characters in a novel. Students do not take a course home with them to read in the privacy of their living rooms, or on the bus, or in the library. It cannot be picked up

---

[1] "Teaching" throughout this paper refers to college-level instruction in American institutions of higher education. Most of what is said applies to all formal group teaching situations in the West. A good deal also applies to historical and cross-cultural teaching situations, although much refinement would be required to make that more general argument.

[2] The audience may or not be induced to become active participants in the event. This does not change the predominance of the performer in structuring the event. The teacher decides the extent and manner in which students are encouraged to participate.

and dipped into at any point or selectively re-read at will. Despite the reality of outside reading, research and assignments, the course happens in the extended face-to-face of the classes. It is performed. Teaching is a performing art.[3]

Teachers need the skills of playwrights, directors and performers. They structure public events (scriptwriting and directing), present prepared texts in face-to-face public situations (acting, stand-up comedy and public speaking), and respond extemporaneously to remarks from the audience (improvisation). In its performance teaching requires the skills and sensibilities needed for all public presentation—articulation, projection, eye contact with the audience, a sense of the ebb and flow of attention and when to tell a joke or review, and self confidence.

The social roles of teacher and student compel the teacher to perform a character. The teacher/student relationship is not intimate and whole, like friendship or marriage. Teachers reveal parts of themselves in class, sculpted or delimited versions of their daily personalities, defining and defined by their classroom behavior. This sculpted personality is a persona, a mask generated for performance effects, which is to say for teaching effectiveness. Like all masks, it both reveals and hides. The classroom persona need not be radically different from one's everydayness, but a wide variety of topics, gestures, behavioral styles and discourses that fill one's ordinary existence simply do not come into the class. Their absence marks the hiding function of the mask. What remains is "character"—the classroom persona of the teacher in action. When students come to office hours or have other official contacts with faculty, they interact with these characters, extending the performative quality of teaching to the entire interaction.

The total environment participates in the performance and shapes the meaningful learning experience of the student. The teacher engages elements of set design, costuming, choreography and blocking, and properties, because space, clothing, and gesture signify powerfully in the extended face-to-face that characterizes performance. This legitimates and necessitates use of the whole performance environment to support teaching—slides, films and video, music, formal performances, student performances, small group working sessions, intentional control of rhythm and pace.

---

[3]Considered by contemporary standards, teaching falls into the category of the "applied arts", rather than the "fine" arts, because it serves a practical end. This links it with graphic, industrial and product design, architecture and landscape architecture, and the crafts—textiles, pottery, carpentry and so forth.

To fully explore the creative potentials of teaching, one must intentionally integrate all the elements of performance into the classroom scene. Poor performance will lead to bad classes and an ineffective course, despite the best syllabus and the clearest and most interesting thought. The formal constraints of performance, including the length of the completed performance and the number of sessions composing it, but also the structure and limits of the well-formed lecture, seminar session, or field trip, and, eg., the acoustics and lighting of the classroom impinge on the content of teaching.[4]

Thought is embodied. It takes place in media—language, textiles, performance, city forms, and so forth. Each medium has its own structures, limits, and symbolisms which play a role in the thinking that occur in that medium. It is one thing to think in stone, another to think in dance, yet another to think in printed words.[5]

Accepting the role of artist and using performance techniques and thought-forms effectively may force teachers to re-examine some of our common myths about art and artists. For example, like all of the arts, teaching can be taught and learned; focused practice in an apprentice context improves results. Neither teaching nor the other arts, fine or applied, is tied in some mysterious way to "genius" or "creativity" or "talent". Like the ability to write and to run and to paint, the ability to teach is variably distributed. Some of us have more potential than others. But as with running and writing and painting, and most other practical

---

[4]Pace is an especially important issue in performance. Pace is not speed, but a more complex temporal phenomenon related to the cumulative effect of preceding temporal experiences on current and future ones. When the pace is either too fast or too slow, boredom and incomprehensibility ensue. Pace problems usually manifest themselves in the latter half of performance. Class may tend to run down near the end of the hour, or the session as a whole may bog down for several weeks shortly after mid-semester, or the last month may seem either terribly rushed or interminably long. Usually pace problems are not caused at the point where they appear, but at an earlier time. Try altering the tempi and rhythms of the earlier parts until you find a combination that works. A key to effective performance is the management of temporality, not just "effective time management" in the task-oriented sense, but effective management of the *experience* of temporality.

[5]See, eg., Jacques Derrida, *Dissemination*, Translated, with an Introduction and Additional notes by Barbara Johnson, (Chicago: The University of Chicago Press, 1981), for a discussion, or perhaps better an exemplification, of the materiality of writing and texts and of the impact of the embodiment of the text on its meaning.

For a discussion of thinking in stone, see Wilson Duff, *Images Stone B.C.: Thirty Centuries of Northwest Coast Indian Sculpture*, Hancock House Publishers, Saanichton, B.C., 1975.

activities, almost all of us can learn how to teach, and most of us can improve it through learning and practice.

Painting, drawing, theater, film, dance, and music are no more (and no less) the result of mysterious unconscious intuitive powers than science, mathematics and philosophy. They are media in which people grapple with the experience/creation of meaning; they are thoughtforms. Great artists are, doubtless, rare and remarkable people. Often they are exceedingly intuitive. The same could be said for the great figures of any area of human endeavor. Many people of varying degrees of ability, intelligence, intuition, diligence, and official repute practice the arts, as, indeed, a similarly varying group of people study religion.

The academic study of religion should not adopt as normative the contemporary western concepts of art and artist. They belong to one among a variety of sets of concepts with which cultures describe, interpret, and effect their creation of material culture and their investment of the cultural landscape with meaning.[6]

"Art" and "artist" emerged contemporary with modernity in the West, beginning in romantic Germany of the early nineteenth century. The figure of the artist took on charismatic qualities formerly associated with religious or political leaders and became decisively associated with "creativity", heretofore a theological concept, and still a key metaphor in Judaic, Islamic, and Christian imagination. These developments were part of the romantic revolt from reason that led to an affirmation of exaltation in Nature (a development of the concept of the sublime from Shaftesbury and Kant), of intense emotional experience, of imagination, of sexual ambiguity and fulfillment, and of intuition.[7] Little wonder that creative artists are now thought to be wild, emotional, intuitive, sexually uncertain, and utterly fascinating (if not disgusting).[8] This is part of the

---

[6]See, eg., Robert Farris Thompson, *The Flash of the Spirit: African and Afro-American Art and Philosophy.* (NY: Vintage Books, 1984).

[7]See, eg., Arnold Hauser *The Social History of Art*, vol. 3, in the chapter titled "German and Western Romanticism", p. 163 - 227. (NY: Vintage Books, 1960). See Lippard, *Overlay: Contemporary Art and the Art of Prehistory*, for one view of how contemporary artists chafe under, struggle with, and try to reinvent the meaning of "art" and "artist". (NY: Pantheon Books, 1983).

[8]In moving to the political and, for some artists in some times, the social and economic margins of society, and by becoming associated with "creativity, change and the new" artists have acquired the social and symbolic characteristics of what Victor Turner called "liminars"—those betwixt and between. See Victor Turner, *The Forest of Symbols: Aspects of Ndembu Ritual*, (Ithaca, NY: Cornell Univ. Press, 1970), especially "Betwixt and Between: The Liminal Period in Rites of Passage" and *The Ritual Process: Structure and Anti-Structure*, (Chicago: Aldine Publishing Co., 1969), especially Ch. 3:

mostly unconscious mythology both teacher and student may bring to the concepts "art" and "artist".

There are other reasons teachers are likely to be biased against non-verbal media. The religious and political history of the American university marks us with a deeply Protestant view of the relationship between words (predominantly printed texts) and truth, especially in relation to such media as art, music, and dance.

In another volume in this series, Lawrence Sullivan speaks out against the tyranny of the text as the sole metaphor for symbolic experience, especially given the fact that most people reflect on their religious and symbolic existence in non-literate media.[9] We do live in a linguistically mediated world; it is also mediated by other forms of material culture such as dress, work schedules, architecture, and music. Language is one powerful medium of material culture; all the media together in dynamic interaction generate/manifest the world.

Texts are best understood, perhaps, as sorts of textiles. The Greek Fates were weavers, threading the weft of consequence through the warp of time. As we follow the weaving of words in a text over the time it takes to read (remarking the time it takes to write), the pattern of the text (the meaning) emerges, woven by the writer/reader from intention, skill, and language. Spoken and written thought are physical artifacts, elements of material culture.

The academy wraps thought in words and has, for the moment, enthroned "text" as the ruling metaphor for understanding systems of meaning. In the study of religion we encounter sophisticated systems of thought and wisdom whose reflections are and have been carried out primarily in media other than words—in dance, plastic representation, music, liturgics, and design.[10] As we learn to understand some of these ways of thought, we may notice that our own material culture is meaningful and begin to apply our newfound hermeneutic skills to our own environment, including the environment of the classroom.

We are also enabled to see texts in their context in the cultural landscape. Text has played a unique and radical role in the West over the past

---

"Liminality and Communitas", p. 94 - 130. Artists (except for the celebrated few) have been moved to the margins of our culture, economically, politically, and in terms of the psycho-social traits commonly attributed to them.

[9]Lawrence E. Sullivan, "Putting an End to the Text as Primary", in the Chicago volume of this series.

[10]See, eg., Lawrence E. Sullivan, *Icanchu's Drum: An Orientation to Meaning in South American Religions.* (NY: Macmillan Publishing Company, 1988).

three hundred years, but that should not blind us to the creative role played by material culture.[11] Judaism, Christianity, and Islam, notwithstanding their scripturality, have been and are profoundly affecting of and affected by art, architecture, and other aspects of material culture.[12]

Like art, religion is directly productive of material culture and is an active force in the maintenance and transformation of shared worlds. As with art, to understand religion one must make it intelligible in its concrete specificity. Ideas play a role, but the whole is physical, material, temporal, and existential. The academic study of religion may share more with the great interpretive enterprises of art criticism and philosophy of art than with the descriptive, analytical, and predictive enterprises of the social sciences.[13]

Religion itself is generative in the fullest sense of the word. Religious actors and institutions generate all levels of material culture from household utensils to worship spaces and urban forms, from personal health habits to widespread patterns of migration and pilgrimage. It is breathtaking to watch in history as a newly developing religious tradition creates itself in the process of generating a new cultural landscape, e.g., in the emergence of Christianity from decadent Greco-roman cul-

---

[11]See Geoffrey and Susan Jellicoe, *The Landscape of Man*, (London: Thames and Hudson, Ltd., 1987), and Yi-Fu Tuan, *Topophilia: A Study of Environmental Perception, Attitudes and Values*. (Minneapolis: Univ. of Minnesota Press, 1972).

[12]For Judaism see, eg., Ed Wigoden, *Jewish Art and Civilization*. (NY: Walker & Co., 1982); Elie Kedourie, ed., *The Jewish World: History and Culture of the Jewish People*; and Gabrielle Sed-Rajna, *Ancient Jewish Art*. (Secaucus, NJ: Chartwell Books, Inc., 1985). For Islam, see, eg., Oleg Grabar, *The Formation of Islamic Art*. (New Haven: Yale University Press, 1973); Bernard Lewis, ed., *Islam and the Arab World: Faith, People, Culture*. (NY: Alfred A. Knopf, in association with American Heritage Pub. Co., Inc.., 1976), Chapter Two—"The Man-Made Setting: Islamic Art and Architecture", by Richard Ettinghausen, Chapter Three—"Cities and Citizens: The Growth and Culture of Urban Islam", by Oleg Grabar, and Chapter Six—"The Dimension of Sound: Islamic Music—Philosophy, Theory and Practice", by A. Shiloah. The role of Christianity in the history of the cultural landscape in the West is so generally recognized that it is seldom written about in its own right, although art history and architecture books routinely trace this role up through some date between 1500 and 1800 after which the influence is supposed to be much diminished. Jane Dillenberger, *Style and Content in Christian Art*, (NY: The Crossroad Publishing Co., 1988), Jellicoe, *The Landscape of Man*, and Tuan, *Topophilia* provide interesting insights into the interactions of Christianity and material culture in the West.

[13]Institutionally it may be that the Academic Study of Religion should be more allied with the arts and less with the social sciences. Certainly scholars of religion should avail themselves of the artists and art theorists at their institutions and in their communities as fellow workers in the arena of meaning.

ture, in the appearance of Buddhist culture (ever so slowly before bursting out in Mahayana), and in the dramatic formulation of Islamic culture in a surge of creativity. Similar moments can be found in the emergence of African religions in the new world and in the transformation of eastern woodland North American religions as they adopted horses and moved onto the plains.

Material culture, the culture of *mater*, mother, is open to creativity from every corner of society. The "high arts and architecture" are often correlated with "high theology" and associated with the privileged elite. There are always also various forms of art, architecture, craft, music, dance, and performance available to those who for reasons of gender, race, class and power are excluded from high culture.[14]

Like gender, race, class, and power, material culture matters in the lives of students and teachers, in the conduct of the classroom, and in religion itself. Teaching about religion must use, reflect on, and take account of the material cultures both of the religions under consideration and of the classroom in which the consideration is taking place.

Material culture encompasses the entire pattern in which a culture manifests in and as the physical world. This pattern is dynamic and temporal as well as static, objective, and spatial. Organizations of time (what might be called calendars) are fundamental elements of material culture, and each culture's handling of time is as unique and significant as its use and experience of space.[15] Time-based arts (performances of any kind, including teaching) order and re-order the experience of time, using the structure of temporality as a medium of significance. Because performance alters and plays with ordinary temporal experience, all performance mimics the tri-partite structure Victor Turner found in ritual.[16] There is a separation from ordinary temporality, a period of altered temporalities, and a return to (a possibly transformed) everydayness. As an arena of temporal structuring, teaching provides a unique point of contact between our professional activity and our topic of study.

The classroom offers an unparalleled theater of experimentation in material culture. Self-consciously engaging theater as performing art leads to improved teaching, mastering the forms and techniques of the

---

[14]See eg., Bernard Rudofsky, *Architecture without Architects: A Short Introduction to Non-Pedigreed Architecture.* (Garden City, NY: Doubleday and Co., 1964).

[15]See, eg. Edward T. Hall's treatment of cultural time worlds in *The Hidden Dimension.* (Garden City, NY: Doubleday, 1969) and Sullivan's treatment of calendars in *Icanchu's Drum,* p. 153 - 227, in the chapter called "Time".

[16]Turner, *The Ritual Process.*

craft for more graceful, stylish and precise teaching. Teaching comes to be a form of thought and self-expression in which one articulates both self and world.

One learns to think in physical terms, to conceive in space and time and matter. Experience thinking physically helps us to develop a hermeneutic to investigate and interpret material culture wherever we encounter it, bringing material culture into the study of religion on its own terms. This hermeneutic opens an encounter with the non-verbal religious thought of indigenous peoples (and of illiterate people within our own cultures), which contains both profound reflections on the human condition, and pointed and insightful critique of dominant western religions.[17]

Practice in performance enlivens us to time as a medium of thought and to event as a dynamic symbolic form. Religion, too, is a temporal form, and thinks itself in rhythms and patterns, interpreting and creating the flow of life through interlocking and succeeding patterns of time. Each day has its shape, and the year shapes its days, and one's stage in life shapes one's station in the events of the year. Following this pattern, pausing to be the center at moments of dramatic transformation—being born, coming of age, marrying, giving birth, dying—gives coherent form, and therefore meaning, to the experience of a human life.

Religion can pattern the experience of the flow of time from the routine of daily events to the cycles of cosmic aeons. Religious events range from the simplest prayer or gesture to ceremonies that span years or even to whole lives. At every point, we are reminded of the performative, dynamic, temporal character of religion. The art of teaching, too, requires us to shape time in order to create and transmit meaning. The practical experience in time based significance this offers can provide key insights for the interpretation of religion.

---

[17]Sullivan, *Icanchu's Drum.*

BIBLIOGRAPHY

Derrida, Jacques. *Dissemination*. Translated, with an Introduction and Additional notes by Barbara Johnson. Chicago: The University of Chicago Press, 1981.

Dillenberger, Jane. *Style and Content in Christian Art*. NY: The Crossroad Publishing Co., 1988.

Duff, Wilson. *Images Stone BC: Thirty Centuries of Northwest Coast Indian Sculpture*. Saanichton, B.C: Hancock House Publishers, 1975.

Grabar, Oleg. *The Formation of Islamic Art*. New Haven: Yale University Press, 1973.

Hall, Edward T. *The Silent Language*. Garden City, NY: Doubleday, 1969.

Hauser, Arnold. *The Social History of Art*, vols. i-iv. NY: Vintage Books, 1960.

Jellicoe, Geoffrey and Jellicoe, Susan. *The Landscape of Man*. London: Thames and Hudson, Ltd., 1987.

Kedourie, Elie, ed. *The Jewish World: History and Culture of the Jewish People*. NY: H. N. Abrams, 1979.

Lewis, Bernard, ed., *Islam and the Arab World: Faith, People, Culture*. NY: Alfred A. Knopf, in association with American Heritage Pub. Co., Inc., 1976.

Rudofsky, Bernard. *Architecture without Architects: A Short Introduction to Non-Pedigreed Architecture*. Garden City, NY: Doubleday and Co., 1964.

Sed-Rajna, Gabrielle. *Ancient Jewish Art*. Secaucus, NJ: Chartwell Books, Inc., 1985.

Sullivan, Lawrence E. *Icanchu's Drum: An Orientation to Meaning in South American Religions*. NY: Macmillan Publishing Company, 1988.

Sullivan, Lawrence. "Putting an End to the Text as Primary," in the Chicago volume of this series.

Thompson, Robert Farris. *The Flash of the Spirit: African and Afro-American Art and Philosophy*. NY: Vintage Books, 1984.

Tuan, Yi-fu. *Topophilia: A Study of Environmental Perception, Attitudes and Values*. Minneapolis: Univ. of Minnesota Press, 1972.

Turner, Victor. *The Forest of Symbols: Aspects of Ndembu Ritual*. Ithaca, NY: Cornell University Press, 1970.

Turner, Victor. *The Ritual Process: Structure and Anti-Structure*. Chicago: Aldine Publishing Co., 1969.

Wechsler, Lawrence. "Taking Art to Point Zero—I", *The New Yorker*. NY: The New Yorker, March 2, 1982, p56-87.

Wechsler, Lawrence. "Taking Art to Point Zero—II", *The New Yorker*. NY: The New Yorker, March 9, 1982, p52-102.

Wigoden, Geoffrey, ed. *Jewish Art and Civilization*. NY: Walker & Co., 1982.

Wolfe, Eric. *Europe and the People Without History*, Berkeley: Univ. of Calif. Press, 1982.

USING AUDIO-VISUAL RESOURCES TO TEACH ABOUT RELIGION[1]

Richard M. Carp

Introduction

Religion involves the whole person and the entire cultural landscape. It permeates the built environment, manifesting in art, music, architecture, ritual, ceremony and pilgrimage as surely as in sacred books and other words. For many, if not most, people, religious experience is a matter of how the world feels and looks and sounds and smells, not of what they think about it. Many religious people do not use texts, whether they are non-literate or illiterate. Visual artifacts may appear to be illustrations of verbal concepts. The truth is often the other way around; texts may be explanations of concepts originally articulated visually, kinaesthetically or aurally.[2]

The material culture of religion, appearing in the built environment, also participates in the education of the senses. Perception seems to be a universal given on which subsequent cultural and individual differences are built. In fact, perception is constructed in a learning process correlated with the built environment, which is permeated with the visual, aural and kinaesthetic creations of religion. This learning process profoundly affects seeing, hearing, speaking, body postures, rhythms, and movement.[3] We cannot investigate religion without gaining access to the

---

[1]Throughout I am indebted to work by Chris Jochim, Barbara Reed, Marcia Hermanson, and Susan Henking at the 1987 NEH Summer Workshop on the Introductory Course in Religious Studies in Berkeley.

[2]See, eg., Edward T. Hall's opus, *Beyond Culture*, (Garden City, NY: Doubleday, 1980), *The Hidden Dimension*, (Garden City, NY: Doubleday, 1969), *The Silent Language*, (Greenwich, CT: Fawcett Publications, Inc., 1959).

[3]Karen McCarthy Brown is convinced that dancing is an original form of thinking and working through life-problems in Santeria (personal communication). See also, eg., Lawrence E. Sullivan, *Icanchu's Drum: An Orientation to Meaning in South American Religions*. (NY: Macmillan Publishing Company, 1988), passim. See also a

modes of perceiving and non-verbal thinking in which the religions participate.[4] To do so we must encounter the artifacts in and through which they think perceptually, in non-verbal media.

Issues in Religious Studies and the Uses of Material Culture[5]

Visual, audible, tactile and kinaesthetic materials are necessary to (re)present religion. When well used they are effective teaching tools, since they engage students' senses and students enjoy them. They also provide forceful and provocative means to raise fundamental issues in religious studies.

For example, examining common ideas about art and artists can clarify how deeply our experience is tied to Western individualism with its roots in the Judeo-Greco-Christian religious complex. Many traditions have no concept of "art" or "artist", and often the act of making is a sacred activity, in many cases one in which the "artist" re-forms herself as well as the raw material that becomes the artifact. The act is often as or even more important than the artifact that results from it. In any case, the traditional artist "is not trying to express himself, but that which is to be expressed."[6]

Arts, musics, and architectures of other traditions often seem bizarre, not only to students but to scholars. Western accounts of African music, eg., often describe it as noise, din or cacophony, while students' first comment on viewing images of Hindu divinities is often "why do they have all those arms?" The difficulty of appreciating the art of other traditions highlights the problem of understanding other religions (or even unfamiliar regions of one's "own" tradition).[7]

---

wide range of feminist cultural criticism, often film criticism. For a good selection see Susan Rubin Suleiman, ed., *The Female Body in Western Culture: Contemporary Perspectives.* (Cambridge, Mass: Harvard Univ. Press, 1986).

[4]As Diana Eck shows for "Hinduism" in, *Darsan: Seeing the Divine Image in India.* Chambersburg, PA: Anima Books, 1981.

[5]This section draws heavily on work by Dr. Barbara Reed at the 1987 NEH Workshop on the Introductory Course in Religious Studies.

[6]Ananda K. Coomaraswamy, *Christian and Oriental Philosophy of Art,* (NY: Dover Publications, Inc, 1956), p39. See also p.80 and passim. The western concept of art as the expression of personal creativity dates from no earlier than German romanticism.

[7]To enter these strange worlds requires being "faithfully available" to the works in which they appear (as Prof. Howard Miller has put it). This faithfulness is not belief, but recognition that experiencing the profundity of these works requires us to be grasped by them. The point is not to grasp them in our terms; their function is to transform our terms.

The unity and diversity of a single tradition can be explored through art, music and architecture. For example in art one can examine the historical transformations of the image of Christ or Mary,[8] or in music one can discuss similarities and differences among, Bach's B-Minor Mass, the Missa Luba, Jesus Christ Superstar, and selections of American urban gospel music.

One can also clarify similarities and differences between traditions, for example by comparing a Gupta Buddha with an Italian Renaissance Christ, or the form and meaning of a Gothic cathedral with a classic mosque.

Issues of gender and power are easily focused with music, art, and architecture. Who is depicted, how, by whom and why? Who composes or performs the music, for whom, in what context? Texts are only fully available to the literate, who are usually upper class men, but all elements of society will have access and recourse to visual and aural media. "Folk" art and music and vernacular architecture are often our only contact with the religion of women and others outside the power elite.

Because art and music are used to create or mark special contexts, they lend themselves to thematic and template courses as well as to a "traditions" approach. Pilgrimage and ritual are marked by special arts, spaces, clothes, and sounds, while gender, divine being, healing, trance and fertility are constructed, effected, ensured and expressed through their own visible and audible forms. Because regions are characterized by a particular, singular conversation among and between potteries, musics, arts, and liturgics, performance, art and craft provide uniquely powerful insights into regional studies.

Where to Find Good Audio-Visual Resources

A surprising number of useful materials are probably already accessible on your campus and in your community; others can be obtained for minimal cost. The first thing to do is to get to know your reference librarians. Your campus probably has a slide librarian working closely with the Art History program and the head librarian. There may also be a music/discography librarian, working in conjunction with your Music

---

[8]For the former, see Jane Dillenberger. *Style and Content in Christian Art.* (NY: The Crossroad Publishing Co., 1988). For the latter, see, eg., Penny Schine Gold. *The Lady and the Virgin: Image, Attitude and Experience in Twelfth Century France.* (Chicago: University of Chicago Press, 1985), and Margaret R. Miles, "The Virgin's One Bare Breast: Female Nudity and Religious Meaning in Tuscan Early Renaissance Culture," in Suleiman, ed.

department. If not, your local public library will have reference librarians familiar with these areas.

These librarians have access to the resources you need. If you have budget constraints, they will prove doubly useful, first by helping you avoid duplicating existing resources and second, by helping you find the least expensive source for materials you want to buy. Also, film distributors, like publishers, circulate publicity on new releases; a friendly A/V librarian will usually pass along to you copies of material relevant to religion.

When you locate resources, whether they have been recommended in this paper, by a friend, or by a librarian, always preview them before using them in class. If you don't like or understand them, or if you think the quality of the sound or sight is poor, don't use them. Appendix One provides a short list of the best available resources and of catalogues and other reference guides.

Using Audio-Visuals Effectively

The following suggestions will help you use any audio-visual resources—film, video, slide, tape, record, CD, or what have you. They will assist you to integrate non-verbal thinking and alternate perceptual worlds in class, generating better and more vibrant teaching and an expanded field of information and insight.

1. Preview your materials. Look and listen closely more than once. Think about how you want to use them, the points you want to make, and the questions that may arise in students' minds.

2. Rehearse. Do you want to make introductory remarks to affect students' "set"? Will you distribute a study guide before the presentation? Afterwards? Lecture and discussion during slide presentations are almost always essential. It is often effective to stop a film, tape, or video to make a point, answer a question, or rewind it to take a second look at something.

3. Use high quality materials that are easy to see and hear. Make sure that an unsophisticated looker or listener can see or hear what you want to teach about. You shouldn't have to explain your resources. They should present information, concepts, or experiences you want to consider further.

4. Take time in class. Seeing and hearing are not as instantaneous as they seem, and a rich variety of information can be packed into one slide or a few minutes of music. Few of us, teachers or students, know how to look or to listen. Give your class time to look at a slide for five minutes and write their observations or questions; listen to a piece of music two or three times and treat films and videos the same way. The payoff is as great as when rereading a text.

5. Practice with the equipment you will use. Your A/V librarian or technician will be happy to show you how to use it and how to trouble-shoot the most common problems. For example, clearing a jammed slide projector requires only a dime as a tool and takes thirty seconds, at most. Knowing how to do it can make the difference between an amusing glitch and a major disaster.

6. Discuss the nature of images with your class. Many of us who rec-ognize the inevitable bias of even the most "objective" text still feel that a picture of something represents it "as it really is". In fact images present point of view, selectivity, framing and aesthetic bending quite as much as words do. Seeing ought not to be believing.

Tips on Using Specific Media

Slides. Slides are the most flexible medium. Although you can pur-chase them in packaged sets with commentary, there is no reason to be limited by someone else's sequencing. Reorder them according to your own teaching objectives, mix slides from different sets, or put together your own sets.[9] When you use slides, you can stop to discuss a question

---

[9]The author is currently working on a new slide resource — *Image Bank for Teaching Religious Studies* — designed for teaching the academic study of religion at the college level. The project, funded by the National Endowment for the Humanities and administered by the School of Hawaiian, Asian and Pacific Studies at the University of Hawaii, will provide an annotated, cross-referenced slide library of about six thousand images with an indexed, illustrated catalogue. The *Image Bank* will have images from around the world and ranging in time from the Paleolithic to the present. It will include both high art and architecture and vernacular art and architecture, incorporating media such as textiles and pottery as well as "fine art". It will have several special emphases such as women and ethnic minorities. The *Image Bank* is composed largely of sequences of 5 - 40 slides: eg. rituals and ceremonies, multiple views of architectural spaces, several varieties of a single kind of artifact, and so on.

Teachers will be able to order slides in pre-packaged sets, singly, or according to index categories. For example, it should be possible to ask for all slides created by or

when it comes up or to make a point when it occurs to you. You can go back to review or jump forward to show an image that has suddenly become relevant.

It is often helpful to use two slide projectors (or more) at once. For example, you can compare an Eastern Orthodox icon of the 12th century CE with a contemporary image of the Virgin of Guadalupe or contrast a Gupta Buddha with a Shiva Nataraja. Or you can show, side-by-side, two girls' puberty ceremonies, one from the African Ndembu and one from the American Sioux. Or you can keep a map up on one screen while showing several images from the region on the map on the other.[10]

Find a way to physically point to features of the image. In some classrooms you may be able to do this manually, in others with elevated screens you may need to get a telescoping pointer (like an automobile radio antenna).

It can be effective to show a few slides and discuss them at length, or to show many slides to give a sense of the experience of, eg., being in an architectural space, a ceremony, or a culture. Be sure, though, if you show a lot of slides in one class, that you have a clear, focused intent. From the students' perspective, such a presentation can become just a "picture show".

On exams, ask students to explain why the image is important or to compare and contrast several images in terms of meaning and role in the traditions to which they belong, perhaps in a brief essay. Most A/V centers have locked, illuminated slide boxes where you can leave selected slides for review and study.

Film and video. Film and video provide a unified audio/visual presentation, capture the dramatic flow of rituals, ceremonies or other events, and lend themselves easily to ethnography and other narrative forms. They are rich, synaesthetic media in which to explore religion. At the same time, film and video have disadvantages that the teacher must counteract. Students are used to watching these media and have a laid back, entertainment mindset that almost automatically kicks in when the

---

showing images of women made in Africa or India between 1500 and 1950. Slides will come with about a page of annotation apiece. Larger sets, such as rituals, will have short descriptive essays. Sets on traditions will have short essays discussing the role of arts and the senses in the tradition. Essays will be available on general issues in religion and the arts and on effective use of slides.

[10]It is not necessary to use a screen. If you have a relatively light wall you can project on that. It is helpful to cover the windows and to dim the lights or turn off a front light, leaving a rear light on so that students can take notes.

projector or VCR starts. A film or video also enforces its own pace on the classroom and is hard to interrupt or to view out of sequence.

Several techniques used in conjunction can maximize students' learning from films and videos. 1) Try to show them for no more than one-half of a class period, even if you have to take two or three classes to complete the piece. Use the rest of class for introduction, discussion or focused writing. 2) Provide students with study guides and specific questions *before* you turn on the media. 3) Ask students to identify biases, points of view and aesthetic choices of the film-makers as they do with text writers. 4) Whenever possible, watch films and videos twice. The second time you may well be able to watch them straight through, particularly if you preface the viewing with questions and observations drawn from the first viewing and discussion. If you don't have time to watch the whole thing, review key passages or those that led to the most heated discussions. Comprehension of film and video can be tested in the same way as you test text, lecture and discussion, and through the sort of direct discussion of image suggested above for slides.

Music. Most of our students are deeply engaged in their own musical worlds; they are probably more musically aware and in tune than most of us. At the same time, most of them are accustomed to short musical pieces. Few have practice listening to music the duration of Bach's B-minor mass or an extended raga. We can use our students' attunement to music as a bridge, so long as we recognize it and do not patronize or talk down to them.

Much of what was said above about film and video applies to music as well. All are time-based media and structure the flow of experience according to rhythm, meter and pace. Students need active referents when listening to music. They need to know what to attend to, how to attend to it, and why. Study guides and questions are indispensable. Providing questions that ask students to compare music from unfamiliar traditions with their own familiar music can be especially fruitful.

Although music is closely tied to affect, generating mood, feeling, and even altered states of awareness, listening to music is learned, since listening and hearing differ from culture to culture just as do looking and seeing. A raga is meant to be heard differently than a song from the Koran and both are distinct from the dramatic/participatory hearing appropriate to a mass.

Discuss this with your class before listening, perhaps providing examples with short musical selections from diverse contexts. Explain the role of sound and music in the religious tradition you are studying before you listen[11] If you use a shorter selection, you may want your class to listen naively at first, then discuss their responses, then instruct them on listening within the tradition, and then hear the piece again. Comprehension may be tested as with film and video.

Art media and processes. Music, dance, art and architecture are original modes of thought. Just as one must be a writer to be an effective reader, so one must be a maker, a singer, a dancer to understand thought expressed in these media. A few simple assignments in one or another of these media will work wonders for students' comprehension. It will also allow bright students who think primarily visually, kinaesthetically or aurally to excel. In his Introduction to Religion class at the University of California at Berkeley, Prof. Mark Juergensmeyer has sometimes divided students into groups and asked each group to "create a religion," and perform aspects of it (a technique described more fully in the next section of this volume). Prof. Catherine Clarke, at Norfolk State University, has students create masks modeled after those of the Yoruba, moving through all the phases, technical and ritual, of the Yoruba mask-making tradition. Karen Voss, at the Graduate Theological Union, at the beginning of a class on Women and Religion, had students make images of their own notion of "goddess," write about both the process and the image, and bring them to class for discussion. At the end of the semester they again created goddess images and compared them with their originals.

If your institution has videotaping equipment for student use (or if some students have their own equipment) they can document a local religious organization, or their own religious practice, or compare several local religious architectures.

It is not necessary to grade these exercises, certainly not on an aesthetic basis. Students should not try to become artists or to compete with one another aesthetically, but to get a brief, direct experience of the difficulties and rewards of thinking in physical media. If you need to grade, written assignments can provide a basis.

Conclusion

Religion is a fully manifest human activity that shapes all the media of material culture—architecture, art, dance, dress, the body, speech, text,

---

[11]Although it is not as effective as a complete presentation, there is some value in playing music simply for mood and color, perhaps under a slide presentation, or during a break, or for the first five or ten minutes of class when students are arriving and things are getting underway.

landscape and urban form. The academic study of religion has tended to focus on text at the expense of the rest of material culture. Interestingly this bias apparently has its roots in religious history, specifically in the Protestant heritage of American higher education. To study religion effectively we need to correct this bias; to represent religion adequately we need all the media of material culture.

Fortunately, mixed-media classroom resources are becoming increasingly available. With some research and imagination, we can create synaesthetic classrooms in which students engage in cross-cultural, intermedia investigations of religion, generating both a vital and dynamic classroom experience and an increasingly broad, subtle, and valid study of religion.

AUDIO VISUAL RESOURCES:
Bibliographies and Catalogues

Abram, Gerald, general editor. *The History of Music in Sound*, 10 Vols. NY: Oxford University Press, 1957. A musical companion to *The New Oxford History of Music*. An excellent source of music and information about it. Volume I includes all of "ancient and oriental music," volumes 2 - 10 chronicle the history of western music.

Bodman, Ellen, ed. *The World of Islam: Images and Echoes.* Second Edition. NY: American Council of Learned Societies, 1989. An excellent critically annotated list of films and recordings.

Cyr, Helen W. *Filmography of the Third World: An Annotated List of 16mm Films.* New Jersey: Scarecrow Press, 1976. A bit outdated but useful for films on third world countries including Africa and Native America. Geographical with short summaries.

Dell, David J. *Focus on Hinduism: A Guide to Audio-Visual Resources for Teaching Religion.* Chambersburg, PA: Anima Books, 1981. The definitive guide, with an introductory essay and good reviews of selected films, slides and recordings, as well as other potential sources of A/V materials. Helpful in the general search for A/V materials as well as those specifically on Hinduism. Hopefully this volume will soon be updated.

Heider, Karl G., preparer. *Films for Anthropological Teaching.* Seventh Edition. Special Publication Number 16. NY: American Anthropological Association, 1983. Brief descriptions of films indexed according to topic and geographical area.

Instructional Development Program for the Institute of Indian Services and Research. *Bibliography of Nonprint Instructional Materials on the American Indian.* Provo, Utah: Instructional Development Program for the Institute of Indian Services and Research, Brigham Young University, 1972.

Jewish Chautauqua Society. *Catalog of Motion Pictures* (about Jews). NY: Jewish Chautauqua Society, ND.

Lomax, Alan, ed. *The Columbia World Library of Folk and Primitive Music, XV Volumes.* NY: Columbia Records, ND. The largest and most complete compilation of local music ever undertaken and still a surprisingly good collection of recordings, with accompanying notes and text. This is truly a world collection, covering musical fragments from ancient sources and folk music from every continent. It treats Australian aboriginal music and Irish folk music with the same evenhanded interest and respect. It is a bit intimidating for the beginner, but your nearest university is likely to have a copy, and it is worth dipping into.

May, Elizabeth. *Music of Many Cultures.* Berkeley: UC Press, 1980. This book, which includes three phonodiscs with text annotations, is a reliable introductory text for courses in Music in World Cultures. A good place to start.

McDermott, Robert A. *Focus on Buddhism: A Guide to Audio-Visual Resources for Teaching Religion.* Chambersburg, PA: Anima Books, 1981. Follows the same format as Dell, above. Similarly complete, all it needs is an update.

National Information Center for Educational Media. *Film and Video Finder,* Albuquerque: National Information Center for Educational Media, 1987. A comprehensive resource of about 90,000 entries with about 50 subject subheadings under the subject "Religion and Philosophy" with over 3,000 entries. Descriptions are brief.

Nordquist, Joan, ed. *Audio Visuals for Women.* North Carolina: McFarland and Co., Inc., 1980. An annotated bibliography including films, videos and recordings focused on women and the church.

R.R. Bowker Co. *Educational Film/Video Locator of the Consortium of University Film Centers and R.R. Bowker, Third Edition, Two Volumes,*

NY: R.R. Bowker Co., 1986, annual. A select listing of holdings in 52 major university film libraries in the United States. Films listed by name, making research difficult, but evaluations are useful.

Schmidt, Roger. *Exploring Religion.* Belmont, CA: Wadsworth Publishing Co., 1988. In an appendix ("Media Guide", pp 375-378) Schmidt provides annotated discussions of selected resource grouped as "introductory," "conceptual," and "social." They are easily applicable to classroom use.

Weatherford, Elizabeth, ed. *Native Americans on Film and Video.* New York: Museum of the American Indian/Heye Foundation, 1981.

WORKS CITED IN THE ESSAY

Coomaraswamy, Ananda K. *Christian and Oriental Philosophy of Art.* NY: Dover Publications, Inc, 1956.

Dillenberger, Jane. *Style and Content in Christian Art.* NY: The Crossroad Publishing Co., 1988.

Eck, Diana. *Darsan: Seeing the Divine Image in India.* Chambersburg, PA: Anima Books, 1981.

Gold, Penny Schine. *The Lady and the Virgin: Image, Attitude and Experience in Twelfth Century France.* (Chicago: University of Chicago Press, 1985.

Hall, Edward T. *Beyond Culture.* Garden NY: Doubleday, 1980. *The Hidden Dimension.* Garden City, NY: Doubleday, 1969. *The Silent Language.* Greenwich, CT: Fawcett City Publications, Inc., 1959.

Suleiman, Susan Rubin, ed. *The Female Body in Western Culture: Contemporary Perspectives.* Cambridge, Mass: Harvard Univ. Press, 1986.

Sullivan, Lawrence E. *Icanchu's Drum: An Orientation to Meaning in South American Religions.* NY: Macmillan Publishing Company, 1988.

TRICKS OF THE TRADE

Compiled by Gurudharm Singh Khalsa

These suggestions for thinking creatively about the media through which the substantive content of the class is transmitted come from participants in the 1987 NEH Summer Institute at Berkeley.

Telling traditional stories helps to explain religious beliefs, customs, and rituals in an understandable and enlivening way. Wisdom stories figure prominently in many traditions and provide an understandable point of entry into the intricacies of spiritual transmission. Humor, detail and local custom enrich any discussion of a religious tradition, and stories often provide the vivid, personal perspective. Telling stories in class holds the attention of students and helps to illustrate difficult abstractions. Huston Smith (Syracuse emeritus) tries not to let an idea go by without providing an a short story or example. Marcia Hermansen (San Diego State University) recommends Paul Reps, *Zen Flesh, Zen Bones* and the Sufi stories in Annemarie Schimmel's *Mystical Dimensions of Islam*. Richard Carp (Kansas City Art Institute) suggests Hasidic tales, particularly early ones associated with the tradition of the Baal Shem Tov as interpreted by Martin Buber and Elie Wiesel.

Visits to local religious communities provide a close up look at the social organization and operating context of living traditions. Interviews with religious practitioners create a human connection with a historic tradition and may communicate the vitality and appeal of an unknown faith. Christian Jochim (San Jose State University) structures an ethnological assignment out of visits to two communities during the semester combined with interviews of the members. He gives students a structural method of taking field notes: theory, practice and social organization. A paper in a chosen aspect completes the assignment. Mark Juergensmeyer (University of California/Hawaii) organizes group visits after discussing the role of the participant observer. He recommends reading Paul Rabinow's *Reflections on Field Work in Morocco* for understanding the process of interviewing and participant observation. William Jennings (Muhlenburg College) suggests longer visits of several days to a community, such as a Benedictine monastery or a Zendo, for a full impression of the religious life. Field visits raise issues of research methodology and may lead to a discussion of the insider/outsider problem of observation and critical thinking.

In order to heighten the awareness of religious roots, Howard Miller (University of Texas, Austin) has students write up their family's religious history from 1800 to the present. This is often the first time that students have consciously reflected on their religious inheritance. James Watt's *Your Family and American History* can serve as a model to frame the assignment. Similarly, Gail Corrington (Pennsylvania State University) has students compose a 500 word essay in which they describe and explain a myth or ritual in their religious tradition, or a major religious celebration in which they participated. Each of these assignments starts a process of reflection in an area familiar to the student, and asks them to articulate their religious influences.

Mark Juergensmeyer (University of California/Hawaii) has fashioned a semester long assignment around the idea that students can create their own religion once they become familiar with the elements that comprise a religious worldview. After dividing the class in groups of six, each student develops one dimension of an imaginary religion: the concept of the sacred, symbol and myth, ritual, community, ethics and relevance to the individual. (See also the components outlined in Ninian Smart's *Worldviews*: experiential, mythic, doctrinal, ethical, ritual or social.) The paper must describe the component, describe its relationship to the other five components, compare the component to one in an existing religion, and analyze the component from a theoretical perspective. The students meet together several times to integrate their ideas and also to prepare a group presentation performed before the whole class at the end of the semester.

Novels with religious themes or characters may spark animating and engaging classroom discussions. For example, Howard Miller uses Harold Frederic's *Damnation of Theon Ware* to illustrate conflict and tension between religious cultures (in this case the aesthetic barrenness of 19th Protestantism juxtaposed against the rich and elaborate rituals of the Catholic Church). Mark Wallace (Merrimack College) enlivens the experience of reading James Joyce's *Portrait of an Artist as a Young Man* by role-playing the character of Stephen. Though the students may not identify with Stephen, still his staged presence in a role playing situation serves as both an ice breaker to discussion and as a "Trojan horse in the camp of preconceived opinion". Barbara Reed (St. Olaf College) also employs role playing and uses both the Book of Job and Peter DeVries' *The Blood of a Lamb* as texts. Role playing can also take the form of imaginary dialogues between students and historical figures or scholars studied in class. The dialogues can be staged or they can become a written assignment that requires the students to interact with the imagined response of the great person. This process develops creative introspection and active imagination.

Teaching techniques which go beyond lecture, discussion and slide show into the experiential realm need to be solidly grounded in the particular expertise of the teacher. For example, Howard Miller (University of Texas) plays Bach's "Saint Matthew's Passion" and other forms of sacred music to evoke a universal language for the expression of the numinous; yet he warns that only a professionally trained musician should attempt this approach. Richard Carp (Kansas City Art Institute) uses guided fantasy and visualization to trigger states of creativity and artistry. Dennis Ryan (College of New Rochelle) asks the students to throw the I Ching then share the questions and responses with the class, a process which often directs the ensuing discussion. Breathing exercises, yoga or meditation may serve as a prelude to reflection or appreciation, but the instructor needs to be keenly conscious of the relationship between the class and the educational community to avoid accusations of "teaching religion" rather than "teaching about religion". Also, there is the danger that the boundary between the teacher as critical thinker and teacher as spiritual leader may become indistinct.

Michael McKale (St. Francis College) employs a heuristic exercise called "Collecting Consciousness and Mapping the World", which involves five steps: 1. Draw a rough map of the world, 2. Locate the world religions on the map and indicate holy cities, 3. Show patterns of expansion and historic overlays of religious culture, 4. Order and reshape vague boundaries, and 5. Indicate areas of religious tension and violence. This exercise defines the extent of students' knowledge, outlines their geographic worldviews, and serves as a starting point for developing a global perspective. Jack Hawley (Barnard College/Columbia University) has sometimes begun the semester by asking students to draw a "family portrait" among characters they portray as the world's religious traditions.

When Jean Graybeal (California State University, Chico) perceives confusion over a topic she assigns a 'free write' where students articulate, for five minutes, their concerns on paper. Sometimes she asks students to begin with, "My biggest confusion in this course is..." Phil Mullins (Missouri Western State College) recommends the two or three page response paper to presentations or readings as an effective way to gauge student involvement and progress. Garrett Green (Connecticut College) requires revision of student papers and finds that, despite the reluctance of students, revisions improve writing skills and further the conversation between student and teacher. Student interest and range of knowledge can be plumbed at the start with a spontaneous writing exercise that elicits students' reasons for taking the class and their concerns with the topic.

Barbara Reed (St. Olaf) has students read each other's papers and write a critique. Then she 'publishes' the best papers by making a collection and handing copies back to the students. The critical review of student papers can serve as a way to learn to write book reviews. Another way to share work is for student groups of three to discuss rough drafts and make suggestions for changes. Jean Graybeal (California State University, Chico) uses a "team journal" where students make an entry every week in response to a previous student contribution. These methods of sharing written work among students improves writing quality, increases class interaction and promotes peer pressure to perform well.

The informal format of letter writing is often more inviting and encouraging to students who are overwhelmed by the formal research paper. Dennis Ryan (New Rochelle) uses creative topics to spur the imagination. For example, a student could write a letter posing as a Buddhist monk or nun writing to a parent whose child has died in an accident. Or the letters can be addressed to great religious teachers from the past or present, posing questions or difficulties.

George James (North Texas State University) uses fifteen minute oral exams to evaluate students. He questions two students at a time and focuses on discussion questions which he has previously handed out. This technique is useful to uncover and correct student misconceptions about the course that have escaped notice. In small classes, Mark Juergensmeyer (University of California/Hawaii) uses the same amount of time for student self evaluation, and discussion about exam answers and grades. In large classes, he uses humor in devising imaginary situations and encounters for students to discuss or explain. Michael McKale (St. Francis) prefers take-home exams which are more conducive to reflection than timed exams. Plagiarism is reduced by asking questions that demand original answers, such as asking the student to take a stand on a controversial issue and relate it to his or her own experience.

RIDDLE ME A RIDDLE: BRINGING THOSE ABSENT INTO RELIGIOUS STUDIES[1]

Susan E. Henking

> Long afterward, Oedipus, old and blinded, walked the roads. He smelled a familiar smell. It was the Sphinx. Oedipus said, 'I want to ask one question. Why didn't I recognize my mother?' 'You gave the wrong answer,' said the Sphinx. 'But that was what made everything possible,' said Oedipus. 'No,' she said. 'When I asked, What walks on four legs in the morning, two at noon, and three in the evening, you answered, Man. You didn't say anything about woman.' 'When you say Man,' said Oedipus, 'you include women too. Everyone knows that.' She said, 'That's what you think.'[2]

This sequel to the familiar tale of Oedipus and the Sphinx speaks clearly to our situation as teachers and scholars of religious studies. Like Oedipus, we thought we had the right answer. Instead, we have answered the questions which emerge in religious studies in an androcentric (male-centered) fashion. We have spoken about man's religions, his symbol making characteristics, his initiations, his myths. Only recently have we heard the voice of the Sphinx and begun to understand the failure of language and of intellectual responsibility associated with our understanding of *homo religiosus* as Man. In excluding women from our purview and, yet, talking about human experience, we have created data and theories, courses and curricula, which are inadequate. We have failed to notice connections between knowledge and power masked by our language and hidden in our naming. Within the context of broader trends which emphasize the social construction of knowledge, the gyno-

---

[1] I am indebted Karen McCarthy Brown for helpful suggestions and to the members of the 1987 Berkeley NEH workshop on the introductory religious studies course who helped to bring gender to the forefront as a key theoretical and pedagogical issue for religious studies and helped create an earlier version of this text.

[2] Muriel Rukeyser, "Myth," in *The Faber Book of Twentieth Century Women's Poetry*, ed. Fleur Adcock. (London: Faber and Faber, 1987), p. 135.

centric (woman-centered) perspective of the Sphinx has blossomed. As Anne Carr has made clear:

> patriarchy, androcentrism, and sexism have so pervaded history, culture, and ideas, the very language with which persons think, speak and write, that nearly everything known is called into question. And this includes the heritage of learning that is prized [i]n the university, scholarship. Less apocalyptically, consciousness of the issue of gender has not only opened new realms of research but has also, in subtle ways, changed the ways we look as the 'same old problems.'[3]

Recognition of the importance of historical, political and cultural forces in the creation of selves and the organization of knowledge has rocked academic discourse. The ideology and intent of liberal education and its expression in universities and colleges, the nature of the academic disciplines, our understanding of theoretical and practical aspects of pedagogy, have each been hotly debated as such new programs as ethnic studies, women's studies, men's studies, African American studies, gay and lesbian studies, have entered the conversations of liberal education and, indeed, of religious studies. Race, class, and gender are increasingly recognized as interlocking aspects of the construction of power which define human experience and the realities of oppression. As Peggy McIntosh has written, the study of women, informed by black studies and ethnic studies,

> makes visible many *men* who were not previously featured in the cur-
> riculum. In fact, about nine-tenths of the world's population suddenly
> becomes visible when one takes the emphasis off the public lives of white
> Western men...and includes those who, for reasons of sex, race, class, or
> national or religious background were defined as lower caste.[4]

As viewed from the perspectives of experts in the varying terrains where women's studies, gender studies and religious studies intersect, religious studies in 1989 is (like english and history) a version of men's studies modified.[5] With other fields significantly responsive to feminist movements within and without the academy, religious studies has un-

---

[3]Anne Carr, *Transforming Grace: Christian Tradition and Women's Experience.* (San Francisco: Harper and Row, 1988), p. 64.

[4]Marilyn R. Schuster and Susan R. Van Dyne, eds. *Women's Place in the Academy: Transforming the Liberal Arts Curriculum* (Totowa, NJ: Rowman and Allanheld, 1985), p. 5.

[5]Dale Spender, ed., *Men's Studies Modified* (NY: Pergamon Press, 1981).

dergone a paradigm shift.[6] Recent work is critical of the religious and anthropological assumptions scholars have brought to the wide range of traditions which we study. Scholarship is burgeoning which examines the roles of women and other silenced persons as religious practitioners; of symbolism relating to power, including the power associated with race, class, gender and sexuality; and of relations between embodied persons and symbol systems. Work has been done, for example, on Buddhist nuns, on menstrual rites, on imagery of the womb, and on the varying ways in which Christians of various races and classes revere Mary.

Following in the wake of extensive methodological and epistemological criticism within humanistic and social scientific fields, recent scholarship within religious studies also includes critique of the theoretical constructs we devise and use. Current scholarship understands religious studies as a historical, cultural and political product of Western patriarchy, especially as shaped by imperialism, capitalism, and sexism of the nineteenth and twentieth centuries. It also includes an assortment of constructive theoretical enterprises which seek to re-vision religion(s) through the lens of analyses which emphasize race, class, gender and sexuality. Whether understood as the study of traditions, texts, peoples, theories, methods, or dialogical fields, the religious studies enterprise in 1989 must be about women *and* men, sex and gender across the vast differences of race, class, sexuality, culture, and religion.

The Sphinx and the Study of Religion

Once awakened to the problematic androcentrism of the original reply proffered by Oedipus, how do we answer the Sphinx's riddle? Do we speak of woman (or women)? of women and men? of humans? Do we try all three? Rukeyser, of course, leaves us to solve the riddle anew. The possibilities in religious studies parallel those developed for bringing currently excluded categories into the liberal education curriculum more generally. We can create specialized courses which focus upon specific excluded categories—courses, for example, on women. As Bowles and Klein have argued, such courses are necessary in a world

in which half the population dominates the other half and 'balance', in the eyes of many, equals women becoming like men....We believe that women have just as much 'right' as men to have courses in which women are at the

---

[6]In this regard see, e.g., Rita M. Gross, ed., *Beyond Androcentrism: New Essays on Women and Relgion.* (Missoula, Montana: Scholar's Press, 1977), p.1.

center of inquiry—and avowedly so and without apology! In an unequal world, courses 'for women only' are of vital necessity.[7]

In a world which has privileged the experience of white middle class heterosexual men, courses organized around race, class, sexuality, and other axes of oppression are also of vital necessity.

We can also incorporate attention to gender, race, and class into more general courses. This can be accomplished, for example, through the recognition of the role of power and ideology in the establishment of the limits of legitimate discourse; the conscientious avoidance of racism, sexism, heterosexism, and class bias in our course organization; and the use of race, class, and gender as analytic categories within our work.

While these strategies have strengths and weaknesses, both facilitate the responsible inclusion of those who stand outside of dominant culture within liberal education. Thus, the Sphinx demands the continued development of specialized courses within religious studies which focus specifically upon women in our vast diversity and in our commonality. She also requires courses which incorporate women's experience and knowledge into other aspects of the religious studies conversation and the explicit development of race, class and gender as analytic principles within our field. Students should *not* emerge from religious studies courses oriented toward such particular topics as the religions of India, mysticism, Christianity, or the psychology of religion without some awareness of the presence or absence of women. They should not graduate as religious studies majors with no ability to reflect critically upon the impact of androcentrism, sexism, racism, heterosexism, class oppression, and imperialism. Nor should students emerge with the view that the experience of others or the study of such topics are irrelevant, trivial, second-class, or of interest only to those who are themselves other. Our students, that is, should take the Sphinx seriously. Like Oedipus, they must learn that to answer riddles by focusing exclusively on Man leads to tragedy, for such answers preclude our understanding of the vast diversity of women and men.

Simple mention of female deities or black preachers or berdache (ritualized cross-gender behavior) among native Americans does not in itself constitute an adequate response to the problematics of gender, race, sexuality, or class within the purview of religious studies. The new riddle posed in Rukeyser's poem is, in fact, complex and the implications

---

[7]Gloria Bowles and Renate Duelli Klein, eds. *Theories of Women's Studies* (London: Routledge and Kegan Paul, 1983), pp. 4, 13-14.

of the Sphinx's conversation far-reaching. Her words remind us of the ways in which power is present in our language and in our theorizing. Like our scholarly work, our courses must be transformed, not simply amended. As Schuster and Van Dyne have written "a transformed course would

• be self-conscious about *methodology* and use gender as a category of analysis, no matter what is on the syllabus (even if all males);

• present changed content in a *changed context* and be aware that all knowledge is historical and socially constructed, not immutable;

• develop an *interdisciplinary perspective*, to make visible the language of discourse, assumptions of a field, and analytical methods by contrast with other fields;

• pay meaningful attention to intersections of *race, class, and cultural differences within gender*, and avoid universalizing beyond data;

• study new subjects in their *own terms*, not merely as other, alien, non-normative, and non-Western, and encourage a true *pluralism*;

• *test paradigms* rather than merely "add on" women figures or issues, and incorporate analysis of gender, race, and class by a thorough reorganization of available knowledge;

• make student's experience and *learning process* part of the explicit content of the course, thereby reaffirming the transcendent goals of the course; and

• recognize that, because *culture reproduces itself in the classroom*, the more conscious we are of this phenomenon, the more likely we are to turn it to our advantage in teaching the transformed course."[8]

As applied to religious studies such a complex transformative impulse requires us to consider anew the goals, course content, format, and teaching style which we bring into the classrooms in which we teach.

New Questions From the Sphinx

Where do we begin? The Sphinx, being wise, whispers in our ears that the introductory course is often the only course students take. That it is our majors' initiation into the field. And that this course is directly linked to our discipline's (and our own) self-identification. "Begin," she

---

[8]Schuster and Van Dyne, pp. 27-28.

suggests, "at the beginning." How? By asking ourselves some of the new riddles which follow from the conversation of Oedipus and the Sphinx.[9]

Most generally, the questions which the Sphinx raises for faculty teaching introductions to religious studies are two: *What have I been doing in my introductory course?* and *How might my course be transformed through the incorporation of those currently made absent or invisible through the allocation of power within religious traditions and within religious studies as an academic enterprise?* These queries can be raised in regard to specific aspects of our courses and curricula, including the goals, subject matter, structure, and pedagogy which we utilize. Though general, these questions truly become riddles as we engage with the complex theoretical and practical issues they raise for our teaching, our scholarship, and our humanity. These questions ask us about our intentions and remind us to consider the consequences we may not intend.

1. How are power, authority, and legitimacy allocated in my course design? As organizations of knowledge, syllabi allocate power to faculty and to students. Less obviously, our courses indicate which scholars, religious traditions, and issues we deem legitimate. Our course design provides our students with a map of "reasonable and appropriate" questions and specifies the nature of authority within our academic field. Its creation involves a decision about whether such issues will be an explicit analytical principle within our introduction to religious studies or will remain implicit. *Are we willing to admit that the map is not the territory and the guide not infallible when the map is our syllabus* and *the guide ourselves?* This broad question underlies many of the specific riddles which follow.

2. Who is excluded from my current course? What are the consequences of the selections I have made in creating an introduction to religious studies? The creation of any course or curriculum involves selection among the vast quantities of available information, texts and artifacts. Making the consequences and the grounds of our choices explicit rather than implicit requires us to consider what it might mean to depict human religiosity as a male activity, a nonwestern activity, an activity of the literate elite. It also requires us to consider the impact of choices which depict the Eurocentric and American, predominantly white, male, upper middle

---

[9]For a series of widely useful questions focused on courses in the humanities, social sciences and sciences, see, Schuster and Van Dyne, "Syllabus Redesign Guidelines," pp. 279-290. For specific questions relevant to race see Johnella E. Butler, "Complicating the Question: Black Studies and Women's Studies," pp. 73-85 in Schuster and Van Dyne.

class enterprise of religious studies as *the* appropriate locus for debate regarding the nature of religion and religions.

Thus, this question has as corollaries an array of riddles about canon and hermeneutics, about the politics of interpretation, and about the ways in which we silence some and, as Nelle Morton has said, hear others to speech. *Whose version of religion—and religions—are presented as authoritative?* Here, we must consider the authority of practitioners versus religious studies professors; our selection of informants and strands within religious traditions; the relative emphasis we place upon literate and other forms of religious expression. We must, in fact, consider which religions we choose to discuss as well as the ways in which we align those we address. *Whose version of religious studies is presented as legitimate?* Here our choice of methods, texts, and critiques is central. Perhaps most important is the issue of how we locate our own position within the vast array of possible stances within religious studies today.

3. *What generalizations do I make in my introductory course? on what basis do I make them?* In addition to inquiring about the general grounds for the brief depiction of religion and religions possible in one course, such questions ask us to consider whether our courses are androcentric, sexist, racist, heterosexist, Eurocentric, or otherwise skewed. In asking ourselves this question, we are reminded that the capacity for critical inquiry which we transmit to our students involves the ability to respond to generalizations about human religiosity by asking "for whom?" "by whom?" "about whom?" Perhaps we also want our students to raise concerns about similarity and difference in their examination of religious experience and institutionalization. In transforming our courses, a useful thought experiment might be to suppose all texts and theory written by men and all artifacts created by men were unavailable. We might then ask ourselves: *could I still teach my introductory course? could I still describe religion? how would generalizations differ?*

4. As these questions have indicated, the identification of conventions which characterize our courses leads directly to consideration of the potentially transformative impact of selecting alternative materials and concerns. This brings with it a vast array of questions about the methods and materials, traditions, texts, and theories which we do select. *Will including topics about race, class, gender, sexuality and power change the body of data? the terminology of the course? the generators of knowledge considered? my use of lanquage? Are the categories of knowledge and rationality used in my class rooted in a dominant culture's vision of the world? Is my emphasis upon*

chronology, periodization, genres, great works, specific rituals, regions, methods, texts, cultural forms such that it privileges men? Are my presentations of other traditions racist? imperialist? Eurocentric? Does the use of such dichotomies as mind/body, culture/nature, reason/affect, theory/practice, public/private support the oppression of subordinate groups? Such queries, of course, remind us that the ongoing epistemological and methodological debates within religious studies reach into our course design. They help us to see that in selecting the methods we choose to discuss, the themes we orient our course around, the texts we order from the bookstore, we also limit our portrayal of religion(s). Feminist theories and the emphasis upon race, class, gender, sexuality, and colonization stand as resources for us in reconceiving the theories and practices characteristic of our field. They remind us in specific ways of the intrusion of power and ideology into the organization of knowledge and into our classroom.

5. *Does my style privilege certain sorts of learners?* Within the limits of the specific constraints of our educational institution, our syllabi and course designs specify the ways in which we expect to teach and in which we expect students to learn. The nature of professorial authority and the valuing of cooperation or competition are, for example, implicit or explicit messages of our syllabi. Like ordinary conversation, classroom speech is about who can speak when, to whom, about what. Like all speech, pedagogical discourse is about power, allocated along lines of gender, race and class.[10] Among the decisions which we make in creating our introductory courses are those about the distribution of silence and the forms of discourse appropriate to liberal education.

6. *What do I notice about my politics and the politics of my department, my institution, my field, when I envision arguing for an introductory course with no men in it? Does the question change if I consider a course with no male students versus a course with no male subject matter?* (Try substituting no white men? no privileged political elites? no women? no nonwestern

---

[10]For those uncertain whether pedagogy per se is "gendered", consider the following illustrative quotation: "Average college students have already been rewarded year after year for superior achievement in elementary and high school classrooms. In many colleges they have had experience in their previous classes with instructors who, *in a more or less fatherly way*, gave information and rewarded those students who could best give it back...." (Wilbert J. McKeachie, *Teaching Tips: A Guidebook for the Beginning College Teacher*, 8th ed. [Lexington, MA: D.C. Heath, 1986], pp. 5-6). For information which considers pedagogical style as linked to issues of power see the work of Paulo Friere and, more specifically, Margo Culley and Catharine Portuges, eds. *Gendered Subjects: The Dynamics of Feminist Teaching* (Boston: Routledge and Kegan Paul, 1985) and the special issue on feminist pedagogy in *Women's Studies Quarterly* XV (Numbers 3 and 4, Fall/Winter 1987).

group? no western group?) What arguments can be made for and against each sort of selectivity in an introductory course? This final question reminds us of the fundamentally political, historical and cultural embeddedness of religious studies and, more specifically, of our own educational endeavors. What we can envision "permitting" ourselves and our colleagues to teach as a introduction to religious studies is, perhaps, a measure of the state of our field. The Sphinx reminds us that we have often introduced our religion through a discussion of Man. Why, she asks, not introduce our topic in a new way?

The Sphinx Concludes

In sum, the Sphinx brings with her the winds of change. Her admonitions expand our horizons beyond their androcentric limits. As we move from Man to Woman, so we must move from Woman and Man to women and men, to an appreciation of people in their diversity and an awareness of issues of race, class, and sexuality. In whatever guise, introductions to religious studies, like Oedipus, hear the Sphinx and nothing is again the same. The transformation of Oedipus has begun. So has the transformation of Rukeyser's reader, a complex recognition process which revisions the world in envisioning women. As the editors of *Unspoken Worlds* have written

> one conclusion to be drawn is that the data on women's religious lives, and, consequently, the interaction of women and men in religious systems as well as much richer and far more complex that anyone imagined when people were content to study 'religious man' alone. In fact, it seems clear that to study religion properly, we must also begin attending to women who have constituted and do constitute at least one-half of almost all of the world's religious communities.[11]

Conceiving of women as symbolizer and symbolized, examining the use (and abuse) of female imagery, moving from woman to women, recognizing the gendered character of male experience,[12] reevaluating our theories in the light of race, class, gender, and sexuality—all follow from hearing the Sphinx's challenge and responding. Our sequel to Muriel Rukeyser's poem requires that we invent ways to understand the

---

[11]Nancy Auer Falk and Rita M. Gross, eds. *Unspoken Worlds: Women's Religious Lives* (Belmont, CA: Wadsworth, 1989, 2nd ed.), p. xviii.

[12]The pro-feminist men's studies movement has turned our attention to the variety of male experiences. See, e.g., Harry Brod, ed., *The Making of Masculinities: The New Men's Studies* (Boston: Allen and Unwin, 1987).

particularities and the common features of our humanity. The vast range of women's religious experience and community, the vast range of men's religiosity, and the diversity of our critical reflection thereon draws us into the future and into a field which is about "the complexity of symbols"[13] and the allocation of power.

---

[13]Carolyn Walker Bynum, Stevan Harrell, and Paula Richman, eds. *Gender and Religion: On the Complexity of Symbols* (Boston: Beacon Press, 1986).

BIBLIOGRAPHIC RESOURCES ON GENDER AND RELIGION

Susan E. Henking

Since the 1979 publication of *Womanspirit Rising,* hundreds of works have been published which deal with scripture, theology, ethics, the history of Christianity, psychology and sociology of religion, and various religious traditions from the perspectives of various feminisms. Such work has appeared both within and outside of religious movements, both within and beyond the academy. The work is both critical and constructive. Some seeks to discover evidence of women's oppression while other work emphasizes the lengthy history of women's agency. The work considers women as religious practitioners as well as symbolisms associated with gender. The methods used and the theories advocated vary, the traditions covered are many, the goals of scholarship diverse. Whatever one's patch within religious studies, the inclusion of women has engendered a new discussion.

The following selections from this vast literature are treasuries which introduce us to significant scholars and issues. They are an essential opening into the conversation, many developed in the past few decades in response to classroom needs and to our own need to begin somewhere.[1]

"Women's Studies," Constance H . Buchanan. *The Encyclopedia of Religion,* Mircea Eliade, ed. (New York: MacMillan, 1987), 15: 433-440. This brief selection locates significant work on women and religion within a conceptual framework which focuses upon critical and con-

---

[1]See, e.g., Carl Olson, ed., *The Book of the Goddess*: "while teaching a course on goddesses in the history of religions a few years ago, I discovered that there was no common source book available to my students. The lack of an adequate source book for classroom use led me to outline a work that would be faithful to the diverse religious cultures and periods of history in which goddesses have played an important role." (p. ix)

structive work. Categories used locate critiques of religious and anthropological assumptions, the reconstruction of historical research, religious beliefs, and ethics, and the development of new religious movements. See also, "Feminine Sacrality," by Nancy E. Auer Falk, 5: 302-312; "Gender Roles," Priscilla Rachun Linn, 5: 495-502; and "Masculine Sacrality," M.H. Klaiman, 9:252-258.

Gender and Religion: On the Complexity of Symbols Carolyn Walker Bynum, Stevan Harrell, and Paula Richman, eds. (Boston: Beacon Press, 1986). This volume serves as a rich, though complex, introduction to central issues which emerge once women are included within the purview of religious studies—questions which center around gender and symbolism. In her excellent introduction to this anthology, Bynum makes clear the two fundamental assumptions of the authors: "that all human beings are 'gendered'—that is, that there is no such thing as generic *homo religiosus*" and second, "the phenomenological insight that religious symbols point men and women beyond their ordinary lives." (p. 2) These essays fall into three groups: "gender as culturally constructed meaning"; "gender as polysemic symbol"; and "gender as a point of view". Taken together, the chapters provide entrance into the worlds of gender symbolism as understood by anthropologists, folklorists, historians of religion, and intellectual historians.

Transforming Grace: Christian Tradition and Women's Experience Anne Carr. (San Francisco: Harper and Row, 1988). This text provides a synthetic overview of much of the discussion within Christian feminist theology. Of particular interest is a chapter entitled "The Scholarship of Gender: Women's Studies and Religious Studies," which locates concerns within women's studies relevant for religious studies. The focus is primarily upon historical methodologies. While oriented toward the Christian West, the chapter raises key conceptual issues of interest for all students of religious studies.

Womanspirit Rising Carol P. Christ and Judith Plaskow eds. (San Francisco: Harper and Row, 1979). Since its publication, this collection has shaped the presentation of women's issues within many religious studies classrooms. Created in response to the experience of its editors, the collection brings together material on feminist spirituality which is both "reformist" and "revolutionary" in scope. Some chapters focus on the transformation of Jewish and Christian traditions from within, while others stress the creation of new movements drawing upon neopagan resources. The editors recognize the limitations of this distinction in their more recent anthology, *Weaving the Vision* Judith Plaskow and Carol P. Christ, eds. (Boston: Beacon Press, 1989). This second collection includes a range of voices—Native American, black and white, lesbian and heterosexual, from various classes and religious traditions. The anthology forces us to recognize that the particularity and commonality of women's voices is now a central area of theological and scholarly inquiry. A reading of the two anthologies together, especially as illumined by the thoughtful introductions to both volumes, will enlighten readers significantly about the shape of feminist religious thought in the past decade.

Unspoken Worlds: Women' s Religious Lives Nancy Auer Falk and Rita M. Gross, eds. (Belmont, CA: Wadsworth, 1989, 2nd. edition). The editors of this volume have compiled texts about women's religious lives from East Africa, India, the United States, Korea, Central America, South America, Morocco, Iran, Japan, China, Tibet, Haiti, and Australia. The articles are diverse both in terms of historical era and religious traditions. Yet, the collection retains coherence because of its emphasis upon bringing women to voice. The authors point to the levels of support which women do (and do not) receive from their religious traditions and to complex tensions between extraordinary callings and ordinary lives in women's religious experience. Sections are devoted to extraordinary women, ritualized rebellion, rituals for wives and mothers, women in male dominated systems, women and men in equity, and mythical models for women's power. In addition, this second edition includes excellent suggestions for further reading after each selection as well as a detailed and up-to-date bibliography which is invaluable.

Beyond Androcentrism: New Essays on Women and Religion Rita M. Gross, ed. (Missoula, Montana: Scholars Press, the American Academy of Religion, 1977). The initial portion of this early anthology addresses the impact of feminism upon methodologies within religious studies. Subsequent sections of the book provide crosscultural and historical studies, including rereadings of biblical material and examinations of female religious imagery across a variety of traditions. Though now somewhat dated, these essays are useful in raising basic issues which more recent collections may take for granted and as an introduction to scholarly voices which have since become powerful proponents of work on women, gender and religion.

Journal of Feminist Studies in Religion. This refereed journal, published by Scholar's Press, is required reading for those interested in issues of gender and religion. The range of material published in this journal is wide. Recent issues have included a special section on women and initiation; a roundtable on racism in the women's movement; work in feminist theology, biblical studies, Buddhist studies, and ethics.

The Book of the Goddess: Past and Present Carl Olson, ed. (NY: Crossroad, 1987). As its title makes obvious, this is a collection which considers the portrayal of female divinities. As Olson notes in his preface, "without trying to be exhaustive or encyclopedic in scope, this book includes examples of ancient and modern goddesses, encompassing Eastern and Western religious traditions, major world religions and tribal religions, living religions and those that have passed into historical memory." (p. ix) The anthology considers the association of goddesses with life and with destruction, the roots of goddess worship in the prehistoric era, the status of such figures in monotheistic religions, and the roles of goddesses as consorts or as independent figures. Among the figures considered are Ishtar, Isis, the virgin Mary, Kali, Kuan-Yin, and Oshun. In addition, two final essays bring historical research on goddess figures into connection with contemporary feminism and the requirements of western spirituality. The range of authors will introduce novice readers to significant scholars and the suggestions for further readings will enable readers to move easily into more detailed work.

Women in World Religions Arvind Sharma, ed. (SUNY Press, 1987). "Men and women equally compose mankind," wrote Dabistan-i-Mazabib in a seventeenth century Indian text which serves as the epigraph for this compilation. The text consists of individual essays on tribal religion, and the "big six" great traditions. The essays are each by a woman scholar with expertise in the particular tradition who uses a phenomenological approach. Each work blends historical with contemporary materials, considers female experience of both agency and oppression within traditions, examines statements in relevant texts which address gender, and explores the roles of female deities. Katharine Young's introduction brings coherence to the text and raises basic questions for the history of religions about women's experience in the world religions.

Bibliographical material makes entrance into the vast scholarly literature on these traditions accessible.

The Politics of Women's Spirituality Charlene Spretnak, ed. (Garden City, NY: Doubleday, 1982). This volume differs significantly from others cited here because it is the product of a new religious movement. Spretnak brings together poetry, historical essays, ritual, thealogical reflection, and related documents. Here the focus is upon goddesses, upon the discovery of an accessible (mythic) history of women's power, and upon the creation of ways to manifest such power within personal and political spheres. The material is significant insofar as it represents a movement with complex connections to feminism and to feminist theology within Western traditions. Work appears here by such figures as Daly, Christ, and Starhawk, whose more lengthy works are significant parts of contemporary reflection.

BASIC READINGS IN THE ACADEMIC STUDY OF RELIGION
Mark Juergensmeyer

In choosing selections from original sources for students to read, it is good to keep a balance among the various disciplinary approaches to the academic study of religion. The following provides a listing of major "schools," along with literature foundational to these approaches.

Anthropology of religion

More than any other group it was the anthropologists of the late nineteenth century who laid the groundwork for nontheological approaches to the study of religion. E.B. Tyler's theory of animism as the basis of primitive culture and J.G. Frazer's thesis that magic precedes religion are as significant for the way in which they were derived—from field work rather than from philosophical speculation—as they are for their logical persuasiveness. The next generation of anthropologists included Franz Boas, who posited that ritual preceded myth in the evolution of religious forms, and also the "functionalists" such as A.R. Radcliffe-Brown, E.E. Evans-Pritchard and Bronislaw Malinowski, who claimed that the most important thing to know about religion was the function it plays within a society. Modern anthropologists are more likely to be indebted to the work of Claude Levi-Strauss and to emphasize the importance of the internal structure of religious acts and myths. Mary Douglas is an interesting example. Her *Natural Symbols* makes a special application of structuralism to religious imagination. Victor Turner takes a somewhat different direction. In his *The Ritual Process* he picks up a theme from van Gennep's *The Rites of Passage* and argues that the liminal aspects of ritual have a community-building characteristic. Other contemporary anthropologists, including Clifford Geertz and Anthony F.C. Wallace, are concerned with the way that religion serves as the ideology, or world view, for cultural systems. A useful overview of these and other anthropological theories about religion is provided in Lessa and Vogt, *Comparative Religion: An Anthropological Approach.*

Sociology of religion

Again, one has to begin with the nineteenth century. The writings of Karl Marx hover in the background, but most sociologists of religion regard their field as having begun with those two giants who recognized that religion shaped society as much as it reflected it: Emile Durkheim and Max Weber. Durkheim is best known for the *Elementary Forms of Religious Life*, in which he argues that the notions of the sacred and the secular are fundamental to a society, and that religion is the name given to the expressions of social cohesion and order. Weber takes a somewhat different tack by arguing that religious concepts and commitments have a formative effect on social structures. For English readers, his essays published under the titles *The Sociology of Religion* and *The Protestant Ethic and the Spirit of Capitalism* are fundamental. In the same spirit is Ferdinand Toennies' *Community and Society*. Talcott Parsons has brought the early European theorists into the context of modern twentieth century organizational society, and his student and colleague, Robert Bellah, a contemporary sociologist of religion (see especially *Beyond Belief* and *Habits of the Heart*), applies the Weberian and Durkheimian concerns to a variety of religious traditions, including the religious culture of modern America. In a somewhat different direction, Peter Berger has explored the relevance of the sociology of knowledge for the study of religion (*The Sacred Canopy* and *The Social Construction of Reality*, co-authored with Thomas Luckmann), and in *The Heretical Imperative* he has shown its usefulness for modern theology. A timely and helpful textbook in sociology of religion is Barbara Hargrove's *The Sociology of Religion*.

Psychology of religion

The pioneer thinker in the field of the psychology of religion is William James, and his *Varieties of Religious Experience* is still essential reading. Freud will occupy a great deal of attention, of course, but it might be useful to balance his more strident views on religion in *Future of an Illusion* and *Totem and Taboo* with those in *Moses and Monotheism* and *Civilization and its Discontents*. Freud shouldn't be made to appear even more reductionist than he already is. The same problem obtains with Carl Jung, who is also easily caricatured. His autobiographical *Memories, Dreams and Reflections* or one of the books on symbols might be a way of easing into Jung, before presenting the mandatory *Psychology and*

Religion. Then there are the neo-Jungians, such as Joseph Campbell. You will make your own decision as to the importance of the contemporary writers who collectively go under the rubric of "transpersonal psychology," but one contemporary psychologist should not be missed: Erik Erikson, whose life cycle and life history studies contain valuable insights for the psychology of religion.

Philosophy of religion

The problem with the philosophy of religion is that one can almost start anywhere with it. Plato,for instance, is always a good place to begin, but if one limits oneself to the modern period, Hegel's *Lectures on the Philosophy of Religion* is an obvious point of departure. (Some think you might also stop there as well.) Schleiermacher's *On Religion* and Kierkegaard's *Philosophical Fragments* are also seminal. It is hard to know what to describe as philosophy of religion for our own contemporary period, but some would employ the writings of Paul Tillich (*The Dynamics of Faith*, for example) as illustrations of the effect of modern existentialism on religious thought. For textbooks, one might turn to John Hick's *Philosophy of Religion* or Ninian Smart's *Historical Selections in the Philosophy of Religion*.

History and Phenomenology of Religion

The emergence of a separate field of religious studies (*Religionswissenschaft*, the "science of religion") out of the welter of modern philosophy and theology can probably best be traced to philosophers such as Schleiermacher and Edmund Husserl (*The Idea of Phenomenlogy*). For beginning students, Rudolph Otto's *The Idea of the Holy* is to be recommended: it has the virtue of being not only historically important but readable. Geraldus der Leeuw's *Religion in Essence and Manifestation*, Joachim Wach's essay in *The Comparative Study of Religions*, and the writings of Rafaels Pettazzoni and Jan de Vries—all twentieth-century works—make important statements in this area, and in the present generation the field is closely identified with the thinking of Mircea Eliade. For theoretical purposes Eliade's most useful work is his *Patterns in Comparative Religion*, but as general statements of his point of view, *The Myth of Eternal Return* and *The Sacred and the Profane* are widely read. The field of History of Religions is defined and defended in the essays in Joseph Kitagawa, *The History of Religions*. For understanding the contemporary discussion of the problem of studying religion in a religiously plural society, students will find helpful the statements of

Ninian Smart in *Worldviews* and Wilfred Cantwell Smith in *The Meaning and End of Religion*. A course might even begin with a probing of the concerns that these authors have about the way religion is conceived as an object of academic study.

Philology and Textual studies

Philology is perhaps more a technique than a theoretical approach to the study of religion, but the fact is that most studies of religion, especially classical studies, are made by textual scholars, so it is useful to inquire into the assumptions they bring to their craft. Can the skills learned in biblical scholarship, for example, be applied with equal success to the texts of other religious traditions? Pioneers in textual scholarship include Julius Welhausen, the father of biblical text criticism in the modern period, and Max Muller, who applied similar methods to Indic texts. For a recent attempt to look at the comparative study of religious texts, see Wendy O'Flaherty, ed., *The Critical Study of Sacred Texts*, and works by Wilfred Cantwell Smith and William Graham on the concept of scripture.

Hermeneutics

There is some debate as to whether hermeneutics is a separate field of study or whether it should be classified a subset of theology, textual studies, philosophy of religion, or the history and phenomenology of religions. Wherever one puts it, one should probably include it somewhere in a basic course on theories of religion because of the influence it currently exerts in the field. One would probably start with Husserl and Martin Heidegger (*Being and Time*), but the major statements on hermeneutics that currently have an impact are those of Wilhelm Dilthey (*Pattern and Meaning in History*); Maurice Merleau-Ponty (*Phenomenology of Perception*); Hans-Georg Gadamer (*Philosophical Hermeneutics*); Paul Ricoeur (*The Conflict of Interpretations*); and Michel Foucault (*The Archaeology of Knowledge*). Useful overviews of this developing field are Robert L. Dreyfus and Paul Rabinow, *Michel Foucault: Beyond Structuralism and Hermeneutics*, and Richard Palmer, *Hermeneutics*.

Theology and Religious Thought

Opinions vary greatly as to what are the classics of Christian theology, and of modern Christian thought. In my Protestant view, Barth, Tillich, and the Neibuhr brothers are high on the list, but a Roman Catholic opinion might insist on Rahner, Kung, and Schillenbeecx. The main point is that students should get some taste of modern religious thinking, and they should taste a variety. This means including non-Christian religious thinkers along with Christian ones. Among Jewish thinkers, the names of Abraham Heschel and Martin Buber are well known, and with some hunting comparable thinkers may be found in other traditions. The same rule of thumb applies to classical, as well as, modern religious thought: if you include Augustine or Aquinas, you should also include Maimonides, Nagarjuna and Ghazzali.

Religious ethics

In ethics, too, the comparative principle applies. There are some interesting recent works of a comparative nature—the studies of Louis Dumont (*Homo Hierarchicus* and *From Mandeville to Marx*) and the theoretical efforts of David Little and Sumner Twiss (*Comparative Religious Ethics*) and Ronald Green (*Religious Reason*)—but a sensitive teacher may wish to look further. An annotated bibliography on ethics that deals with each of the major religious traditions will soon be published as a reference work by Cambridge University Press.

Course Syllabi

Syllabus #I: The World Religion Survey Course
Mark Juergensmeyer

This is perhaps the most commonly taught course in the religious studies curriculum. It is also one of the most maligned, for it is easily taught as an unrelieved series of snapshots of ideas and historical developments of the major world religions. There are several ways in which this pattern can be avoided: one is to show the interconnections of religious traditions in a single history of world religion; another is to provide opportunities for experiencing the distinctive world views of peoples of different times and places; a third is to pursue a thematic connection that ties various traditions together at the same time that it illustrates their differences. The following syllabus incorporates all three of these elements: it traces the history of world religion chronologically through related cultural regions; it offers field trips and slide shows and visits to religious figures; and it provides a sub-theme of gender perspectives on religion. Other sub-themes that might usefully be employed are pilgrimage, scripture, and the transformative self. (See my article, "A Brief Argument For an Endangered Species: The World Religion Survey," elsewhere in this Sourcebook.)

The reading for the course could include sections from a world religion textbook such as Ninian Smart's *The World's Religions* or Niels Nielsen, et al., *Religions of the World*. Or one might create a sourcebook especially for this course. The readings below indicate some of the myths, stories, sacred texts, and essays that could be utilized to provide a counterpoint to a textbook and present some of the living aspects of faith.

Schedule

1. INTRODUCTION: The elusive notions of "religion" and "tradition." Reading from W.C. Smith, *The Meaning and End of Religion*.

2. THE RELIGION OF EARLIEST HISTORY: A consideration of theories about the origins of religion. Readings from Freud, *Totem and Taboo*; Levi-Strauss, *The Savage Mind*.

3. RELIGION OF THE ANCIENT NEAR EAST: Ancient river cultures, including Egyptian and Mesopotamian. Readings from the Gilgamesh Epic; Neill, *Rise of the West*; Frankfort, *Before Philosophy*.

4. THE GODDESS IN ANCIENT NEAR EASTERN CULTURE: Readings from mythology and slide showing of ancient iconography.

5. RELIGION OF ANCIENT ISRAEL: Readings include selections from the Hebrew Bible (OT); Bright, *A History of Israel*; Neusner, *There We Sat Down*; and Trible, "Depatriarchalizing in Biblical Interpretation".

6. THE RISE OF THE JESUS CULT: A discussion of social unrest and religious ferment in colonialized Israel and the rise of the Jesus cult. Readings from the NT Gospels; Bornkamm, *Jesus of Nazareth*; Brandon, *Jesus and the Zealots*.

7. WHO WAS JESUS?: A panel discussion of the film, "The Last Temptation of Christ". Readings include film reviews and press reports of the controversy; Schweitzer, *The Search for the Historical Jesus*.

8. THE EARLY CHURCH: Readings from NT Acts and Epistles; Meeks, *The First Urban Christians*.

9. THE RISE OF RABBINIC JUDAISM: Field trip to a Jewish synagogue. Discussions of historical developments after 70 CE and demonstrations of Jewish ritual. Readings include selections from the Talmud; Neusner, *The Way of the Torah*.

10. EARLY EUROPEAN CHRISTIANITY: The early church fathers, Constantine and after. Readings from Peter Brown, *Augustine*, *The Cult of the Saints*.

11. THE RELIGION OF MEDIEVAL EUROPE: A discussion of pre-Christian European religion and the evolution of Christendom; Readings from Latourette, *A History of Christianity*; Leff, *Medieval Thought*; Bynum, *Jesus as Mother*; and *Holy Feast, Holy Fast*.

12. MONASTIC CHRISTIANITY: A field trip to a Roman Catholic monastic community or a priory.

13. THE RELIGION OF EUROPEAN JUDAISM: Readings from the Zohar; Scholem, *Major Trends in Jewish Mysticism*.

14. MUHAMMAD AND THE RISE OF ISLAM: Readings from the Qur'an; Fazlur Rahman, *Islam*.

15. RELIGION OF ISLAMIC EXPANSION: The rise of the Caliphates and great Empires and the development of Muslim philosophy. Reading

from Fazlur Rahman, *Islam*; Brinner, "The Examplars of Islam" (in Hawley, *Saints and Virtues*).

16. ISLAM IN THE MODERN WORLD: Guest speaker from local Muslim organization. Readings from Malcolm X's pilgrimage to Mecca. Smith, *Islam in Modern History*; Geertz, *Islam Observed*.

17. RELIGION OF ANCIENT INDIA: Indus valley and Vedic religion. Readings include selections from the Vedas; Basham, *The Wonder That Was India*; Renou, *Religions of Ancient India*.

18. THE BUDDHIST AND JAIN HETERODOXIES: Teachings of the Buddha, the early Buddhist sangha and Jainism. Readings from selections from Jain and Buddhist texts; Jaini, *Jaina Path of Purification*; Conze, *Buddhism*.

19. INDIAN RELIGIOUS TRADITIONS: The development of Hinduism from the Upanishads through the Epics. Readings from the Ramayana; the Bhagavad Gita; Zaehner, *Hinduism*; Embree, *The Hindu Tradition*.

20. HINDU DEVOTIONAL RELIGION: Bhakti and the rise of Sikhism. Readings from Sikh scripture and bhakti poetry; Eck, *Darshan*; Hawley and Juergensmeyer, *Songs of the Saints of India*.

21. HINDU TEMPLE WORSHIP: Field trip to the Hare Krishna Temple. Readings on the Hare Krishna movement.

22. MODERN HINDUISM: Film and discussion of the life and teachings of Gandhi. Reading from Gandhi's *Autobiography*.

23. THE RELIGION OF BUDDHIST EXPANSION: The rise of Mahayana and the development of Theravada cultures. Readings from later Buddhist writings; Suzuki, *Mahayana Buddhism*; Beyer, *The Buddhist Experience*; Keyes, "Ambiguous Gender: Male Thai Initiation," and Richman, "Female Renouncer in Tamil Buddhism," in Bynum, *Gender and Religion*.

24. RELIGION IN CHINA: Strands of religion in Ancient China, including Taoist, Imperial and Confucian elements and how they interacted with Buddhism. Readings from Waley, *Three Ways of Thought in Ancient China*; deBary, *Sources in Chinese Traditions*; Black, "Gender and Chinese Cosmology," in Bynum, *Gender and Religion*.

25. RELIGION IN JAPAN: Strands of religion in Japanese culture, including Shinto, Joto Shinshu, Shinran and Zen. Readings from Anesaki, *History of Japanese Religion*; Earhart, *Japanese Religion*.

26. RELIGION IN MODERN ASIA: Field trip to a Japanese new religious movement, or slide show of religion in modern China.

27. THE RISE OF MODERN WESTERN RELIGION: The religious impact of the Enlightenment and the Renaissance; the Reformation and the growth of Protestant denominations. Readings from Dillenberger and Welch, *Protestant Christianity*; Ahlstrom, *A Religious History of the American People*.

28. NATIVE AMERICAN RELIGION: Guest Native American speaker. Readings include a description of the vision quest; Native American songs and poems; Capp, *Seeing with a Native Eye*.

29. INFLUENCES FROM AFRICA ON THE WEST: Yoruba and other African traditions; their influence on Caribbean and Afro-American Christianity. Readings from Raboteau, *Slave Religion*; Ray, *African Religion*; Mbiti, *African Religions and Philosophies*.

30. RELIGION IN CONTEMPORARY AMERICA: The variety of contemporary religious choices; tension between religious community and secular society. Readings from Bellah, et al, *Habits of the Heart*; Glock and Bellah, ed, *The New Religious Consciousness*; Needleman and Baker, *Understanding the New Religions*.

Syllabus #II: The "Religious Experience" Course
Mark Juergensmeyer

This course is a thematic introduction to the study of religion. It posits that there are major elements of religious systems—such as the concept of the sacred, the practice of ritual, religious community and sacred persons—and it tries to understand how they fit together in integrated views of the whole. It takes examples of these elements from various religious traditions, and shows how scholars have debated over the appropriate ways of studying them.

While this template course is in some ways simpler to teach than the world religions survey—one does not have to teach the history of every religious tradition in the world—it has its own problems. The teacher has to show how the themes are integrated into a whole, and how they are lived in the real experience of peoples in various parts of the world. And in this course more than most the teacher is in danger of projecting his or her own view of religion onto the subject matter. Visits to religious communities and presentations by spokespersons of various religious persuasions will help to cut through the teacher's biases. Students' projects—such as studying a religious community in their neighborhoods, creating their own religion, or constituting the whole class as a religious community—might help show the integration of themes. This is a highly personal course, but there are some textbooks that might be appropriate. The readings suggested below might also be used in creating a sourcebook.

Schedule

1. INTRODUCTION: Questions of definition, and the relation of religion and experience. Theories of the origin of religion. Readings from Freud, *The Future of an Illusion*; Wallace, *Revitalization Movements*; Karl Barth.

2. THE SACRED QUEST: The idea of religion as openness to the sacred. Readings from T. S. Eliot's *The Waste Land*; St. Theresa; Muhammad's vision; and the Vision of Subud.

3. THE IDEA OF THE SACRED: The concept of ultimacy and the sacred as common to all traditions. Reading from Tillich.

4. GOD AND THE GODS: Readings include myths and stories of Native American, Hindu divinities, praise of God in Islamic, Jewish and Christian writings, and descriptions of a divine-like Buddha in Mahayana Buddhism.

5. THE POWER OF SYMBOLS: The notion of symbol as representation and manifestation of the divine. Readings from Jung and Tillich.

6. THE SACRED IN ART: Field trip to University art museum. Reading from Jaffe on circle symbol.

7. THE REALITY OF MYTH: Theories of myth from Kluckhorn to Jung; examples of creation myth in Vedic, African, Native American, Japanese, Greek, Babylonian, Zoroastrian and biblical narratives.

8. EPIC MYTHS OF THE WEST: Dramatic readings from the Gilgamesh Epic and Homer.

9. EPIC MYTHS OF THE EAST: Videotape and film clips from the Ramayana and Mahabharata.

10. SCRIPTURE AND THE SACRED WORD: The idea of sacred text and how to analyze it. Readings from Welhausen and W.C. Smith, and excerpts from Zoroastrian, Jewish, Hindu, Buddhist, Islamic, Chinese and Christian scriptures.

11. THE RITUAL PRESENCE: The relation of ritual to myth and the concept of liminal space. Reading from Victor Turner, examples from Navaho ritual.

12. PILGRIMAGE AS RITUAL: Film and discussion of pilgrimage as a ritual event. Readings of pilgrimage to Cantebury, Mecca, Benares, Brindavan and the Wizard of Oz; Eck, *Benares*; Hawley, *At Play with Krishna*; Malcolm X.

13. COMMUNITIES OF FAITH: The concept of sacred community. Readings from Durkheim and Troeltsch, and from texts on Buddhist and Confucian social values.

14. A COMMUNITY OF WORSHIP: Field trip to a Jewish synagogue. Discussion of liturgy as community building. Readings from Hassidic writings.

15. THE DISCIPLINE OF PRAYER: Discussion of the Islamic concept and practice of prayer as paradigmatic of essential liturgy, the link between private and collective religious activity.

16. SACRED TIME: The meaning of festivals and holidays. (Class meeting should correspond with a religious holiday to be used as the focus for discussion).

17. TRANSFORMATION THROUGH MUSIC: A demonstration lecture on the evolution of church music from Gregorian chants to the present, and/or a presentation-discussion of Bach's St. Matthew Passion.

18. SACRED PERSONS: Readings include accounts of biblical prophets, Chinese sages, African kings, and Indian gurus; Heschel, *The Prophets*.

19. PRIEST AND PASTOR: Discussion of the contemporary role of the religious specialist. Guest panel speakers include a Roman Catholic priest, a nun, and a Protestant Evangelist.

20. THE TRANSFORMATIVE SELF: The concept of the self in various traditions, and the possibilites for transformation. The contemporary search for spiritual consciousness. Readings from Ignatius, Conze, Castenada.

21. UNDERSTANDING MYSTICISM: The problem posed for academic analysis by the study of religious experience. What are the limits of rational knowledge? Readings from Schleiermacher, Streng, Kaatz, Staal, Proudfoot.

22. LOVE: Love as a metaphor for mystical union; the devotional genre of religious love in tension with law. Readings include Plato's Symposium; legal codes, bhakti poetry, Marriott's "Feast of Love."

23. THE INTENTIONAL SELF: Living righteously as a personal religious goal. Readings from Gandhi's Autobiography, Niebuhr, Pirsig.

24. RELIGION AND SOCIAL RESPONSIBILITY: The religious motivation for social betterment. Reading from Martin Luther King, Jr. and liberation theologians.

25. INTENTIONAL COMMUNITIES: Visit to a monastic or new age religious community. Readings from *The New Religious Consciousness*, Needleman and Baker.

26. RELIGION ON THE CONTEMPORARY CAMPUS: An analysis of the moral vision and religious life of modern young Americans. Readings from Bellah, et al., *Habits of the Heart*.

Syllabus #III: Approaching Human Consciousness
William Darrow

This syllabus attempts quite self-consciously to read a set of short classics in the field that work well in the classroom. It is admittedly a demanding set of readings, but all these tend to be works that appear over and over again on syllabi (one might even dare to suggest that they are a kind of canon in religious studies). They are also deliberately selected to collapse any easy distinction of primary and secondary texts and to present obliquely the categories of analysis in religious studies. Admittedly and sadly one main problem connected with such a syllabus is the cost of books, but most if not all are readily available in paperback.

Schedule

Week 1	Eliade, *The Sacred and the Profane*
Week 2	Niehardt, *Black Elk Speaks*
Week 3	Turnbull, *The Mountain People*
Week 4	Freud, *The Future of an Illusion*
Week 5	Geertz, *Islam Observed*
Week 6	Turner, *The Ritual Process*
Week 7	Fingarette, *Confucius: The Secular as Sacred*
Week 8	Herrigal, *Zen and the Art of Archery* and Suzuki, *Zen Mind, Beginner's Mind*
Week 9	*The Bhagavad Gita*
Week 10	Castenada, *A Separate Reality*
Week 11	Vidal, *Messiah*
Week 12	Tillich, *The Courage to Be* or *Dynamics of Faith*

Syllabus #IV: Introduction to the Phenomena of Religion
William Darrow

This syllabus develops a template of themes in the experience of most religions, and stresses the readings of primary texts. The course generally follows the categories of Mircea Eliade and employs a reader of his works edited by Wendell Beane and William Doty, *Myths, Rites, Symbols: A Mircea Eliade Reader*. It uses Eliade's *From Primitives to Zen* (printed in four volumes), *Gods, Goddesses, and Myths of Creation* (GGMC), *Man and the Sacred* (MS), *From Medicine Men to Muhammad* (FMMM), and *Death, Afterlife, and Eschatology* (DALE) as the main source book with some additional primary and secondary texts also employed.

A course such as this initiates students directly into both the textual content of religious traditions and also into some of the central categories of religious studies. The obvious problem with the course will be the difficulty of reading the short selections contained in the Eliade reader and with placing them in a context meaningful for the student. The reader does not provide such a contextual setting so the instructor would have to. This can only be done, however, for a portion of the material at hand. On the other hand the breadth of coverage and the care with which the materials have been selected can give a coherent introduction to religious expression as seen through the interpretative framework of Eliade.

Schedule

Week 1   Religion and Magic
           Bellah, "Religious Evolution"
           Malinowski, "Magic, Science and Religion"
           Douglas, *Purity and Danger*, chapter 1

Week 2   The Holy and the Sacred
           Beane and Doty, 32-92, 140-163
           Selections from Durkheim, *Elementary Forms of Religious Life* and Otto, *The Holy*.

Week 3   Supreme Beings of Sky and Earth
           GGMC, 3-80
           FMMM, 164-210
           Beane and Doty, 352-406

Week 4   Symbolization
           Geertz, "Religion as a Cultural System"

Levi-Strauss, "The Effectiveness of Symbols"
Douglas, *Purity and Danger*, "The Abominations of Leviticus"
MS, 3-24
Beane and Doty, 341-351

Week 5   Myth
GGMC, 83-151
Beane and Doty, 2-31, 92-129

Week 6   Ritual: Rites of Passage
MS, 135-165
Beane and Doty, 164-189; 407-431
Turner, "Betwixt and Between: The Liminal Period in Rites of Passage"

Week 7   Ritual: Sacrifice and Worship
MS, 49-105
Beane and Doty, 133-140, 200-218, 243-255

Week 8   Death and Afterlife
DALE, 3-101
Beane and Doty, 218-230, 431-451

Week 9   Sacred Personages: Shamans, Prophets and Founders
FMMM, 3-70
Beane and Doty, 257-282

Week 10   Ascetics and Mystics
FMMM, 71-107
Beane and Doty, 283-339

Week 11   A Case Study in a Mystical Tradition
Herbert Weiner, 9 $1/2$ Mystics: The Kabbala Today

Week 12   Comparative World Views
FMMM, 111-163

Syllabus #V: The "Introduction To Religious Studies" Course
Mark Juergensmeyer

As I have argued in my essay in the first section of this sourcebook, one of the most interesting ways of introducing the subject of religion— and perhaps the most useful way of showing how religious studies is linked with other areas of the liberal arts—is the introductory course in the study of religion. There are several textbooks that cover the various theoretical approaches to the study of religion. Lessa and Vogt's *Comparative Religion: An Anthropological Perspective*, gives a useful sampling of recent theories. For the historical development of religious studies as a field, Claude Welch's *19th Century Protestant Thought* is a useful reference work, especially the chapter on the history of religions, and the article by Robert Bellah on "The Sociology of Religion" reprinted in *Beyond Belief* gives a good sense of the intellectual climate surrounding the emergence of social scientific approaches to the study of religion in the late 19th century.

Schedule

1. SOCIOLOGY OF RELIGION: Readings include Bellah, "The Sociology of Religion"; Durkheim, *Elementary Forms of the Religious Life*; Weber, *On the Social Psychology of the World Religions*; Parsons, "Religious Perspectives in Sociology and Social Psychology"; and Geertz, "Religion as a Cultural System".

2. PSYCHOLOGY OF RELIGION: Readings include James' "Healthy-Mindedness and World-Sickness"; Freud, *Totem and Taboo*, "Obsessive Acts and Religious Practices"; and Jung, "The Autonomy of the Unconscious."

3. HISTORY OF RELIGIONS: Readings include Otto, "Religion as Numinal Experience"; Wach, "Development, Meaning, and Method in the Comparative Study of Religions"; Kitagawa, "The History of Religions in America"; and Eliade, *Patterns in Comparative Religion*.

4. WESTERN THEOLOGY: Readings include Tillich, "What is Faith"; Buber, *I and Thou*; Barth selections from *Evangelical Theology: An Introduction*; and Kung, selections from *On Being a Christian*.

5. EASTERN THOUGHT: Readings include Jose Pereira, "An Overview of Hindu Theology"; C. Humphreys, "What Karma Means"; S. Radhakrishnan, "Hindu Dharma"; Needham, "Correlative Thinking and its Significance: Tung chung-shu"; and Conze's "Introduction" to *Buddhism: Its Essence and Development*.

6. TEXTUAL STUDIES: Readings include Edgar Krentz's "The Methods of Biblical Scholarship"; Shemaryahu Talmon, "The Old Testament"; selections from Bornkamm's *Jesus of Nazareth*; introduction to Conze's *Buddhist Scriptures*; and Paul Ricoeur, "The Sacred Text and the Community."

BIBLIOGRAPHY OF TEXTBOOKS AND OTHER RESOURCES

Gurudharm Singh Khalsa and William Darrow

There is no accepted, standard introductory textbook in religious studies, though there are many well-respected texts in widespread use. The most prevalent type of textbook is the survey of traditions which separates the major religions into chapters and then proceeds to describe the most characteristic elements of each faith. A second genre of textbooks are those that arrange chapters by themes, dimensions, or expressions, forming a template of categories to explain religious life. A third type is the anthology: some anthologies provide articles by specialists in the histories and ideologies of major religions; other anthologies give samples of theoretical scholarship on the study of religion; and still others provide primary source material in the form of myths or sacred texts along with brief commentary. The following is a selection from each type of textbook, followed by a list of other bibliographic resources for the teacher: bibliographies, dictionaries, and encyclopedias.

I. World Religions Textbooks

Bush, Richard C. et al. *The Religious World: Communities of Faith.* New York: Macmillan, 1982. 396 pages.

Material contained in this introductory text has been intentionally shaped by questions most frequently asked by the author's students. The text focuses on the "world's living religions;" that is, those traditions that still attract followers today. Special emphasis is placed on "religion and the question of meaning" and "religious meaning in a pluralistic society."

Carmody, Denise L. and John T. Carmody. *Ways to the Center: An Introduction to World Religions.* Belmont: Wadsworth, 1981. 408 pages.

The book is divided into major sections on Ancient Religions, Asian Religions, and Near Eastern Religions.

Comstock, Richard, W., ed. *Religion and Man: An Introduction to World Religions.* New York: Harper and Row, 1971. 676 pages.

An introductory text which divides the religious map of the world into five sections: Indian, Far Eastern, Judaism, Christianity, Islam. Emphasis is placed upon anthropological and phenomenological notions of ritual and symbol in defining religion and religiousness.

Ellwood, Robert S. *Many Faiths: An Introduction to the Religious Life of Humankind.* New Jersey: Prentice Hall, 1987. 356 pages.

This is a study book that covers the major traditions and comes with chapter objectives, summaries and useful glossaries of key terms. It has a lively and informed style.

Hopfe, Lewis, M. *Religions of the World.* New York: Macmillan, 1987. 460 pages.

This recently published introduction to world religions is arranged in classic format: the divisions are as predictable and focused as a slide show presentation. Each religion gets its own chapter (thirteen in all), followed by study questions and further reading suggestions.

Ling, Trevor. *History of Religions: East and West.* New York: Harper and Row, 1970.

Ling makes a case for the study of comparative religion in this sophisticated survey and interpretation of world religions. His work is rooted in the sociological perspective of Max Weber. The text traverses the field both chronologically and geographically. An erudite book, not for the beginner.

Nielsen, Niels C. et. al. *Religions of the World.* New York: St. Martin's Press, 1983. 688 pages.

This textbook on the history of the major religions, written by well-known scholars, is visually appealing with many excellent pictures, time lines, and "boxed features". This text is designed for undergraduate students; although the language sometimes sounds patronizing, the scholarship is first rate. The highly successful single volume is now available in two separate volumes: one for the Religions of the East, the other for the Religions of the West.

Noss, John B. *Man's Religion.* New York: Macmillan, 1984. 589 pages.

This widely used textbook, now in its umpteenth edition, herds world religions into compact chapters that read like encyclopedia entries. Though the text is well edited and contains many passages from primary textual material, the tone of the work is lifeless and dry.

Parrinder, Geoffrey. *World Religions*. New York: Macmillan, 1984. 589 pages.

This textbook dwells in more detail on ancient religions than most survey books. The articles are well written, though their authors go unnamed. Pictures highlight the text.

Smart, Ninian. *The World Religions*. Englewood Cliffs, New Jersey: Prentice Hall, 1989. 576 pages.

Ninian Smart has created his own alternative to the conventional world religion textbook that goes from tradition to tradition, as in his *Religious Experience of Mankind*. This book moves through cultural regions chronologically, from the religions of primitive people to the conflicting worldviews of today. It is a lucid and commendable alternative indeed, one that may soon become the standard.

_____. *The Religious Experience of Mankind*, 3rd edition. New York: Scribner, 1984. 634 pages.

A history of religious traditions throughout the world from prehistory to the present. Highlights the major traditions but also includes African and Native American experience and rivals to religion, such as Marxism and Humanism.

Smith, Huston. *The Religions of Man*. New York: Harper and Row, 1958. 328 pages.

A personal essay on what the author feels is the heart of each tradition. This book has remained a popular pick of college instructors for thirty years because of its brevity, its insight, and its eloquence in conveying the essential aspects of the various traditions it surveys.

Yates, Karl M., ed. *The Religious World: Communities of Faith*. New York: Macmillan, 1988. 394 pages.

Seven authors have written a fresh-looking text with beginning students in mind. The text is enlivened with pictures, time graphs and helpful glossaries. The editor has included only "living religions" which makes the text shorter and less comprehensive than many.

II. Template Textbooks

Carmody, Denise L., Carmody, John T. *Shamans, Prophets and Sages: A Concise Introduction to World Religions*. Belmont: Wadsworth, 1985. 320 pages.

This textbook divides the phenomenon of religion into three "personality types": shamanic, prophetic and sapiential. It includes appendices which survey historical and philosophical aspects of nine religious traditions. Each chapter includes a summary and study questions.

Ellwood, Jr., R.S. *Introducing Religion from Inside and Outside*. Englewood Cliffs, NJ: Prentice-Hall, 1983.

A lively and intentionally personal introduction to the study of religion from the inside (the experience of believers) and outside (description of various features "common to all religions"). Geared toward the elementary college level, with study aids (chapter objectives and summaries), glossaries and annotated bibliographies.

Hall, William T. *Introduction to the Study of Religion*. New York: Harper and Row, 1978.

A multiauthored work. It deals with myth, belief, ritual, scripture and art as means of religious expression; and it contains a general classificatory essay that introduces world religions. It also deals with the religious issues of belief in God, death, suffering and salvation.

Kaufmann, Walter. *Religions in Four Dimensions: Existential, Aesthetic, Historical, Comparative*. New York: Readers Digest Press, 1976. 492 pages.

This book deserves praise for the author's abundant photographs, many in color. Quotations from sacred scriptures appear throughout. The author is outspoken and his views are reflected in the writing. The treatments of Christianity and Islam are especially controversial.

King, Winston L. *Introduction to Religion: A Phenomenological Approach*, 2nd edition. New York: Harper and Row, 1968.

A more advanced textbook organized in terms of phenomenological categories such as sacred space, time, devotion, community, and revelation. While probably too advanced for introductory undergraduates, it is useful to have at hand in preparing the first syllabus.

Monk, Robert C. et al., *Exploring Religious Meaning*. New Jersey: Prentice Hall, 1987. 357 pages.

A highly eclectic thematic presentation of religious issues and their impact on the individual and society. Cartoons and abundant quotations make this book inviting; the focus is on the artistic expression of religion.

Needleman, Jacob, A.K. Bierman and James A. Gould. *Religion for a New Generation*. New York: Macmillan, 1973. 572 pages.

An anthology focused primarily on the religious scene in contemporary America with special attention to the contemporary crises of war, racism, ecology, sexism and social action. Methodological selections provide a set of different judgments on the foundation and reality of religion. Following sections include texts considering spiritual discipline, cosmology, scripture and death.

Novak, Michael. *Ascent of the Mountain, Flight of the Dove.* New York: Harper and Row, 1971.

An invitation to religious studies focusing on the story character of religion, in the context of both myth and autobiography. Develops many of these in reference to Sam Keen's *To a Dancing God.*

Raschke, Carl A., James A. Kirk and Mark C. Taylor. *Religion and the Human Image.* Englewood Cliffs, NJ: Prentice-Hall, 1977.

An introduction focusing primarily on four human images contained respectively in the Hebraic, Christian, Indian and East Asian traditions. An introductory methodological chapter and two concluding chapters explore the religious landscape of the modern world.

Schmidt, Roger. *Exploring Religion.* Belmont: Wadsworth, 1988. 523 pages.

This text separates religious expression into three broad categories: the conceptual (doctrinal aspect), the performative (practical and moral aspect), and the social (community and tradition). It can be used in a philosophy of religion course as well as an introductory course in religion. Contains a valuable media guide.

Sharpe, Eric J. *Understanding Religion.* London: Duckworth, 1983.

An invitation to the study of religion written for the new student. It distinguishes religious studies from theology, while affirming that the two activities are complementary. Four modes of religion are presented: existential, intellectual, institutional and ethical. The concepts of sacred space and the nature of transcendence are also examined. Concluding attention is given to the process of secularization and to the relationship between religion and culture.

Smart, Ninian. *Worldviews: Crosscultural Explorations of Human Beliefs.* New York: Scribner's, 1983.

This effective introductory text collapses the distinction between religions and ideologies and attempts to provide the student with an introduction to the analysis of symbolic systems. Six dimensions are explored: experiential, mythic, doctrinal, ethical, ritual, and social.

Streng, Fredrick. *Understanding Religious Life*. Belmont: Wadsworth, 1985. 276 pages.

An introduction to the ideas and concepts of religious experience one encounters in studying religion. Includes "Ways of Being Religious," "Modes of Awareness Used to Express Religious Meaning" and "Approaches to an Objectified Study of Religion."

Wentz, Richard. *The Contemplation of Otherness: The Critical Vision of Religion*. Macon, Georgia: Mercer, 1984.

A invitation to religious studies that stresses the stance of religious studies as a continuing encounter with alternity, be it with the singular, representative or wholly Other.

III. Anthologies

Capps, Walter. *Ways of Understanding Religious Life*. New York: Macmillan, 1972. 399 pages.

An excellent anthology of writings of major scholars in the study of religion, including sociological and phenomenological perspectives.

Dye, James and Forthman, William, eds. *Religions of the World: Selected Readings*. Appleton, 1967. 636 pages.

The editors have gathered significant documents belonging to the Hindu, Buddhist, Chinese, Judaic, Christian and Islamic traditions. They include writings of poets, mystics, moral philosophers and theologians, as well as scriptural texts.

Eastman, Roger. *The Ways of Religion*. San Francisco: Canfield Press, 1975. 597 pages.

This introductory anthology collects the writings of exceptional authors and primary sources which convey the "essential spirit" of the religions. Includes contemporary and ancient sources.

Eliade, Mircea, ed. *From Primitives to Zen*. New York: Harper and Row, 1977. 645 pages.

A well-known sourcebook of primary texts of many of the major non-Western religious traditions. It is especially valuable for its selections from the various primal traditions of Africa, the Pacific and the Americas. The volume was prepared by Mircea Eliade for his course in the History of Religions at Chicago, and reflects the methodological framework of his "Chicago School."

Hall, William T., ed. *Introduction to the Study of Religion*. San Francisco: Harper and Row, 1987. 357 pages.

Includes articles on the study of religion, varieties of religious expression and religious issues. Study questions, projects and bibliographies follow each chapter.

Hinnells, John R., ed. *A Handbook of Living Religions*. New York: Viking, 1984. 528 pages.

Sixteen scholars contributed their expertise to this collection of essays on the religions of the world. The articles in this handbook read like expanded encyclopedia entries.

Lessa, William A., and Vogt, Evon, Z., eds. *Reader in Comparative Religion: An Anthropological Approach*. New York: Harper and Row, 1972. 572 pages.

Includes selections from well-known anthropologists and other social scientists writing on religion and presented under chapter headings such as symbolism, myth, ritual, shamanism etc.

Needleman, Jacob; Bierman, A.K.; and Gould, James, A., eds. *Religion for a New Generation*. New York: Macmillan, 1977. 572 pages.

Cited above under "Template Textbooks." The selections range from Meher Baba to Carlos Castenada, from Nietzsche to Tillich.

Smart, Ninian., and Richard Hecht, eds. *Sacred Texts of the World: A Universal Anthology*. New York: Crossroad, 1982. 403 pages.

This reader serves to draw excerpts from the major representative sacred writings of the world religions into an organized presentation. A good companion volume to a survey course.

Streng, Fredrick J.; Lloyd, Charles L. and Allen, Jay T., eds. *Ways of Being Religious: Readings for a New Approach to Religion*. New Jersey: Prentice Hall, 1973. 627 pages.

A companion volume to *Understanding Religious Life*. Includes first person accounts of spiritual experiences and scholarly investigations and reflection. Thematically organized around the dynamics of religious experience.

IV. Bibliographies

A. General Bibliographies

Adams, Charles J. ed. *A Reader's Guide to the Great Religions*, (2nd edition). New York: Free Press, 1977.

Although a bit dated, this is a comprehensive and well researched collection of bibliographic essays on each of the major world traditions, each written by a leading scholar of that tradition. Meant for the serious scholar and researcher as well as the introductory student. Includes a section on the history of religions.

Karpinski, Lesek M. *The Religious Life of Man: Guide to Basic Literature.* New York: Scarecrow Press, 1978.

As the title implies, this work is devoted to the basic, though by no means pedestrian literature of the field. Entries fall into six categories including a general overview of the Religions of Mankind, Religions of the Past, The Asian Religions, The Beliefs of Native Peoples, The Occult, Judaism, Christianity, and Islam. With a general index, this work should prove helpful in organizing an introductory course.

Mitros, Joseph F. *Religions: A Select, Classified Bibliography.* New York: Learned Publications, 1973.

Although now out of date, this is a well organized bibliography of the major world traditions, with emphasis on Christianity. Written specifically for students of philosophy, but of use to those teaching an introductory course. Author index.

Wilson, John F., and Thomas P. Slavens. *Research Guide to Religious Studies.* Chicago: American Library Association, 1982.

This work includes an introduction to religious scholarship, with general comments as well as a list of sources on the study of religion and the history of religions, and a well-annotated list of reference works including atlases, bibliographies, guidebooks, encyclopedias and dictionaries, as well as works on specific traditions. Author, title and subject index.

B. Topical Bibliographies

Burr, Nelson Rolin. *Religion in American Life.* New York: Appleton-Century-Crofts, 1971.

A selective but dated bibliography of the many facets of American religious life with an emphasis on the sociological aspects of religion. Despite the somewhat specialized nature of many of the listings, the breadth of this work (twenty-two subject headings) should render it of some use. Author index.

Carman, John, and Mark Juergensmeyer, eds. *A Bibliographic Guide to the Comparative Study of Ethics.* New York and London: Cambridge University Press, 1990.

Covers the primary and secondary ethical literature of the world's major traditions. An essay introduces each tradition, and a subject index provides a useful tool for comparing ethical themes across traditions.

Dell, David J., et al. *Guide to Hindu Religion.* Boston: G.K. Hall and Co., 1981.

This guide forms one of an ambitious series of works sponsored by the Project on Asian Philosophies and Religions. Designed specifically to familiarize teachers and others who are not specialists with the basic resources of the field, this volume is divided into 12 categories treating the Hindu tradition from a wide range of perspectives. Annotations are crisp and critical. The work of top scholars, this guide should prove very useful. Index.

Ede, David. et. al. *Guide to Islam.* Boston: G.K. Hall and Co., 1983.

Another work sponsored by the Project on Asian Philosophies and Religions. Annotations are succinct and critical, listing sources covering Islam from a range of perspectives. One shortcoming of the guide is that it does not list sources published after 1976. A supplementary work, we are told in the preface, is under way. Author and subject index.

Homan, Roger. *The Sociology of Religions: A Bibliographic Survey.* Westport: Greenwood Press, 1986.

Although the majority of books and periodicals listed in this survey will be too specialized for the introductory course, it may prove useful in treating such seminal topics as religion and ethnicity, social class, and politics. The twenty-four subject headings display a slight North American and Christian bias. Author, title, and subject index.

Reynolds, Frank E. with John Holt and John Strong. *Guide to Buddhist Religion.* Boston: G.K. Hall and Co., 1981.

Designed specifically for undergraduate teachers of religion. In keeping with the other volumes in the P.A.P.R. series, the scholarship of this work is of a consistently high quality. Twelve sub-headings list sources treating the Buddhist tradition from a wide range of perspectives. Author, title and subject index.

Smith, Ron. *Mythologies of the World: A Guide to Sources.* Illinois: National Councils of Teachers, 1981.

A geographically organized guide to the mythologies of the world. Written in essay form, this bibliography lists a wide variety of works pertinent to the study of myth including cultural, historical, and archeological treatments. Suitable for cursory as well as in-depth studies.

Yu, David C., and Laurence G. Thompson. *Guide to Chinese Religion.* Boston: G.K. Hall and Co., 1985.

Religious elements indigenous to China (thus excluding Buddhism) are treated from a number of perspectives, comprising 11 categories. This volume is another in the series of guides from the Project on Asian Philosophies and Religions. Emphasis is placed on the religious entities themselves, the philosophical aspects of the various traditions being treated in Yu's companion volume, *Guide to Chinese Philosophy.* Author, title and subject index.

V. Dictionaries and Encyclopedias

Brandon, S.G.F., ed. *Dictionary of Comparative Religion.* New York: Scribners, 1970.

Whereas the Abingdon and Penguin dictionaries deal primarily with "living" traditions, this volume is considerably broader in scope. It is, however, slightly outdated, and less accessible than its counterparts—the frequent use of abbreviations makes it at times difficult to follow. Still, the often detailed entries and the inclusion of bibliographical suggestions will render this work of use. General and Synoptic index.

Crim, Keith, general ed. *The Abingdon Dictionary of Living Religions.* Nashville: Abingdon, 1981.

This "authoritative guide to the historical development, beliefs, and practices of religions in today's world" is a useful reference work. One volume (830 pages) including comprehensive articles on four main traditions: Islam, Christianity, Buddhism, and Hinduism. References are lengthy, encyclopedic, and readily accessible. Several color maps. Cross-references but no index.

Eliade, Mircea, ed. in chief. *The Encyclopedia of Religion.* New York: Macmillan, 1986.

This authoritative 16 volume encyclopedia is now the standard reference work in the field. In addition to its comprehensive coverage of the histories and ideas of the major traditions, it also covers minor and non-literate traditions, crosscultural themes, and general aspects of religious experience.

Gray, Louis Herbert, and John Arnott Macculloch, general eds. *The Mythology of all Races*. New York: Cooper Square Publishers, 1964 [c. 1916-32].

Although originally undertaken in the early 1900's and republished in the 60's, this work still serves as a comprehensive treatment of myths and legends. In thirteen volumes, divided geographically by peoples, it covers the whole gamut of myth in essay form, rendering it less of an encyclopedia than a collection of small books on the myths concerned. A general index for the entire series, however, gives it an encyclopedic range.

Hastings, James, et. al. *Encyclopedia of Religion and Ethics*. Edinburgh: Charles Scribner's Sons, 1908-22.

Although this work has been superceded by the work of Eliade, et al., it deserves to be mentioned as a classic in the field. For years the definitive (and only) encyclopedia of religions, it contains many topics not covered in the Eliade work, and some that are duplicated are superior in the Hastings.

Hinnels, John R., ed. *The Penguin Dictionary of Living Religions*. London: Allen Lane, 1984.

Although in dictionary format, the entries of this one-volume work are substantial, crisp and very readable. The work of 29 scholars from a variety of disciplines, this affordable and portable paperback should prove useful as a quick reference work.

Parrinder, Geoffrey. *Dictionary of Non-Christian religions*. Amersham: Hulston, 1971.

Though somewhat dated, this one volume work is nevertheless useful in its brevity and conciseness. Less comprehensive in scope than either the Abingdon or Penguin dictionaries, it does offer considerable treatment of a great many topics in the non-Christian traditions, devoting special attention to Hinduism, Buddhism, and Islam.

Smith, Jonathan Z., ed., *Dictionary of Religion* , New York: Harper, (forthcoming).

This special project sponsored by the American Academy of Religion promises to be the "state-of-the-art" compendium of articles written by the best-regarded specialists in the field. It should be available in the mid-1990's.

Zaehner, R.C. *The Concise Encylcopedia of Living Faiths*. London: Hutchinson, 1971. 435 pages.

The Judaic and Indian traditions represent for Zaehner the two primary streams of religion: that of Western religion originating in the Near East, and of Eastern religion springing up in the Indian milieu. In spite of its limitations in scope (native traditions are excluded), it remains a scholarly source book with major articles by A.L. Basham, E. Conze, A.C. Graham and others.